Seumas MacManus, poet, novelist and play-
wright, was born in Mountcharles, County
Donegal, in 1869, the son of a small farmer. He
qualified as a pupil-teacher at the age of sixteen,
and after having taught at Enniskillen Model
School and Kinawley National School, County
Fermanagh, became principal of Glencoe about
1888.

At the age of eighteen his professional career
began with verse and humorous sketches which
appeared in the Donegal Vindicator. But his true
metier was to be the rich store of folklore in which
he had steeped himself since boyhood — sitting
entranced at the hearthsides of the old storytellers
— the shanachies — of his native Donegal hills.
With scores of these tales set down in penny
notebooks and hundreds more to come, he
resigned his teaching appointment in 1898 and
left to seek his fortune in the United States. There
he found almost-overnight success with leading
magazines of the day, followed by the first of his
many book publications. In 1901, back in Irelnd,
he married Ethna Carbery (Anna Johnston), the
Antrim-born poet and nationalist, but she died
only a year later. In 1911 he married Catalina
Paez, a Venezuelan-American, and settled in the
U.S.A. where his popularity as a writer, master
storyteller, lecturer and interpreter of Irish life
and 'the Irish Cause' spanned many decades. On
his death in 1960, Padraic Colum described him
as 'the last of the shanachies'.

THE ROCKY ROAD TO DUBLIN

Seumas MacManus

THE ROCKY ROAD TO DUBLIN

with a foreword by IRVIN S. COBB

First published 1938 by MacMillan & Co Ltd, New York
This edition published by
Moytura Press, 73 Clarence Mangan Road, Dublin 8.

BRITISH LIBRARY CATALOGUING IN PUBLICATION DATA
MacManus, Seumas
The rocky road to Dublin: the story of
Seumas MacManus of Donegal. — 2nd ed.
1. (County) Donegal. Social life, 1900-1921
Biographies
I. Title
941.7082'1'0924

ISBN 1-87130-500-4

This edition was printed by
The Guernsey Press Co. Ltd,
Guernsey, Channel Islands.

Evening Light on Greenport Rocks, a painting by Derek Hill
reproduced by kind permission of the artist.
Cover design by Jarlath Hayes.

TO THE MEMORY
OF A NOBLE FATHER
PATRICK MacMANUS
AND A RARE MOTHER
MARY MULLOY
THIS BOOK IS DEVOTELY DEDICATED.

Contents

Foreword

It has long been my contention that every proper Gael is, down inside of himself, a poet. He might not write poetry but, by heavens, he thinks it.

It took a poet to write such prose as one finds in this book. Page on page, the lines carry with them a rhythm as limpid and gracious as the voice of the summer wind in a rippled field of Irish barley. Yet to me no chapter, no passage even, is clogged by the feeling that emphasis has been laid on style rather than on coherent and ordered narrative. The story marches, nor halts for dress parade. That sacrificial sweat which goes into all authentic and honest pen-work has been absorbed in the sheer joy of creation. Here is no labouring word-smith more intent on the vanity of rounding out a phrase than on speaking his piece. First and last, for better, for worse, here is a teller of tales whose sentences sing with beauty, whose paragraphs scan like balanced versifying, only because, by reason of this natural man's racial inheritance, it's his natural way of writing.

The Rocky Road to Dublin is the tally of its author's own life — almost from conscious babyhood to the time when a measure of real success first came to him as an author. It is told in the third person, thinly disguised. Which is not a bad trick. Many autobiographical accounts, dullish and self-centred to start with, are so thickly studded with capital I's as to make me think of a picket-fence around a vacant lot. By speaking of himself as the 'child,' the 'boy,' or, progressively, as the 'scholar,' the 'master' — since he was for awhile in his youth a schoolteacher — then as the 'traveller,' or as the 'writer' — yet keeping unbroken always the thread of his own individuality, he has avoided burdening this account of his adventurings along the way with the weight of the most weighty and arrogant of the pronouns.

If you set off with this shaggy, hard-headed, sensitive, high-tempered, mountaineer lad of the back-country of Donegal, you cannot tear away from him until he himself waves you a goodbye at the end of his book. For he shows you the intimate life of a people — members of perhaps the most picturesque race, temperamentally speaking, and certainly the most unpredictable and contradictory, beneath the sun. He takes you into the homes — yes, into the hearts and the passions — of the true Irish people, with all their sweetness, their bitterness, their sentimentality, their prejudices, their vain-glory, their unquenchable patriotism, their memory for old wrongs, their melancholy which is part merriment, and their merriment which often is so deeply melancholy; their hospitality, their generosity, their poverty in things material and wealth in things spiritual; and, most precious heritages of all, their sense of humour, their sense of romance, and their everlasting hope and belief that someday, somehow, their land would be free. The composite picture of his own breed as Seumas draws it shows us creatures who might be mired in a ditch which for deepness and darkness was like a grave, but still looked up to behold a star. The mud of the bogs was on their thighs but it rarely soiled their souls. And the sharp flints of their native hills might cut those naked feet but never it failed to hone to keener edge their mother-wit. Certainly those hard stones, which he likewise trod, sharpened Seumas MacManus' perceptions to the point where he not only could paint a fair likeness of himself but could people the background of the portrait with a multitude of fascinating and colourful bye-actors. The strain of Irish blood in me is pretty well thinned by other Celtic lines, such as Scotch and Welsh, but reading The Rocky Road to Dublin made me, of a sudden, all Irish — and powerfully proud of it.

Irvin S Cobb
Santa Monica

CHAPTER ONE

Jaimie — and the Marquis

The lad who lilted along this cogglesome road, and whose life and memories this book is built around, was Jaimie.

In Glen Ainey he grew — Knockagar of Glen Ainey. Which, as all the world knows, is the heart of Donegal. And the same world knows again that Donegal is the real heart of Ireland — even though 'tis in its high shoulder.

Throngs of pictures crowd the lad's far memory.

The very earliest are of Donegal Bay. One, of a ride on a jaunting-car wedged between his mother and an aunt, and driven by one of the warmest-hearted, most crabbed of uncles, by the waters of the bay, glimmering and shimmering like sheets of tin on a tinker's back — a dog asleep on the pebbles at the lapping water's edge, and a singing burne close by, emptying itself and its song into the shining sea. — Another —linked with the same deceiving bay — is of two drowned fishermen, stiff, and smelling of sea-wrack, laid out on planks in the village market-house, the short, stout man's left shoe gone, showing a darned grey sock, with a square big toe sticking through — the taller man with a scapular straggling from the neck-open of his grey-wool shirt. The strange emotionlessness of the men, and absolute indifference to the awed glances, whisperings and head-shakings of people who stood and moved around, sorley perplexed the child.

But the most impressive of the lad's very early memories was his misfortunate meeting with the Marquis.

The Marquis's grand demesne adjoined Jaimie's father's little farm. (The Marquis would probably have put it the other way round). The Hall House with its thousand blazing windows — anyway there must have been two dozen of them — was a fabled castle to the boy, fascinated by distant glimpses of it when on furtive expeditions in the woods. Yet, as he afterwards learned, it was only a shooting-box for the Great Man, who lived here parts of summer and harvest. (In those years the boy's mind was troubled sore for thinking where or how the poor man and his wife cowered through the bitter winters.)

His Donegal was a wild and rugged, barren country, its only trees in infrequent fertile valleys that the great lords chose as their summer shelters. So, small wonder that our wee *gasúr* — very wee then — a dreamer and a roamer, was infatuated with the Marquis's waving woods, their mysteries and treasures, their rabbits and hares, birds and birds' nests and pheasants' lairs, their sloes and their nuts, haws, blackberries and wild cherries. Always was he roaming and exploring them — always, that is, when a slave-driving father didn't have him kibbing potatoes, stoning meadows, herding cows from the corn, or some other of the hundred persecutions invented for the blighting of young lives and wasting of invaluable days. The hours that the boy saved from servitude he invested in these magic woods which the Marquis, at great expense, maintained for *his* delight and pleasure. For, though it must have cost the Great Man's grandfather thousands of pounds to grow them, and himself a purty penny to game-keep and upkeep them, the great outlay was not for himself, but just for behoof of a certain *gasúr* with patched coat, scratched shins, and muddied bare-feet. The lad, in his constant collecting of the woods' lavish bounty, had never once met their supposed proprietor searching out a bird's nest, climbing a cherry-tree, chasing a rabbit, or packing his pockets with sloes. Altogether, Marquises, though in their own way useful enough members of a community — since without them there would be no woods, and woods-wealth — were yet objects of sincere sympathy : for the child had learned from Jack Hegarty (who ran the messages for the Hall) that Marquises got no dinner at dinner-time, like Christians, but had to wait for it till seven in the evening! Which being the case — even aside from other big drawbacks —Jaimie wouldn't take all the money in the Mint and be a Marquis.

The boy's delight in these woods of his was always tempered by dread of running into the arms of the big, round, rough, gruff, Scotch gamekeeper, Hector McCurdy, the fearful 'br-r-r-r' on whose tongue could, like a buzz-saw, cut into two exact halves the palpitating heart of any little boy surprised in the woods by this ogre.[1]

But, worse than the ogre, it was the Marquis himself that wee Jaimie met on this dread day — the first time and the last that he had ever encountered *him* in the woods. The *gasúr* was raiding a rich sloe-nook that none but himself knew. His pockets were bulged to bursting, and he was trying to fill also the last available hold-all, his stomach when the sound of *brosna*, breaking underfoot told him he was caught. As no mad bull's bellowing was put up behind him, he knew it wasn't the game-keeper. But, to his terror, when he turned around it was worse. There was the Marquis himself, gun under arm, standing square in the neck of the sloe-nook! — a big langling, gangling Marquis, his steely grey eyes boring right into the little boy's breast in front, and out between the shoulder-blades behind!

The frightful Giant of the Castle and his brave little victim — brave, but quaking — stood eyeing each other, that way, without sound or move for a full year — anyhow at the very least a full half-minute — and then the Marquis, who had never before been known to split lips to anyone

4

lower than Esquire,[2] shot at the boy, 'What are *you* doing here?' and on the *you* his terrible eyes were encompassing, from muddy toe to ragged poll, the cowering object before him. The lad opened his mouth but sorra a word would come. Then, after a year — it was surely a year this time — the enraged noble, saying, 'Answer me, you dam little runt!' got hold of his gun in a way that jerked the lad out of his dumbfounder and drove him to sudden action. Now, of course, the Marquis did not intend to shoot.[3] But the *gasúr*, not being sure, made feint to dive past the Marquis to the right; and when, as expected, the man blocked that move, he made dive toward the left. The Marquis, spreading his long legs, frustrated this effort, too; and, not knowing boys very well, considered he had won. But the *gasúr*, despite two hands tied, so to speak — covering the mouths of his bulging coat-pockets to hold the plunder in — made his third and quickest move, always his master-stroke — 'Under the Bridge' he called it — he dived between the Great Man's legs — to freedom!

Unfortunately, it wasn't the clean dive he had intended. Though head and shoulders got through, the lad's hind-quarters, far more than grazing the arching legs, pushed out of balance and over threw the noble gentleman. On a fearful glance over-shoulder the lad beheld a pair of heels kicking high in air; and, worse, immediately heard heart-stopping report of a gun gone off! Protecting hands jerked from his pockets, to grope the hinder part of his pants — which, thank the saints, were found to be as comparatively intact as usual.

In his mad retreat from the Terror, that day, the *gasúr* harvested more cuts, scratches and bruises than normally fell to his lot in six months' unlawful roaming of the woods. And when he sat him down in security on top of Formaoil Hill, applying magic docken leaves to his torn shins, he paused in the medical labour to cast regretful look at the waving woods with castle chimneys above them peeping, and shake his head over the selfishness and cruelty of Marquises who couldn't enjoy their woods, to little boys who would. He vowed that if he should ever become a Marquis, which, to be sure was very, very unlikely — but *if* — he only said *if* — he ever should become one, then for sake of *gasúr* who hungered and thirsted for woods, their treasures and mysteries, he would hang them around with signs reading 'All persons, particularly little boys, are forbidden to NOT trespass, under penalty of the law.'

He never told at home about his fearful adventure and narrow escape. His father would be as mad as a Brocach badger, and there would be sad results. But for a week, he dreaded, day and night, the coming of a regiment of British red-coats with guns and bayonets, in search of the murdering villain who had upset the great Marquis. When he ventured, at length, to confide in and question Jack Hegarty, he learned the sequel: the shot from the gun that had discharged itself when its great owner was upset, missed, by a few feet, the Marquis's heir, Lord Francis, who was on the other side of the sloe-nook — and, still stranger, brought down a pheasant that had been risen by the rumpus! Lord Francis, running to the rescue, found his father recovering his posture — but not his poise. He was in terrible temper and had to be held from going after the escaped lad and giving him the contents of the gun's still-useful barrel. As the old man was the most famous worst shot in the world — couldn't hit a haystack unless he put the gun muzzle against it — and sorely knew that his sporting friends secretly made merry over his marksmanship — his wrath was hell-raising when he learned that his unintended shot had brought down a bird!

The joke-loving Lord Francis — who, by the way, singular in his class, loved the people, and was beloved of them — lost little time telling every servant around the Hall of his father's brilliant shooting that morning! And, during days after, every frightened one of them found it sore to keep a straight face when meeting the Old Marquis — who well suspected what his chase-grace son would be doing. Jack Hegarty told our lad that Lord Francis, when he set the servants roaring with description of his father's miraculous shot, announced, 'If any of you can discover for me the *gasúr* who upset my father, and if you find that he's hire-able at any price within reason, I want to engage him to run in and out among my father's legs, during the shooting season.'

Jaimie weighed the proposition as seriously as he believed it to be meant — but, after due thought, decided to reject it. It mightn't at all be the bird the Marquis would hit next time.

NOTES

1 Throughtout his boyhood the lad learned to know that all stewards and gamekeepers of all lords in Donegal were Scotch — brought over from Scotland because these lords wanted trustworthy people.After he had become a man, and, travelling abroad, went to see the residence of one of the most famous of Scotland's aristocracy, Abbotsford (where Walter Scott's descendants now dwell), he was non-plussed to find that their steward was O'Flynn from the County Leitrim — brought all the way from Ireland because this great Scotch family wanted a trustworthy person!

2 The statement is not literally true. The Marquis did not speak, once before, to a plain man. Very early one morning, he met the rascal Hughie Dougherty — a noted poacher — prowling too close to his woods. 'May I ask, sirrah,' deamanded the Marquis, 'what's taking you abroad so early in the morning?' The rascal Hughie had the boldness to reply, 'And might I ask what your honour's self is doing abroad so early in the mornin'?' Snapped the Marquis, 'I'm out to get an appetite for my breakfast'. Replied Hughie, 'A meself's out to get a br'akwist for me appetite'.

3 For full generation before the boy's day, it had come to be considered not only uneconomic, but almost immoral, to kill a tenant — even to cripple him. The very government had now come to advocate their preserving.

CHAPTER TWO

The Fair

But the boy's *very* first recollection is of a fair — of his sitting on a chair in the window of a little house that was his home — stuck on a knowe above the village street — viewing a street packed with all the people in the universe, milked with cows and yowes, dogs and pigs and donkeys, apple carts and dilisk-stands — everything that mind of man could imagine; and hearing the mighty hub-bub of people shouting, cows rowting, pigs squealing, sheep bleating, dogs barking, donkeys braying, sheep- men whistling, hucksters yelling — *roolye-boolye* such as never before on earth was heard, and never could again. He saw the sudden uprising, above the crowds' heads, now here, now there, of clumps of sticks, waving, flourishing in the air, sometimes crossing and clashing, sometimes not, before subsiding and disappearing again.[1]

Fairs were to furnish the big excitement for Jaimie's young life. The fair-day was a wonderful day, for him, entirely — and for all of Glen Ainey. It was supposed to be for buying and selling, but that was small part of it. For people like him, who viewed fairs in the right way, while there was fun to be sure at the bargaining for pigs and mooly cows, far more was the joy of beholding light-hearted crowds come together, men, women, boys, girls, meeting and treating, sporting, courting, sometimes matchmaking — and, still more, the hucksters and the gamesters gathered from all airts and parts to make the countryside a holiday. Everyone came dressed in his best, and anyone who hadn't any best, for that day borrowed it.[2]

Our boy watched the fair-goers crowd in — the mountain men, in blue broadcloth, or grey homespun — mostly their own hand- woven — the women, the well-to-do of them in long, blue, deep-hooded, deep-fluted Spanish cloaks, the majority shawled and white-capped — beautifully white, and beautifully frilled and starched caps that framed sweet, clear-skinned, deep-wrinkled faces — the shawled girls, with lovely heads of well-combed shining hair be-ribboned, and a bright ribbon around the neck. Nearly all the females carried shoes in hand till they reached the Lazy Bush — great, ancient thorn-bush by the town's edge — where they sat down on the road's green marge and donned them — after rinsing their feet in the near-by burne. The men, however, despite the inconvenience, walked in unaccustomed shoes — all except those from the Fall of Sru-Aill who, refusing to suffer for seven miles, carried their shoes over-shoulder. Well did the child know the grand riddle so often posed among

7

the little ones by the fireside, 'Where do the shoes first blister a Sru-Aill man?' — and the answer 'Between the two shoulders.'

But the sight that pleased the boy best was that of the more prosperous mountain couples who rode their nags to town, the old man in bright-buttoned blue swallow-tail, tall hat, tight knee-breeches, grey stockings and low brogues — his wife, blue-cloaked, deep-hooded, pillioned behind him, a basket on one arm, and the other clasping for support her good man's waist.

A treat to our *gasúr* was the hargle-bargle in the cow-market, where asker and bidder would seem, at beginning, as unlikely to meet as Cruach Owenach and Cruach Conallach, the pair of mountains menacing each other across Barnish Mor Gap — and would wrangle and rage at each other like the west and the east winds meeting and beating in that wild gap on March's first day. Excited, he watched men hold them, collar and elbow, from clashing one minute, and from separating forever the next — till, the mediators in general and the Split-the-differ in particular, bringing them inch by inch nearer, got them to meet exactly half-way between the first asking and first bidding. Then everybody, heartily satisfied, clumped to the nearest public-house, to cement the bargain.

Little Jaimie had more than one early bargaining experience of his own in the fair. He couldn't have been more than six or seven when he tried to help Eddlie Cuinn dispose of the old horse that time out of mind had served him for cadging fish from door to door the country over. A likely buyer was disputing with its owner the animal's mystical age, the latter asserting, 'The baste's only in his teens,' while the other, swearing his years were beyond count, called Eddlie a liar. Here our child indignantly intervened — 'You're calling good Eddlie a liar, and you knowing the horse less than five minutes, while Eddlie knows him thirty years.' 'right you are, *avic-0!*' (0 son) replied the stranger. 'And 'twould be mortal sin to part a lovin' pair that have grown anshint together.— Good luck to him and his ould ruin !' — flicking the animal with his rod, and marching off. Eddlie, for all that he was rough-appearing, had a very gentle streak in his nature: his sole reprimand was, 'Chile, dear, while I'm selling this baste take care if ye open your mouth again not to put both your feet in it, and then plump yourself afther.'

But if he wasn't a remarkable salesman, he proved himself an in-genuous buyer. Once, he bought four black-face sheep from a mountain man after cleverly beating him down from twenty-five to twenty-two shillings and six-pence for the lot. His complete capital, a penny, he then put in the surprised man's hand, saying, 'I'll pay you this much now. You take the sheep home till they grow up, and when I sell them then, I'll pay you the other twenty-two and fippence' — an entirely new, ingenious plan for amassing riches which, curiously, had never been thought of in

8

Donegal fair before. Like most mountain people this man was again' all new ideas: he threw his penny at the boy, and got of a string of Gaelic that not the densest Beurla speaker (English) could possibly mistake for a prayer.

The lad saw the shy Glen Ainey girls form rows on both sides of the street, whispering and blushing when the boys and young men in twos and threes, very straight and stiff, paraded up and down past-casting side-glances at the blushing rows. Most all of them as brave, usually, as the badgers on their hills, the boys were now as frightened as sheep, before the batteries of beauty. But after a time he saw the boys surmount their shyness, and the girls discard their aloofness, while they paired for a happy fair-day.

On the Stannins (canvas-covered street-stands) one bought for a penny or tuppence — that is, of course, if one had a penny or tuppence — any *fairlie* that the heart of man could desire. Always the Stannins drew Jaimie's heart and held it. Along with their thousand *fairlies*, they tempted (in days a little later) with infinite variety of fascinating literature — at least a dozen tuppenny and thruppenny chap-books, put out by Publisher Warren of Dublin Quays. There were, the Harp of Erin Song Book (itself worth a guinea if it was worth a penny), Valentine and Orson, The True History of Freney the Robber, Paul and Virginia, Hibernian Nights, Irish Rogues and Rapparees, The Seven Champions of Christendom, Old Moore's Almanac, and others equally entrancing. From these classics, the Stannin's literary exhibit for years without end, Jaimie, after he was able to read, got infinite intellectual pleasure. He didn't buy the books, couldn't buy them — their possession was for the wealthy who had sold a cow or a pig. On many fair days he had a penny to sport and spend — which, in presence of all the million allurements of the fair, entailed budgetting that was brain-racking. But the chap-books were ever beyond his financial ability. Yet not lost to him for all that: by persistent industry he got to know the contents of all the books. Of the constant crowd that lined the front of Paddy MacBrearty's Stannin, viewing with wonder its wares, our *gasúr* was perhaps the most constant unit — his place always at that left-hand corner where the world's literature was displayed. Posing as a potential investor, he availed himself of a buyer's right to sample the goods; and would snatch the contents of a page, sometimes three, before being driven away by the ever-haunting dread that Paddy would next minute be demanding to know if his intentions were honourable — but in phraseology somewhat less polite. In very busy hours, when Paddy's attention was engrossed by nimble business, and that, besides, the great merchant was then well-pleased with the world and indulgent to its denizens, the boy could, by breathless gulping, devour ten or twelve pages without undue strain on his nerves. On winter fair-days his bare feet, to

9

be sure, would get frozen and numb from standing in the snow-slush; but he could always run home and thaw out the provoking underpins in the heart of the flame of the turf fire — and be quick back to his duty. So, by fearfully-joyous snatches down the years of his childhood and early boyhood Jaimie managed to get practically by heart the treasures of the dozen chap-books of C. M. Warren, may God rest him! And rest poor Paddy, the Stannins man, too!

The yelling, shouting, jesting apple-hucksters drew him — aloft on their carts counting loudly the great penny-worth of apples that they piled on hands and arms — 'Here's wan (one) for Rosie, wan for Biddy, and two for the cat, wan apiece for Micky and Sheila and Pat, wan for your brother, wan for your mother, three for yourself, and wan to carry ye home! — Sold again ! Sold again! to the wee woman in the big bonnet, and five purty daughters at her elbow that she intends to fortune with thirteen pence apiece and a row of corker pins!' — 'Sold again! Sold again! to a squint-eyed, string-halted gintleman with a bad spavin, an income of three hundred a year and a private tailyer that he keeps drunk from Christmas to Christmas!' — 'Sold again! Sold again! to the hand-somest, winsomest, purtiest *cailin* walks the fair — if she only didn't have flappin' ears and flat feet!' — 'Roll up! roll up! and open both your pockets and your mouths for another big penn'orth!'

And there were the games and gamesters — enthralling always. 'Pick the thimble, gintlemen, and win a fortune. Just missed! But no blame to you, my brave young sport: the most masterful minds the world ever knew make mistakes and many of them; but there's few of them such splendid sports as you, me little hairo, who are always willing to try, try, try again. We'll give you another chance to win back your money. Faint heart never won fortune. There it goes again — in there. Now a quick eye and an open purse — them's all ye want and all ye need to win fame, name, and fortune besides, at this board, which is patrionized by born ladies and bred gintlemen, and the crowned heads of Europe, Asia, Africay, Australiay, and the County Tipperary. — To do all things fair, square, and above board is our motive; for although we're poor we are dishonest, and pay all winnin's in goold; exceptin' large sums, for which we give a cheque upon Taigy Raigan's turf-bank. — And now, again, sir, I'll wager ye any bet, from one shillin' to the Bank of Ireland, that ye don't find the pea.'

This gamester, to be sure, had a little of the Black Art. Jaimie's mother often told him of the Black Art Book which initiated God-forsaken ones — but which, despite its devilish intent, must, on its very title-page, warn the sinfully curious,

> *'You may peruse me, but do not use me,*
> *Or Hell will be your end'* .

10

In a fair, later, the lad was to see a complete Black Art man, who before everybody's eyes did a thousand things that it was impossible for earthly man to do. — He chewed and ate and swallowed fire, and after smacking his lips over it, blew it out of his mouth and nostrils again (which after all was natural enough for a bad man in colludher with the One that he was in colludher with). He made old Micky Manachan sit on a box and lay six duck eggs. He threw half a crown in the air, made it disappear, and then from the skirt-pocket of poor Molly McGrady — whom everybody knew to be as honest as the sun — took the same half-crown — in view of the whole fair ! It was the thrillingest exhibition of the Evil One's power that our boy and the whole fair had ever witnessed. The man gathered hatfuls and hatfuls of pennies ; for though it was sinful to pay him, none dared refuse. 'You have your choice,' he told them plainly, 'either to contribute a free-will penny or have me call pounds from your pockets into my own. I'm a good-hearted man even if I do work through me good friend, Lucifer, and not greedy, and would ten times sooner have a penny with your good wish on it than a pound with your grudge.' They all jostled to get their pennies into the hat, quick. Only Jaimie, who having just one bare penny to lose might as well take a chance: he held tight grip on the coin, in his pocket — and the Black Art man entirely forgot it!

For long time after, Jaimie was distressed for thinking of the fate ahead of that unfortunate man. He wondered how hatfuls and hatfuls of money, although they gave him command of all the world's pleasures just now, could yet give him any real joy, with hell's gates waiting wide for him the instant he died!

But one of the *gasúr's* greatest joys in the fair was the ballad- singers. When they appeared, he was always in the thick of the crowd that listened absorbedly to their chanting the story of the latest murder, or fishermen's drowning, or the wonderful deeds of great Daniel O'Connell —

> *'O'Connell, our hairo, he planted a tree,*
> *Sayin', 'Irishmen, whack away! die or be free!'*

And, at a ha'penny apiece the ballad-singer was putting his ballads into scores of eager hands. Yet, with the traditional caution of all sound financiers, our lad listened to all the ballads in the fair before investing. But if his treasury was exhausted when a particularly good ballad rang out, he followed the ballad-singer up and down the fair till he had it by heart.

In the boy's mind there always lingered one mournful incident linked up with fair memories. On a bright May morning that was a fair-day of Donegal village he was sitting on a stone at the Knockagar crossroads, watching a game of handball between two bigger *buachaillíni*,[3] when a

11

little country-boy driving his father's cow to the fair, asked which road he should take to Donegal. Tom McGrady, who was a vagabond anyway, directed the boy to take the Doorin road — leading away from Donegal! Our *gasúr*, grieving, would have run after the boy, but the vagabond Tom threatened him, 'I'll knock your two eyes into one, if you don't hunker down again, and stick your advice in your stomach.' So he had to sit in sad silence, watching the boy drive his cow out of sight on a road that could never, never bring him to Donegal!

For years after, Jaimie, awakening in dead of night, would wonder, In what part of the world, now, is that poor boy, with his cow? — wandering on, and on, and on, hoping that round the next turn he'll surely see the Donegal that, alas, he is next to find!

NOTES

1 Later, the lad would learn that these were casual demonstrations from the backers of both parties, at a sale where buyer and seller struck a snag in their long hard bargaining over a cow or a yowe (ewe). When Jaimie came to know more about people and fairs, he found that the age of real stick-fighting had passed just before his arrival, and that now only a few veterans were left to lament the loss of a heroic sport. Supple Sweeny, one of the proudest of these relicts vividly pictured to our lad the enthusiasm at the old fair of the Purt — 'If ye flung a sciach (flat wicker basket) from the top window of Tom Meehan's public house 'twould take a hour to find the ground, for all the sticks that were in the air. — Ye can see for yourself a granite rock on the road-side by Partholan MacKaye's, a hundred yards this side of the Purt — every mountain man comin' to the fair tried his blackthorn on this rock, and if it broke, he went home'.

Fighting was high-spirited sport then as boxing is today, and, as in boxing, accidents sometimes occurred. Of a poor man's trial for head-breaking at this famous fair, the story is told how when a doctor had testified that the victim had an extraordinarily thin skull, what doctors know as 'a paper skull', the prisoner's counsel, turning to the judge, indignantly asked, 'And I ask Lordship what possible business a man with a skull like that could have at the fair of the Purt'?

2 There was a neighbouring district, Doorin, peopled by Protestant descendants of the Scotch Planters on whom James 1 had bestowed every fertile patch amid Donegal hills — after driving the Irish to the moors, bogs, and barren cruachs. Here was a colony of struggling Methodists, very earnest, worthy people much joked about by their fellow-Protestants. On a night before a fair of Knockagar, the itinerant preacher who from time to time served them, visited and was lodged as usual in the poor cottage of Jane Anne McClay and her good man Wullie John. (Half of Doorin always knew when the preacher was arriving, for they could hear the great-lunged Wullie John from the top of Dhrimgarman Hill — where he was digging his potatoes — announce it to Jane Anne a quarter of a mile below — 'Put another herrin' on the tongs, Jane Anne, I see the praicher comin' down the road'.) When the preacher, awakening on this fair morning, would hurry on to his next little isolated flock, twenty miles away, he couldn't find his trousers. After searching till his bare legs were chilled, he covered himself properly in bed again and called for Jane Anne. 'Mrs McClay, I regret to tell you that a most mysterious occurence has transpired. I left my nether garment on the chair before I got into bed last night, but now it is nowhere to be found'. 'Arrah,

praicher sir', Jane Anne answered, 'lie snug in the bed for a couple of hours and I'll bring you your brakwist, and your Bible to entertain you. Wullie John hadn't a pair o'trousers fit to be seen in the fair, so borrowed yours to stand in. He'll have them home in good time, for my man's a jenny-wine Methodist who never lets night find him in a fair'.

3 A buachailín is a little fellow. A big fellow is a buachal. Gasúr is the equivalent of buachaillín.

CHAPTER THREE

At the Tullen-A-Grainne Wedding

His first wedding was, to the child, not only a sight for sore eyes, but fed him adventures within an adventure

The bride, Nelly Glacan of Tullen-a-Grainne, was the lad's own third cousin. His mother, going to the wedding, fetched him with her. They went the seven miles on the jaunting-car of his uncle, Billy MacAteer. Jaimie was stuck in the car's well behind, legs dangling over — for there was more than a load on both sides. Molshie Logan, a widow woman lively as a cricket, who would give a year of her life for a wedding spree, was left for want of room — though she begged hard to be let double herself in the well and nurse the boy. But Billy, a crabbed man, gave Molshie an unsweet bit of his mind — 'In troth and it'll do your soul good to miss one weddin' for a change. Stay at home, sweep your kitchen corners that haven't seen a besom for seven years, and comb the cobwebs out o' your hair'.

As the *gasúr's* party sighted Litir Barra bridge they found there, not alone their own groom's party, but a pair of grooms' parties — awaiting two brides' parties. For it was the Monday at Lent's gate when many wedding parties would be thronging the ways. The two grooms' parties had mingled and exchanged drinks; and to the music of their fiddlers, they were, each boy and girl of one, footing the dance on the bridge with some girl and some boy of the other, crowd.

Our lad's friends — who were headed for the wedding-house, not the Chapel — drew up for the fun on the bridge — and weren't long there till Jamie saw his cousin Nelly's party descending a distant hillside, fording the Ainey Water at the Steppin' Stones, streaming over the meadows and along a by-way to the bridge. It was a thrilling sight to him. A fiddler led them, diddling his elbow for all he was worth: and to his music boys of the party stepped and skipped and swayed, relieving themselves now and then of a shout and a cry — but some of them whistled to keep the fiddler company. The boy liked to observe one low-set little man with beard like a hill of whins, a short leg that made him go hipplety-hop, hipplety-hop, when he walked — who every now and then jumped in the air, and for joy at every jump put out of him a *screagh!* that could be heard the other side of Carn-na-Maoin. Dinny the Smith, they called him.

The girls carried shawls, folded over arm, and showed bright colours, brightest of which were the ribbons that bound their lovely heads. All of them were bareheaded, even the bride herself, a black-haired, blushing *cailín* who had a cashmere shawl on her arm, and with her bridesmaid, headed the procession following the fiddler. Her fiddler was the famous Donal a- Thoorish, beloved of seven parishes. On either side of the procession marched men carrying whiskey jars and, each of them, an eggshell — for the treating of everyone in every house they passed, and of everyone who ran cheering down the hills. When the crowds met upon the bridge each one in each party, must take a sup — or at least touch the shell to his lips — from the other party's stewards. After Nelly Glacan's party came, the second bride's party streamed in sight, down a steep slope to the left, headed by a piper, whose skirling music rolled down the hill and echoed up the valley. And the sight and sound drew, from the crowd on the bridge, cries and shouts and cheers that swept the moors for miles away! For Jaimie, who had never before, even at a fair, seem or heard anything like it, it opened a world that was stirring to his soul.

To the piper's playing, now, all the weddin'eers began dancing. And when the piper had had his fill, three fiddlers took up the music for a gathering growing every minute greater — for, down the hills and up the valleys the lad beheld boys and girls, old men and little children, who deserted their homes — and women who left their work undone — thronging to swell the crowd, and share the fun, congratulate the brides and grooms, and lift a cup to their long life and good health.

After watching the united parties dance their fill on the bridge and then set off for the Chapel, Jaimie's car and car-load headed on to the wedding-house. The Glacans, well-to-do, and making great feast for their daughter, had put three houses under it — their own home where terrific cooking was going on, both in its kitchen and two rooms, their big barn which was cleared of its everything for the eating and drinking, and a neighbour's house, Linty MacRoddy's, borrowed for the music and dancing.

Through all three houses the *gasúr* had the time of his life, himself and a yellow mongrel which made up to him on his arrival and didn't part with him till he left. In Condy Mór Glacan's kitchen — where chiefly was the cooking — over a great turf-fire on a wide hearth that could roast a cow, a sheep and a pig at one time — was a throng of people getting in one another's way and provoking a dozen cooks who were dashing this way and that, each with a dish, a spoon, or a knife in her hand. The cooks were tripping over, and putting bad prayers on, everyone, alike guests and beggars (for all the beggars of the barony were there congregated). There was shouting and talking and laughing and drinking and calling and cooking, and the Lord only knows what else, making an immortal hub-bub, enough to delight any youngster's heart — or any oldster's. Indeed, the lightest-hearted that the lad saw there, and the most jubilant and at times most obstreperous, was Conn of the Hillhead, a little man who counted a hundred and two years behind him, and who, later, at the dance

15

in Lanty's, challenged the bride to face him in a jig, put her to shame for nimbleness, kissed her and planked her on the groom's knee — and then dared thee next conceitiest girl in the house to dance him a planxty. And when his challenge had daunted the best of them he sat down to wild cheering.

The feast was served on half-mile-long tables that filled thee big barn from door to gable and nearly from side to side: yet, even at that, the diners had to sit down in relays every hour, so many were the wedding guests. It was during the progress of this dinner that there happened to the *buachaillin* the things that made most memorable his first mountain wedding.

Whilst, close followed by the faithful mongrel, he was busily trying to miss nothing, but keep under observations the activities of three wedding houses, Jaimie discovered, laid to cool, on a low stone-wall between Condy Mor's and the barn, a dish of some tempting concoction wherewith he had never before made acquaintance. It was — he was long afterward to know — a rare dessert that the chief cook, Susie Kincaid, had learned to make in America, and now specially prepared as surprise for beloved old Father Mick, who would preside at the feast. All unsuspecting the jealousy with which cooks guard the integrity of their dishes, and finding that no matter what was this food it smelt good, Jaimie decided to sample it. By a coincidence, not startling, the ashy mongrel made the same decision at the same time. And both of them fell to it. The lad, for want of a spoon, found fair substitute in a trowel that stuck from a near-by wall. The dog did very well with his nose. Agreeably they began at opposite ends of the dish, and — for both of them found it remarkably tasty — were giving good promise of meeting in the middle when Jaimie suddenly felt himself grabbed by the neck and his nose stuck deep in the dish — not nose alone, but mouth, eyes, whole face bogged in it. In the same instant he heard his table-companion squattering off, leaving in his wake a line of fearful yowls, which told he had been well kicked. — 'Sweet bad luck to you, ye young divil's imp!' an angry woman was praying above the quaking lad — 'Ye've gone and destructioned the beautifullest combustible Susie Kincaid ever boiled or baked — Father Mick's blue- mong!'

Jaimie, tearing himself loose, and tearing off after the dog — blindly, for his eyes were sealed and whole face plastered with the combustible in three leaps landed in the encompassing, unfragrant mire of a du'ghill!

Amid the uproar of the main wedding house the *gasúr* was, by two patient old women, rinsed and washed and rehabilimented in odds and ends of apparel collected from generous guests and surrounding houses. And, when renovated, he found himself ready for his next adventure — which indeed was not far to seek.

The immortal hullabaloo which had held the kitchen all day happened

16

to be heightened at the moment the boy found himself newly arrayed —
only made still more confounding by a quarrel sprung up between two of
the multitude of beggars, voluntary wedding-guests — the Bacach Rua,
a long red-headed marteen-legged fellow, and a spiteful old hussy, well
named Biddy the Pite. The lad, always of an inquisitive turn of mind, drew
to the scene, seeking enlightenment. Across a stool on which sat a cup of
yellow liquid, plainly the cause of the wrangle, he beheld the Bacach and
Biddy berating each other, threatening, daring, denouncing — whilst their
stout sticks flourished, and sometimes clashed. Noting that the contents
of the disputed cup looked like a beautiful drink which he called goose-
lime (plain people called it lime-juice) — delightful drink whereto Tom
Kelly, the publican, often treated him — the boy stepped between the
disputants, took a *shlug* of the disputed liquid, only to find that it wasn't
goose-lime at all, but something that burned and tore his mouth and throat,
causing him to eject it again — while, in impulsive disgust, he flung the
cup and its contents into the fire. Two sticks that had been in the air,
instantly descended on the boy's back, fetching from him a wild, wild
yell!! Through the door he dashed — and across the yard, hotly pursued
by two scolding, storming, cursing ex-disputants, now ardent allies, who
had quickly elected as common enemy the boy whose skull they strove to
crack. Always a champion sprinter, Jaimie out-stripped them as far as the
barn-door — but, alas, inside there was little chance of further escape!
The tables that nigh filled the floor were jammed with eager eaters, and
the side-walls jam-packed with rows of voluble unseated guests; between
and among whom dozens of women attendants, carrying tea- pots, toasts,
roasts, piles of empty dishes, were almost vainly trying to shoulder,
squeeze, scold, and fight a passage. At a glance the boy took in the difficult
situation; but seeing a momentarily vacant chair at end of the table next
the entrance, bounded on it, from it to the table, and, thence, as best he
could pick his steps among lakes of soup, hills of potatoes, and mountains
of roasts, fry, and boils, stumbled and ran the long table's center toward
his mother who sat close by the presiding Father Mick at the table's head.

Because of the eating and drinking and joking and laughing, general
merry-making and up-roar whereto the guests abandoned themselves,
even the flying *gasúr* was taken little notice of by anyone in the populous
lines betwixt which he swept — or stumbled — in break-neck flight. His
mother, who in all her life never missed anything that was ludicrous, saw
him, and set up hearty laugh at a lad — whom she didn't yet recognize
because of his new habiliments — tearing his way up the table-top. Father
Mick, who likewise seldom missed a good thing, joined her enjoyment,
and shouted to the oncoming one, 'Stop, stop, *mo bhuachaillin!* This place
is too public for coming to confession.' The lad's foot struck a dish of
potatoes that staggered him; but would have regained his balance if some

17

good-for-nothing jokester at the left hadn't reached out, grabbed his ankle, and given it a jerk that threw him completely off balance, and plopped him head down and heels up in his mother's lap in which humiliating position he hearkened to a thunderous roar of laughter from a million diners who had turned to enjoy the sight of a pair of dirty heels kicking high in air!

When he got right side up, again, he beheld the Bacach Rua and Biddy, far down at the door, brandishing sticks at him and roaring vows of vengeance that would be wreaked as soon as ever they'd get their 'tin commandments,' on him. And the boy still recalls the curious words of the Bacach when, after Denis Lafferty, the kest Man, had risen angrily and shouted at them 'Get out, you ill-mannered divils, or I'll go down there and throw yous out!' — he answered back, through his teeth, 'You think yourself a consaity fella, Dinis Lafferty, but just come outside with me and throw me out, if you dar'.'

That both the beggars were more venomous against him than they ought to be, was — though the lad didn't then know it — because of misfortune they met at start of their dash. They had jundied in the kitchen-door, and upset, Susie the cook, entering with a pot of tea in one hand and jug of milk in the other; and when she, in revenge, dealt Biddy a real scalding of the hot tea, and smashed the crockery over the Bacach's skull, their sufferings the enraged ones would lay at the innocent lad's door.

But Jaimie's little mishaps were forgotten in the deep sleep he had, doubled up in the car-well, on the way home from a wedding that everyone else on Billy MacAteer's car — if he could only have heard them — were loud-praising as the proudest wedding they ever went to.

CHAPTER FOUR

School

Jaimie's school was famous among its mountain fellows, for its roof was of slates. Besides, it was more than six foot to the eaves, and had windows that opened. It was eleven yards long, and half as wide; and its population varied from sixty bare-foot boys in the summer — when for most there was work to be done at home — to ninety, and a hundred, and a hundred and ten, in the winter. Its Master was the envy of the mountains: he drew a salary of twenty-four pounds a year — and school-pennies over and above.

The first inkling of school in Jaimie's memory is in connection with a tea-party given in it by kind Lord Francis, the first such feast ever known in Glen Ainey — and the last for long years. Our boy was too young to go to it, but he well recalls the luckier, larger youngsters, each with a tin porringer, joyously thronging there. And he well remembers the news brought home again, that while every other youngster had his tinpandy for the tea service — cups, though, in the case of a few aristocrats whose fathers kept shops — Paudyeen Haraghey, from Drim-a-Loscy, fetched a wooden noggin.

On his first school-day the terror that sight of such an edifice would naturally inspire in the breast of a would-be-student of five, was augmented by a roar from it which, even five fields away, out-roared the waterfall of Sru-Aill Mountain. The lad was to find that the noise came from four-score of throats strenuously swallowing the lore dispensed in Glen Cuach National School. The great big Master, with spectacles on nose and rod in hand, soothed the lad and put him to warm his hands and toes by the turf bonfire that was blazing on the hearth. Like his brother, and every other boy, Jaimie had carried under arm two turf, the daily tribute to the school-fire. For, he knew that bringing turf every morning was as important as bringing books; and the rare one who defaulted was denied five minutes hand- warming by the fire. Our *gasúr*, an honest boy always, was to learn that wicked ones who lived three and four miles away, and put ease above honesty, often waited for their turf till they came nigh the school, and then helped themselves from the turf-stacks of decent, hard-working people. Such boys usually burst into school breathless — oftentimes pursued by an outraged, scolding, bellowing man, who proclaimed that the fellow he followed held a devil as big as a hedge-hog.

Many of the scholars — for scholar was the modest title bestowed on every pupil from his first school-day — came distances of four, and even five, miles to school — almost all of them bare-footed both summer and winter. A few puffed-up lads, of whom Jaimie was one, owned winter shoes, but, regarding the honour as not worth the handicap, saved them for going to mass on Sunday. Neither Jaimie nor any of them was clothed in luxury — but the want didn't worry them: there were often more air holes than anything else to their clothing, and more than one could boast, without strain, that the smallest hole in his britches was the one he put his leg through. Yet, it was long, long years later before it struck Jaimie as strange that scores of light-hearted lads from far mountain valleys came, soaked to the skin from rain, snow, and sleet, and by their own body-heat dried themselves out, complete, during school-hours. Our lad and the other lads had heard of overcoats, but the rare sight of one on a man's back told them at once that the wearer was a doctor, a school inspector, or a king in disguise. Jaimie was soon to learn that the lads who came from the remoter glens — each as full of deviltry as an egg was full of meat — lads who, coming or going, raided turf stacks, turnip fields, gardens that grew beans, and laid flags atop of chimneys to choke the inmates — were as hard and hardy as the flint of their own hills: and though our boy's comrades of the lowlands and by the seashore had no mean opinion of their own hardihood, these rascally mountaineers regarded them as *girseachs* (little girls).

Jaimie laid on the Master's desk, that first Monday morning of his school-career, a big brown penny — along-side a heap of sixty brown pennies, already laid down by sixty other lads — weekly tribute to the Master. The great heap of gold dazzled a little boy who, till then, didn't dream there was so much money in the world. Indeed the Master, fearing rumours of his too-great riches, took pains to explain to the school that morning — as he did on many Monday mornings — that he wasn't at all the wealthy man people thought, for between feeding and clothing and rearing a family of eight, and buying a weekly paper, and paying a ha'penny every Sunday at the Chapel-gate, he needed all the money he got. Even, he said — but this was plainly for rhetorical effect — he could use more if he had it!

That the Master was a most learned man, Jaimie realized when he heard him in the class that day, teach Spellins-and-Meanins to lads who, already a couple of months at school, were advanced scholars — and though the neophyte hadn't known any letter of the alphabet except *a*, he mastered, complete, three Spellins-and-Meanins before school was let out — 'R-a-t, rat, a species of vermin.' 'C-a-t, cat, an animal of the tiger kind.' 'C-o-w, cow, a quadruped.' He also learned, that day three other alphabet letters whose fine sound he liked — Haitch, Jaw, and Izzed.

But the alphabet was mostly taught by the Master's son who, Jaimie was to find, was a more popular teacher than his father: for, grudging a minimum of time to an unexciting subject, he devoted most of his hour to guesses, and two popular class competitions — 'Whoever tells the funniest story goes up head,' and 'Whoever tells the biggest lie goes up head.' Jaimie recalls that the man who went triumphantly to head of the class in the latter competition, was Anthony McAnulty, the Marquis's gardener's son — who told, 'There aren't nineteen rats at the Hall.' Since everyone knew that the Hall rats, if they ever made up their minds to move away, could carry with them on their backs the Hall and all in it, no child grumbled at Anthony's getting the prize.

The boy's artistic career began when, his class sitting down in the desks with slate and pencil, he was set to copy off the blackboard a headline of Pothooks-and-Hangers — the loops and crooks and double-crooks to which all literary aspirants spent their apprenticeship before daring the mysteries of the twenty-four Phoenician symbols. When the Master, examining his Pothooks- and-Hangers, named Jaimie an ignoramus, he was feeling mighty proud — till an envious neighbour told him that iggerammis was a scolding word, meaning he would never learn to write while there was a bill on a crow.

On that very first school-day our lad tagged on one of the mountain boys a nickname that stuck to him ever after. In the seat behind Jaimie one of these mountain vags, whom he heard people call Charlie, skewered a pin through the tough underskin of his big toe and gave our *gasúr* a stab behind that made him yell. 'What's the matter with you?' the Master yelled back. 'Charlie stabbed me with a pin in his big toe.' 'Charlie who?' Our *gasúr*, unacquainted with his enemy's cognomen, but noting the loud pattern of the boy's distinctive habiliment — the slip that covered all petticoated country-boys from neck to ankle — answered, 'Charlie with the checker slip.' That fellow's real name was in one uproarious moment tacitly declared extinct by four-score loud-yelling scholars, and in time forgotten; but Charlie-with-the-Checker-Slip is still remembered in Glen Ainey though in his early manhood, long ago, he quitted Donegal and Ireland forever.[1]

On that day, too, our *buachaillin* earned his first fee as a *shanachie* (story-teller). A youngster who, from somewhere in the back regions crept under the desks, plucked our lad's tail, and offered him a broken, but very alluring, bit of blue glass — that made all the world beautiful when you looked through it — to tell him the story of Murroghoo Mór and Murroghoo Beag. Here our lad was at home, for though there were in school that day more than four-score other youngsters who could make a hare of him in many accomplishments, there weren't five of them could hold a candle to him at story-telling.

And he learned that the school's submarine activities — as they might well be named — were the most flourishing and most fascinating of school life. Underneath the desks, not only were fairy stories and fables exchanged, and ballads traded, but there was a rich commerce in trogging of all the varied merchandise transported in boys' pockets — even to their *bit* (lunch), which changed hands for a whipcord or a handball or a young hedgehog complete in the glory of his three hundred spikes. There, too, on this day, our lad paid — with his blue glass — for tuition in the monkey-dance, a difficult, but enchanting performance done on one's hunkers: there, too, were formed combines for robbing orchards and bean fields: and after-school fights were arranged by ambassadors, on stomach crawling to and fro between likely combatants. The *gasúr* was matched to fight Bernie Griffin, a boy he had never before seen or heard tell of — and whom he wasn't to see till they faced each other in the fighting field, when he found Bernie half as big again as himself. Indeed, Jaimie wasn't a fighter by nature, and didn't want to fight, but only from fear agreed — fear of losing regard from his fellows, and being dubbed *coward*.

The boy was yet to learn that individual fights, a minor joy, were put back on a day when that major joy, a stoning match, was arranged — always between the boys who should head home for the mountains, and those who should head for the sea. Two-inch roadstones were the ammunition; and since, from persistent practice, the combatants had marvelous power of arm and accuracy of aim, the nimbleness of mountain goats and vision of hawks were in order when, the rage of battle possessing the combatants, the deadly missiles began *whooming* through the air. The mountaineers, of tougher fibre, prevailed over the fishermen, and drove them deep into their own territory — sometimes to the very sea, in ignominious rout. Our *buachaillin*, of the shore side, was, in days yet ahead, to do his bit on many a hard-fought field, and win a host of battle scars that were mighty useful for hardening of his head.

But it was that first school-day of our brave *buachaillin* we were dealing with, and its reserved, individual private fights — in contradistinction to the general public ones free to all comers. The matches were staged in Cormac Keeny's field, just beyond the Lazy Bush — which marked the limit of the Master's domain. Oftener than there were hairs on his head was our lad to hear the Master drive it into the boys, and when necessary rivet it with a stick, that every scholar must hold in his heart the peace of God as far as the Lazy Bush. 'After you have put that mark behind you,' he would say, 'you're welcome to eat one another alive, leaving only a thighbone to tell the tale. And from the bottom of my heart I pray God to hurry that blessing.'

After school, this day, at the foot of the Brown Knowe, our boy fought his brave fight — and got thrashed by a much bigger boy. Though the battle blows were painful and he was hoping in his heart each blow would be the last, he dare not, would not, let the joyous baiters know that he suffered. But oh, it was a relief from Heaven when, after he had got one closed eye, a lip split, a nose spurting blood, and five knock-downs, big Dinny Moohan (who favoured him) pulled Bernie Griffin off his back, declared it a drawn battle, and shouted for the next pair of glory-contenders to step into the bloodied ring.

Though hardly was there a boy at Knockagar who hadn't a nickname — our lad had come to school that day without one — yet did not undistinguished go home. He had a hedge of reddish hair then; and when the fights were fought, and that the rascals must have further fun to pass the time profitably between there and home, one knave, his roving eye taken by Jaimie's red mane, shouted 'Lookit the Madairín Rua !' (Wee Red Fox). The boys, quick to catch the spirit of divilment, came barking and bouncing around him, crying 'Madairín Rua! Madairín Rua!' started the scared little fellow on the run, themselves after him in full cry, some of them barking terrifyingly and others keeping up, 'Madairín Rua! Madairín Rua!' Jaimie, running for his life like any hunted little fox — but, unlike the real fox, crying loudly — managed to swing in off his father's door just half a bound ahead of the foremost hound. And 'Madairín Rua! Madairín Rua! Madairín Rua !' was the last sound ringing in his ears as he buried his head in his mother's lap — his first adventurous day at school ended!

From that day our *buachaillín* was the Madairín Rua to the country-side.

Yet we should not leave the subject of School without recording that the Madairín Rua was not long going there till a hero he became. Even if a hero by accident. On a day of his early school career he went with some bigger boys over the moors, bird-nesting. These , finding him at length more of a hindrance than a help, sat him by the side of a deep pool while they pushed farther. When he saw them disappear, and realized that he was alone on the lone moor — alone, that is, except for the serpent which, all youngsters knew, was guarding in its coils a pot of gold at the black pool's bottom — he, seized with fright terrified, raised a howl that might have been heard the other side of Barnes Mór, and ran for his life. The boys below the horizon heard him, came galloping after, overtook him ere he reached school, and asked what had happened. Now, suddenly seized with shame for having to tell nothing at all had happened, he — with shame to be recorded — calling imagination to his aid, told that after they had gone the great serpent came out of the pool and chased him; and, finding itself unable to overtake him by its natural mode of motion, had put its tail in its mouth and whirled wheel-fashion after him! From feeling he was a coward he found himself a hero! As a hero he was led back to school, and when school skailed that day, all of the children walked around

23

and around him in fascinated wonder, feasting their eyes upon the distinguished one. And for years after, on the very rare occasion when a new boy came to the parish and was being shown its wonders, one of the first and greatest that he was brought to gaze upon was this hero who had never been chased by the serpent.[2]

NOTES

1 Long years after the occurrence here set down, when our gasúr had become a writer, and was, on tour, lecturing in a town in the Green Mountains of Vermont, there came to speak to him after the lecture a dark-visaged, curly-headed, meticulously dressed gentleman, who said, 'I wonder could you by any chance recognise a Donegal man, right from your own parish'? After studying his features the lecturer said, 'No, I'm sorry — What is your name'?

'I used to be Charles Haughie, a boy from Drim- a-Loscai. Now a foreman in the mills here'.

'Surely not Charlie-with-the-Checker-Slip'?

Through a burst of laughter the dark gentleman did his best to reply. 'Just Charlie-with-the- Checker-Slip — no other'!

2 The crock of gold referred to was, of course, some of the Danes' gold. One of a multitude of such treasures that the Northmen, ere they were driven out of Ireland a thousand years before, left behind under many a hill and fairy rath, and at bottom of many a pool through the length and breath of Donegal. The boys often searched for the Danes' gold and always lived in bright hope of finding it, dressing in shop clothes, and living carefree lives of luxury forever after. For this they often eavesdropped at the hen-roost at night — for the hens know of where every crock of gold is hidden, and preserve it for the Danes when they come again: and the murmurs which now and again during the night pass through a henhouse are the fowl telling the secret hiding place, one to another, to make sure none will forget.

The boy knew, besides, that the Danes, when they were driven out of Donegal, after robbing its people and holding the people's farms for nigh two hundred years, never resigned their robber- title to the Irish lands they had grabbed and worked: for, from that day to this, every Dane in Denmark before he dies wills his Irish farm to his eldest son. Our lad knew well the story of the servant boy from Largymore who, long ago, in a fair in Killybegs where a Dane had come to buy Irish cattle, was by the buyer employed to help with a ship-load of them to Denmark, from Killybegs Quay. When they reached the foreign land, and the cattle-trader's home, the trader's old blind father asked to speak with the Donegal youth. His employer, who had taken a liking to the lad, picked up a bone, a horse's tigh-joint, and gave it to the boy, saying, 'If my blind father asks to shake hands with you, let him clos his fist on this bone'. To the boy's surprise the old fellow asked him, 'What townland in Donegal are you from'? He replied, 'From Largymore'. Then to his amazement, the old fellow queried, 'Who's now occupying the Limekiln Farm in Largymore'? 'Why', said the astonished boy, 'it's Cnochar MacGinnis. — That farm has always been in the MacGinnis family'. 'Has it'? says the old fellow, bitterly hissing the words through his teeth. — 'Tell me, how is MacGinnis caring it'? 'It's the best cared farm in the barony', says the boy. 'It had better be', says the old fellow. 'Some day his seed will have to a sharp accounting to my seed for how they cared that farm of ours and for every penny they ever earned of it. — And now', says he, 'I want to shake your hand, and show you the warmth of my wish for my Donegal subjects'. The boy, remembering, reached him the bone — on which the old man closed his hand, crushing it to powder.

CHAPTER FIVE

His Day

When the boy was put out of bed, a fortnight before breakfast- time in the morning, he must either hie him to gather *diarcan* for scalding for the cows' breakfast — or carry the cows to Glen Cuach meadow, there to herd till milking time and his own meal time. For Glen Cuach he put in his pocket a farl of oat-cake that his mother had left him on the dresser last night, with sore warning that he mustn't eat it for common hunger, but save against the *feur-gortach*.[1] He was fortunate, however, through his boyhood — but in later days, on the mountains, the *feur-gortach* got him three times — only, luckly for him, each time help and food were near at hand.

The worst that happened him in the morning herdings in Glen Cuach was from stones that bruised his feet when he scampered the meadow to turn the cows from the corn. But yes — worse still were the cold autumn dews and sharp white frosts that in early mornings covered everything in Glen Cuach and put a knife-edge on every grass-blade. Ah, yes, those break-o'-day frosts in Glen Cuach were heartless with little boys who'd never do no harm to nobody!

There were times, however, when he loved the lonesomeness for something that was real grand about it — as when the red sun, rolling over the shoulder of Barnes Mór, steeped in glory Glen Cuach and all the glens and hills as far as one could see; waked to song the woods of Boe;[2] and started showers of silver light jigging and dancing on Donegal Bay. But best of all to the boy the lonesomeness was when it set him dreaming his dreams and up-building his castles. Oh, the bright beauty of the dreams that the *buachaillín* dreamt! and oh, the dazzling, glittering, gorgeousness of the castles he reared, in realms that arose betwixt the night of the day, when the lonesomeness lay on the Glen! In all the world again were no such dream mines, gold mines, as discovered themselves to barefoot boys herding near the fairy rath on the uplands of Glen Cuach!

The *gasúr* came home to breakfast — with the cows — when the sun got just three feet high . (He had a peeled and notched ash-stick for making measure). Then small slight he put upon the gorgeous breakfast of oatmeal stirabout and buttermilk — with a spill of sweetmilk added by way of special reward to a labouring-man. And on the heels of the stirabout, to wash it down, a bowl of tea! and a farl of his mother's pan-bread! this even buttered sometimes! Tea after stirabout, unusual in Knockagar, gave local rank to Jaimie's family. Our *gasúr's* recalls a lamentable accident that befell a little lad from Sru-Aill mountain, who came all the way a message one morning about a heifer that Jaimie's father had at grazing, there, with the Gasúr Mór. The mother made the little fellow sit down to breakfast — though, more by the same token, it took mighty little making. The stirabout was of oatmeal particularly sweet, because it had come home from the mill only the week before: and moreover, the mother had mixed sweetmilk plentifully with the buttermilk. The little stranger worked wonders at that rare meal — ate, and ate, and ate, and ate — till he astonished, in spite of them, people who bravely fought the bad manners of being astonished. All hands had to wait their tea till the wee fellow finished his stirabout. When filled complete, and, not able to take another spoonful, the mountain lad pushed his bowl away from him, and the mother brought on the bowls of steaming brown tea with butter-cappered slices of fragrant fresh pan-bread, the wee fellow — who, to be sure, had never dreamt, nor heard, of such luxurious climax to a feast — looked about him bewilderedly, laid his towhead on the table, and sobbed sore.

But to our own lad. — When his morning banquet was ended, he got two turf under one arm, slung his books in a string over-shoulder, and raced the hills to school where he first presented to the Master his hands and face for inspection. If he was unlucky, the Master — a dread, dry wit always — would admonish him to the school's thunderous delight, 'Tell your daddy to stop sending you out to hoke with the other pigs in the morning' — and to shrills of new delight, command, 'Trot yourself down to the quarry-hole and get a spade-deep of dirt dug off you. — Neil a-Cunnihan!' to a boy three times as big, 'You go with him as washer-woman. If you find his face — which I doubt — be sure you wipe it well on the grass before you bring him and it into the school again.'

With a heart-and-a-half went the favoured Neil, for, to rinse and wipe a little boy unmercifully was better to him than bread and butter thick covered with sugar. The school had its climaxing joy when Neil, returned with the laundry, presented it for inspection to the Master — for that caustic man would then say, 'Upon my soul, Neil, and was it the Wee Red Fox you found under the dirt?' If he had only thrashed a boy for dirty face and hands, that would have been by comparison a treat. Though he had a powerful arm, the Master's tongue was ten times sorer, in a school where fourscore vagabonds were breaking their hearts to find someone to laugh at.

Small wonder that when a boy found himself late, he was strong-tempted to scheme school rather than provide the fun that the scholars were ever hungering for. Often, boys did so scheme — but only once in his career Jaimie. He was persuaded by three bad boys to join them: but found it the most melancholy joy of all his experience. It was a day of

26

storm and sleet when Christians needed shelter of a roof : but these four outcasts, beyond benefit of clergy, aroused unwelcome — sometimes silent, often-times violent — wheresoever they tried to push in their heads. Their unwelcome chiefly came from mothers of families, one of whom expressed it with a besom and three with potato-beetlers. Shiela Brishlan, a withered little woman with a large limp, amazed the lads by the toe-to-heel chase she gave them over five fields, taking every ditch like a steeple-chaser. When she gave up, and they stopped to gibe her, she flung at them the beetle, winging it with a curse, and by less than an inch did it miss braining Conal MacDaid the gang's headsman. After the schemers found themselves debarred from all human habitations they tried cow-byres, where the very beasts tied at the stake turned heads to look at them, with — as our lads saw plainly and painfully — infinite disdain in their slow eyes. Even at that, they weren't long in the cows' company till a man, coming in to feed the cattle, discovered them, and accusing them of trying to rob his hens' nests, denounced them as 'dam pickpockets,' and chased them over three hills and three hollows with a pitch-fork. It was a real relief to Jaimie to get home at last, and take the beating that was waiting him — and which he was all the happier after. He would take the Master's cuttingest joke ten thousand times rather than scheme school in his life again. The way of the wicked is a hard way.

School, anyway, was terrible thralldom to a man who loved the hills and the woods and freedom, a man of roving fancy as well as roving foot: and a divine day to him was always the day his father said, 'Jaimie, son, you can't go to school thi' day, for there's a big day's work for you footing turf in the bog.' At the glad news his heart bounded !

To be sure, mighty little joy was in his heart at hearing of work on a day that was not a school day. Less still a day on which all normal Christians went to Donegal fair — or the even greater day, that of the Races on the Holmes's Strand. One such occasion particularly and pain-fully lingers in his memory. This was a bright and beautiful Races day, one of the brightest ever fell from the skies, and in the morning the boy was out with his father in Glen Cuach, breaking clods on the corn-ground. 'Father,' the boy said, 'you're letting me go to the Races thi' day, of course?' His father, hurrying with work that was already belated, didn't lift his head as he answered, 'Sonny-boy, break clods and you'll go.' At the good news the boy went breaking with such vim that the clods surely thought he had a spite on them. After an hour he said, 'Now, father, can I go to the Races?'

'Sonny-boy,' said his father without lifting his head, 'break clods and you'll go.'

The boy looked about him, to see all the world streaming down the hillsides dressed in the bottom of the trunk. But he buckled to the breaking

27

again. After a time — 'Father can I now go to the Races?'

'Sonny-boy, break clods and you'll go.'

After still shorter and shorter spells he would pause in his performance on the poor clods, and ask his plaintive question — alas, every time to get the same reply ! When at length the sun, from his highest heaven of the day looked down at the lad asking the old question — and getting the old answer — he gazed first afar off to the Holmes's Strand black-circled with happy crowds, next to the sun, and then to his father, and cried in despair, 'But, father, 'tis so late now there'll be no Races when I get there.' The amazing reply of his father to his desperate appeal still sticks in the boy's sore heart, and still puzzles him — 'What matters that, son-O? Even if there's never any 'Races, there'll always be plenty of clods to break!'

The breaking clods on the turned ground, for corn-sowing and potato-setting, was one of many jobs before the little boy when he'd got home from school. After school field-work depended on the time of the year, and had variety enough for displeasing of any healthy boy's heart. When the meadow began to grow in May he picked stones off it — to save the scythe's edge, and the mowster's soul, come mowing time. He dropped potato-seed for the kibbing; he broke *seuchs* for the potato shovelling; he spread manure; he sometimes handled a man's spade and dug and planted like the biggest of them. Sorest work of all on the *gasúr* was the cutting of the wrack on spring-tide days in February, when at high-ebb the farther out rocks and heavier wracks were laid bare. This was hardest, not only because it held the little fellow continuously and back-breakingly bent two-double. Nor yet because, since tides wait on no man, he had, with his big wrack-knife to but and hack and hew with lightning speed, treading the tail of the outgoing tide, and then, at the tide's turn, turn with it, and cut and hack and hew his way inshore on the mane of the inrushing flood. But more because February's frosty winds buffeted and bit him, and its sleety rains slashed and cut him, while the flying salt spray whacked and whipped him and soaked him to the pelt.

After wrack-cutting, the next hardest work, footing turf in the bog, though it was the dickens's own work, almost seemed easy. Yet, here, to be sure, when came in the day's middle the welcome stop for eating your farl of india-bread and drinking your bottle of milk, you needed first to get someone to stand and stamp on your back — while you lay out-stretched — to straighten and take the *cruit* out of it; whilst in the evening, when the day's work was done, you'd thought nothing less than an elephant dancing a hornpipe on it would be any benefit. Sometimes, from the bog to which he had come in the morning a lithe-some lad, the boy would start home in the evening a bent old man, with no other prospect in life than two stout sticks to hobble by, and a black pipe and straw-bottomed chair in the chimney corner. But lo and behold! ere he covered half of the four miles home, he would be finding himself, to his surprise, skipping ditches like a goat, sowing finger-stones over the landscape, and cheerily 'hallooing to comrades who were herding three hills away. He intended to stay young for another year yet.

Harvest work he loved — the winning of the hay and cutting of the corn in sunny August and September days — with dinner for a king, served in the day's middle, bottles of milk, whole cans of tea, great farls of sweet bake-bread, buttered, and gorged by a group of sweating, happy, hungry men huddled in a comfortable ditch. This, the day's crowning joy, delighted the heart of him, in harvest — while yet he took no thought of the sore days coming in bleak October when he would be chilled to the bone by snowwinds, and his fingers numbed by the frosts, as, following the diggers, he picked the potatoes from the muddy, sleety ground, and with them filled baskets, creels, sacks and pits, for the winter's storing.

But every evil in this world has, by God's decree, it's compensation — as he well realized, when, getting home at candle-light from perishing potato-gathering, he was greeted, and had his heart lifted, by the bonfire of turf blazing on the hearth and supper-stirabout bubbling and blowing and puffing in the crane-hung pot above. The sight filled him with a gorgeous glow; for the blood that had evaporated entirely from his body in the drear, drooky, frosty potato-field, now flew back from the grey sky to which it had gone, through the door after him, and rushed, gushing, into and through his veins again. While the fire was good and bright and blazing he must get his spelling book and his geography and, stretched on his stomach on the hearth, learn the morrow's lesson. Later, when the fire was lower, and the candle, of course, put out after supper, his father would light him through his lessons with the light of a thin, long spail torn from the heart of an ancient fir block dug out of the bog's bowels — a pack of which spails was always kept seasoning in the chimney corner to answer for candles in emergency.

After October — after Hallowday — life was easy. The boy attended the thatcher, carrying up the ladder to him the sheaves of straw and bundles of scollops that were constantly a-calling for as the man thatched his way along the roof. Then attending the thresher in the barn, throwing down the sheaves of corn to his flail, and drawing and wapping the threshed straw — play made doubly pleasant by the fact that threshing always attracted a crowd of the leisured whose interesting tongues loosed to the thud of the flail and made discourse that was better than dinner (the idlers frequently refused to go home for it), and started stories, the best of them coming from the thresher himself between strokes. Oh, threshing days were such delightful days that the boy wished and longed that the thresher instead of finishing his work in a week, might draw it out till the sun began warming the world in March again.

And after the threshing the milling was every bit as good — just as leisurely and pleasant. Maybe more so. The thundering of the wheels and the thumping of the hoppers, made music grand — grander still because there, too, gathered the leisured, the most talented conversationalists and the best story-tellers of the countryside, seeking outlet for their spirit on stormy winter-days. Story-telling was continuous in the mill, and more especially in the kilns — the warm kilns where the corn was drying, and where, by the welcome hot fire the idlers and story-tellers, while they let their bodies bake, often talked and told till morning.

By the fireside, at home, it was happy to sit on the creepy-stool seeing this neighbour and that drop in on their nightly ramble, sit in the circle, and help along the excitingly-interesting discussions which held the household on the long winter nights. When finally his mother, putting aside her patching, lifted her rosary of its nail on the wall and commanded the household to its knees the boy would be feeling so ready for bed that when it came his turn to lead a *diccat* he'd be needing a big pluck by the tail, or a sharp jundy of his mother's elbow, to startle him to it.

Once in a while he'd be enough awake after the rosary to watch his mother rake the fire; pulling the red coals and ashes to one side, to give place for three damp black turf stood up to the back-stone, and against them piling the half-burned coals, and with loads of ashes burying all — to await the morrow- morning's resurrection. (For always the new day's fire was coaked from the seeds of the old.) He liked to watch the raking, and to see his mother, after she had finished, and swept the hearth tidy, with the tongs cut a cross on the ashes in front, 'In the name of Father, Son, and Holy Ghost, bless the fire seed and our seed, this night and forever, Amen' — then carefully lay the tongs lengthwise across the hearth — thus all evil barring from house and household till God should again send His blessed daylight.

Mostly, however, the boy had crept under the blankets before the fire-raking, and his eyes had closed for a wink or two. And when he opened them again to find if his mother had begun the raking, behold ! a new fire was burning, the cock was crowing, and an impatient father calling from his bed, 'Isn't that young vagabone out of the bed-feathers yet and off to his herding?'

Alas, in Glen Ainey there was no rest for the innocent. No, never.

NOTES

1 Well the lad knew that this, the dread fairy-hunger, suddenly prostrated everyone who by mischance stepped on a patch of hungry-grass — the paralysing grass that always grew on spots where some greedy mortal, eating, had neglected to leave behind him a bit for the Good People (fairies). So like every wise one who went on the hills, he safe-guarded himself

30

with a pocket of hard-bread — and would endure the pangs of hunger all morning rather than eat his bit and risk the feur-gortach.

2 Memory of the beauteous hour was, later, to wake the boy himself to song —

THE LITTLE LINNET OF BOE

When I was young my life was glad as Murlo's crooning stream,
Each moment was a sparkling joy and every day a dream.
Oh, many and many an hour I sat, while yet the sun was low,
And listened to the linnet green, that waked the woods of Boe.

I knew the mavis of Monea, the blackbird of Sthragar,
I loved the leverock of Caroo, the gooldie of Glenvar;
But of all the birds in bush or sky that sunny long ago,
None could compare the linnet rare that charmed the groves of Boe.

Oh, wander west or wander east, oh, fare me far or near,
That little linnet's piping voice is pleading in my ear;
Still calling, calling, calling, 'Oh, why will you wander so?
Why leave these happy, happy woods? Come back! Come back to Boe!'

Ah, weary's me on wanderin' and weary's me on gold!
It sours the nature in the breast, it turns the warm heart cold;
It chokes the lilt that lightened life, it drowns the gladdening glow
I felt what time my linnet green awaked the woods of Boe.

Please God, I'll tie my bundle up, I'll take my stout blackthorn,
And the risin' sun will meet me on the road the morrow's morn.
'Farewell'! I'll cry, and wave my hand — 'Farewell to gilded woe!
'Tis wealth I seek — a singing heart, and the linnet's lilt in Boe'.

I know a red-lipped cailín there, as bright as May-morn beam;
I know a white-walled cabin 'longside a purling stream;
I know a hundred, hundred joys that o'er our days will flow,
While the lovely little linnet green makes glad the graves of Boe.

— From Ballads of a Country Boy.

CHAPTER SIX

These Stirred his Imagination

Certain things and people awakened and stirred Jaimie's imagination in his childhood days, and oriented it for life.

First was the Mount — high, steep, lovely hill which, rising right from his father's door-step towered into the skies three hundred feet at least — from the top whereof one could see the whole wide world. That is, if one wasn't too busy holding hard by the grass-roots to save from tumbling into the sea, far below. The Mount was not only an infinite wonder because of its own self, but was haloed with magic; for of all the hills in Donegal it was the fairies' favourite — crowded nightly with troops, armies, multitudinous assemblages of the Little People. To be sure, Jaimie never trespassed at fairy-time — after dusk began sifting down: but from the security of his father's door his ear often caught bars of the fairy music, the skirling of the pipes and plaining of the fiddles; and again and again his eye caught glimpses of coat-tails, coloured petticoats, bright shawls, when, at this hour They were whirling, twirling and jigging on the hillside. He never could say he saw the figures, exactly, of the Little People — only just what his mother called *wafts* of them. Of course, he knew many who had seen them complete: but he never ventured near enough. If he had curiosity, he had caution likewise. He was a wise child.

Again, through every one of his young days he observed the whole world ringed in, some miles off, by a range of real mountains, grey, brown and purple, that climbed the sky. Three-quarter ways, to be accurate, the world was ringed by this protecting wall. The gap that broke the ring was filled by the ocean — where the broad mouth of the Bay was all day alternately drinking and disgorging the Atlantic that either glowered or glimmered outside. That water-gap was just to give the sun a place to sink in, at night. (Strange to say, though, the sun, for all that he went down in his ocean-bed every evening without fail, couldn't have taken any rest to him there but — must have busied himself, while everyone else was asleep, getting back to where he came from: for in the morning the child, to his surprise, would see him rolling up over the shoulder of Barnes Mór mountain again — on the very other side of the ring — and just as casual as if he had, all the time, been sleeping his honest sleep at Barnes Mór's back.)

Yet it wasn't the trick the sun played, but that line where the mountains met the sky, that so stirred the child's imagination. His eyes constantly sought that mysterious line, wondering, wondering: and his heart fretted for the day when he should be grown up enough to travel away to those hills and climb up to that line — and look over ! The idea thrilled him to the soul! Would he be looking down, down, down bottomless cliffs that, far as human eye could carry, disappeared into shuddery nothingness? Or maybe at the foot of a finite cliff — maybe only two or five or ten miles down — he would see Heaven! Or see — Ah no, he always tried hard to shut his mind to the less pleasant possibility. But the fascination of the thing always put him feeling pity — mixed up with some other feeling that could not be called contempt, but might be contempt if it was grown up — for the torpid grown-ups around him — creatures who, though both able and free to go and see for themselves what lay beyond — and get the thrill, not of a lifetime, but of eternity — yet loafed away their lives digging and sowing and mowing.

It must have been in the very first month of his school life that, coming home one day, the Madairín Rua was dumbfounded to find sitting in his father's kitchen the loveliest lady he had ever beheld — the loveliest, in fact, that could be in the world — she dressed grander and smarter than he had ever before seen anyone dressed — with the possible exception of the Marquis's gentry. Though it was doubtful if even any of them was so grand. But certainly none even of them was a hundredth as lovely. Yet he believes it wasn't the grand lady's gold dress, or her extraordinary loveliness, that enchanted him entirely. It was the beautiful sound of her speech, and the bewitching words she used, that clinched his enchantment, and chained him to the creepy-stool, drinking every lovely syllable falling from nice lips that were used like he could use his fingers. There wasn't a word in the language that the boy knew better than the word *guess* — for, sure, they had guesses every night by the fireside, hundreds of them — but when this lovely one said 'I guess' — and often returned to it — it was a new discovery and a magic word, more deliglitful than any he had ever listened to. Then the sound she put in her voice — what he heard his mother afterwards call her accent — was so entirely-and-entirely different from any voice sound he had ever heard before, that it bathed his soul in a glow of glory. He had heard the gentry of the Hall speak, half-a-dozen times; but though theirs sounded different from, and much nicer than, the talk of Glen Ainey, it couldn't at all compare in delightfulness with this beautiful lady's speech — before which he sat long and open-mouthed. She was Mary O'Gorman. She was a Come-home Yankee — come back from a beautiful, and beautiful-sounding, city called Philadelphy. She had been for eight years maid in a grand house in that grand city — house with four upstairses, everyone above another. And her beautiful speech, it seems, was just the way that everybody in Philadelphy spoke everyday and Sunday. From the enchantingness of Mary O'Gorman's talk, and the fascination of its phrases, the boy, in his mind, built Philadelphy — a fabled city with houses of gold, streets of silver, rainbow skies, and peopled by ladies all very near as lovely as Mary O'Gorman, and grand men the least of whom would shame the very Marquis. And he conjured up the picture of a day of the far future when the Mount fairies (who could do anything they liked), rewarding him for some good turn, would whisk him through the skies, over the oceans, and plank him right down on one of the solid silver streets of gorgeous Philadelphy !

Though it was years and years and many many years — aeons to the eager boy — before that fairy miracle was performed, still, there scarce passed a day of those years that there wasn't echoing down the corridors of his memory, a haunting music, the bewitching Yankee words and enthralling Yankee accent of lovely Mary O'Gorman of lovely speaking in his father's kitchen in Knockagar.[1]

Tim Griffin, most famed ball-player of the Ruas — whom he one day saw in the Knockagar ball-alley matched against the best handball player of Knockagar — came, a new face, new figure, and new ideal, into the boy's life. Tim's manliness, handsomeness, suppleness, easy grace, his thick-curled, dark-red hair — and then his marvellous skill in turning, shooting, and killing the ball — flashed a new feeling into the boy's soul, and gave him his first inkling of what people meant when they spoke of a hero. It plainly signified a man whom the world wanted to fall down before, and worship. Only twice again did he see him till he heard of his going to America — where he got enveloped by the unknown — but, through the years after, Tim Griffin walked, a welcome ghost, in the boy's memory — there after meeting and crossing Mary O'Gorman — worshipful in his easy casualness and laughing eyes that could lay spell on any girl: and the boy could never again hear of a hero without wanting to put him into Tim's supple frame, and give him the handsome face and bush of curly auburn hair which once, in a Knockagar ball-alley, had laid upon him a spell that was never to be lifted.

Through all his early memories, still our *gasúr* sees the boys and the girls of his parish, in twos and in groups — once in a while singly — waving good-bye to the world, as down the Glen road they headed for the hiring-fair. The girls were bare-headed and shawled, with rolled up skirts showing red petticoats, and each of them carried in their hand a little bundle, red-handkerchief-wrapped. The brave boys mounted their bundles on the end of their stick, and bore them over-shoulder. These gallant ones were going twelve, and twenty, and thirty and forty miles — out over the mountains — into the fat lands of Fermanagh and Derry and Tyrone where farms were big and farmers wealthy and wanting both a boy and a girl. Watching these wayfarers go to walk the world and push their fortune, our lad's soul filled with adventure, and oh! how he longed to be grown up to the size of four feet that he might mount his own red-handkerchief over-shoulder and go push his fortune in a world full of thrilling mystery and enticing adventure. And hordes of gold, too — for he knew that every girl of these, coming home again at the end of each half-year, would bring two pounds and three pounds with her, and every boy four pounds or five — to their fathers and mothers. Moreover, they would have explored new countries, and seen strange peoples, outside the hills. And oh! the stories they would bring back with them of all the big towns that were there, with houses having up-stairs, and hundreds of people, many of whom went with money in both pockets. These blessed boys and girls, great travellers, world adventurers, he clothed with glory — when he wasn't envying them.

But other boys and girls there were, going from Glen Ainey to push their fortune in a farther world, who drew from him a little envy only, but much pity. It was those who sailed away to America — some of them for seven years, most of them, alas, forever. Their going stamped itself deep, deep, on a tender mind — and sore it was in the stamping. Each year they began going in the late autumn — after the harvest work on the little farms was finished — and, week after week, in crowds, kept going till the spring work began again.[2]

In the week before their sailing, Jaimie was accustomed to see the emigrants-to-be journey to every home in miles of ground, bidding good-bye to man, woman and child. Often and often went he to the going-off party, the Convoy — where friends and neighbours gathered to the home of the departing boy and girl, and sat through the last night with them whom they might never sit with again. A fiddler fiddled, dancers danced, singers sang, and to the boy and girl and grieving family everyone spoke the word of cheer that no one felt. Always, everyone prophesied that they would all yet meet and dance and sing and lie happy together again. But ah, Jaimie knew, so sorely was needed at home in Glen Ainey the little money they'd make in America that it couldn't be wasted on voyaging back.[3]

The big Americay ship sailed from Derry on Fridays. Jaimie's home was by Knockagar cross-roads where the jaunting-cars loaded the emigrants for the long, last journey — away from Glen Ainey, through Barnes Mór Gap, to Stranorlar railway station more than twenty-five miles away. It was the scenes at the going away which stamped themselves so sore on the boy's mind that never could he, can he, erase the poignant memory. — In the middle of the night the departing ones set out from home for the Knockagar Cross, accompanied by their own and their friends, a band of twenty or thirty, sometimes fifty or more — little Jaimie himself sometimes one of them. Quitting of their father and mother's roof was sorest — and the *gasúr* a hundred times saw heart-broken ones kiss the door-posts, saw sobbing girls get on hands and knees at cabin-doors to kiss the door-step that never would feel their foot again. Too often these same cabins were oh, so poor! but when Jaimie would see a girl kissing the threshold of the very poorest of them, he knew it was greater than the King of Spain's castle. — And often he strained his imagination trying to picture to himself how awesomely noble must be those fabled Americans to whom such girls would be but serving-maids.

The jaunting-cars were waiting at the Cross, by the boy's own home, and there all the Convoys came together. And at the meeting of the girls who were to be sisters in exile, these threw their arms around one another, and kissed, and mingled their tears. Then every girl embraced and kissed and mixed tears with every one of her Convoy. The going-away boys made great pretence to be gruff and brusk, and mad with every-one sorely straining themealves to hide and hold in. Many of the party wept in silence; but always there were some whose heart-broken cries could be heard hills away. And at the off-getting of the cars, finally, the boy often saw car-drivers who were naturally kind- hearted thrashing and slashling with their whips to break the hold of the left-behind ones who wanted to cling to the cars, and to the skirts and embrace, of them whom they would never see more.

Small wonder such sight, so regularly seen round all his childhood should, with others, leave deep impress on the lad's imagination.[4]

NOTES

1   To this incident there was to be a wonderful sequel — which will be recorded later. It may be noted here that any Donegal boy or girl who returns home, after one year, or years, in any corner of America, is, henceforth, a Come-home Yankee.

2   Then, America was ten thousand times farther from Ireland than it is today. And far, far more surely then, than now, it meant, between those who were going and those who were left, everlasting separation. Among a fearfully fond people it signified something a little less than death.

3   The money would come home in the 'Americay letter', month after month, year after year — would pay a shop debt, the rent to the landlord, clothe the family, re-roof the house, make happy the old father and mother, young brothers and sisters left behind in Ireland. For, then, the Glen Ainey boy and girl, gone to America, never forgot. And never were forgotten.

4   Emigrants going from Donegal a good generation earlier still — in the boy's mother's young days — during the decade of vast emigration that followed the famine years — went away under conditions harder far. They sailed out of Donegal Bay in little ships of two and three and four hundred tons, each emigrant carrying his own provisions packed in a barrel —potatoes oaten-bread and butter to last him twelve weeks: for these little schooners, though they sometimes made America in six and seven weeks, occasionlly took three months in the crossing. Then the boy's own uncle, Billy MacAteer already mentioned, sailed from the Green Islands in Donegal Bay for America, and after a fearful nine weeks' voyage, was rejoiced to make land — but disappointed when he found that it wasn't the New World loomed up, but the hills round Killala in the County Mayo — sixty miles from his starting point. The uncle walked home, on dry land, satisfied that he had voyaged enough for one lifetime, and content to leave America to the brave ones who had already reached it.

The boy, in his day, spoke with men who had made the long, long, crossing; and, besides, heard stories from old Joe Peary, of Ballyweel, who piloted these ships out and in of Donegal Bay. By the Green Islands the waiting ships rode at anchor — receiving the emigrants with their belongings the day before the poposed sailing. Their Convoys came aboard with the departing ones. The boy's mother, then a very little girl, went on some of these Convoys — and often told him of them. There fiddling and dancing and singing all the day and all the night, by all the crowds that could find foothold on the ship. Waiting for favourable winds, frequently the ship would not sail on the announced sailing date, but delay from day to day, sometimes from week to week.Evening after evening boat-loads of emigrants'friends returned to renew the festivities that should lift the lonesomenes off the hearts of the departing ones.

As an applicant for passage was never refused, these little ships were sometimes packed and jammed with creatures destined, in stormy passages, to spend weeks and weeks bolted down in a crowded hold. No wonder it was that ship fever and famine-fever carried off not tens but hundreds of thousands of Irish voyagers then. Affairs were at their worst in the famine years when, in the case of some voyagers on record, less than one-half of those who embarked reached the American shore alive. In his Story of the Irish Race this author gives more detailed particulars of that awful time.

Among hundreds of stories of voyaging in those days which the boy listened to by the fireside, were those of Barney the Sailor, who, from being a coastwise navigator in small way, light-heartedly undertook an enterprise which Columbus had faced with prayer and fear. The story went that after Barney, with his human cargo, sailed out of Donegal Bay into the Atlantic, he would heave to, awaiting a west-going-vessel — after sighting which, navigating Atlantic was easy. Even should Barney the Sailor, as sometimes happened, lost his guide ship by night or in a storm, he just slacked the sail — but kept going westward — till God sent him another ship. He put his passengers ashore at St. John's, Halifax, Boston, New York, Baltimore, or Charleston, South Carolina — whatsoever port his guide-ship happened to be going to. Any port was all right, as long as it was in the Land of Promise. For setting their foot on any portion of America's far-flung shore-line, his passengers were only too glad to thank both God and Barney.

The only record that Barney ever in his voyaging endangered, was that of the longest passage. He once made America, they tell, in eighteen weeks. Grumbling passengers he consoled with the reminder that, 'For the spendin' a couple o' spare months there's a healthier place in the worl' than the sae'. And, to meet the complaints of passengers who, Americanised by anticipation, spoke about lost time, he had an apposite and silencing proverb, 'Thanks be to the Lord, the man who made time, made plenty of it'.

And These Moulded His Mind

Far-varying factors that moulded the boy's mind and shaped his life were work, loafing, roaming, and his mother's fireside.

As escape from that penal servitude called school, work was delight; but the delight dropped out of it entirely when it had to be done mornings before, and evenings after, school. Every kind of labour on his father's little farm he did; and from his early teens forward a grown man's stint was expected of him. Working with his father side by side, he had to keep pace with him — and did. The hardest day's work of his young life was one shearing corn in Drim-a-Loscai — him, a little fellow clearing his own *hintin* foot for foot with four big men. As the work was for a widow, they sheared double-speed; and a score of times that day the lad, either too 'shamed or too spunky to drop his scythe-hook and give in, somehow, from some mystery place, borrowed a strength that carried and kept him in line till welcome evening fell, and the four men, trying to straighten themseves, pronounced, 'You're a man afore your time, God bliss you!'

When weather was not too *hascaigh* — or raw — he got positive pleasure from working in the field that topped Dhrim-an-Aran Hill — whence he saw the whole world round him, together with the occasional carts that passed, a quarter of a mile below, on the road to Donegal. Moreover, had worked on Dhrim-an-Aran top, where mountain and sea airs came to grips, had grand compensations: one, the beautiful relish it added to relaxation, afterward, by the night-fire; another, the appetite it whipped into you, putting on potatoes and salt a glory that the King of Spain with all his gold couldn't bribe for his banquet.

But never did any other of all the many meals made glorious by a hard-earned appetite, gratify his gluttony as did a particular one that he'll look lingeringly back to the day he's dining off the gold dishes of Heaven — a meal of potatoes, *bainne romhair*, and *meascán* of yellow butter, that himself and his appetite sat down to in Mary MacCailin's cabin, at the Ainey Steps. The appetite he had taken from a hard, hard day's turf-footing in Litirtraina bog. Than footing turf there's maybe no sorer labour in a sore world — and surely no hungrier. He had been bent to the play from early morning, with a bare few minutes in the day's middle whilst he swallowed his bottle of milk and farls of hard bread. Flying for home in the evening with, hot on his heels, a ravishing hunger, he'd just hopped the rocks which are the Ainey Steps, when Mary MacCailin, may God bless her! coming out of her cottage, halted him, and with an unmerciful scold for trying to hurry by her door, dragged him within, and set him in front of a big beechen dish full of still-steaming 'tatties that were laughing at him through their jackets, a *meascán* of butter that would make gold look green, and a bowl of thick-milk deep enough to drown a ploughman. Almost the sight brought tears of joy to the ravening little man! Although he was ever after — is now — ashamed of how he ate that day, and how much, he yet loves to let his memory linger on that glorious meal at Mary's. And many a time in manhood years when he sat down to banquets gorgeous his table-neighbours hearing him sigh must have wondered for why. Poor Mary's body, from the Ainey Steps has long since gone to Dhrim-a-Srone graveyard — but oh, she lives — Mary lives!

A bigger brother, Padraic, laboured with the boy and his father, but, unlike our boy's case, labour and himself never loved each other: he would scheme when he could, leaving the *gasúr* to work for both. Padraic's love for books was even more passionate than our lad's. He knew the location of every book that was within a radius of ten miles; and if a new one was smuggled in, anywhere, he heard of it before its owner opened it — and was hot-foot on its trail. When both boys must report for labour on the hill, Padraic might or might not have his spade or graip with him — very often not — but he never missed having a book. 'Hagh!', his mightily-provoked father would cry, on seeing him jump the ditch into the field. 'Here he comes, with his bible under his oxther!' And for the remainder of the work-day, at every chance — which is to say every time that his father's attention was elsewhere — Padraic was at the back of the ditch with his bible, while the *gasúr* laboured for both. Yet he refused the joy of reading to Jaimie, when evening came and leisure: but though he wouldn't share the book in its physical form, he would, even after one galloping perusal, unfold to Jaimie — indeed, to anyone in the world whom he could coax to listen — everything worth while that tried to hide itself anywhere between the book's two covers.[1]

Our lad's lightest labour was the herding — not so light when done alone in the mornings — but easy enough with comrades, whom almost always he could bribe in the evenings. Because his head was crammed with fairy stories, and he had by heart a host of ballads, it was easy work luring three or four or more lads with him to the hill. The first ballad he loved and learned — and declaimed to the boys at the herding — the one, also, that gave him and them their first glow of patriotic ecstasy — was that of 'Donnelly and Cooper, who fought on the Rakes of Kildare' — the never-to-be-forgotten boxing-match between the great champion who stood for the glory of Ireland — and won — and the great English boxer who in that famed contest on the Curragh of Kildare, gave England's tarnished glory to set with the setting sun.[2]

Before long, however, the boy thrilling for native land, could rouse his comrades with ballads of still nobler patriotism about Irish heroes of rank above brave Donnelly. And stories of great deeds done for Ireland soon vied with the folk-tales for enticing comrades from their homes to the herding. By these ballads and tales to such a pitch of patriotism was wrought the group, that, when rumour ran of England's going to call up all men to help her win a war against France, this patriotic band sat in debate on top of Dhrim-an-Aran — crying pee-weets circling over-head — planning to save their fathers from eternal shame. Smothering them in their beds the night before they were to shoulder an English musket, was suggested by one wild fellow, The Vagabone. Though this was a simple solution, and effective, these boys, loyal sons of good fathers, almost unanimously rejected it; and felt, under Heaven there must be a worthier way out. From Dhrim-an-Aran, those anxious days, they often strained their gaze to sea, hoping against hope for sight of a French frigate sailing into the Bay — just as, for the '98 Rising, such a frigate (whose awe-inspiring anchor and chain still lay at Donegal) had sailed in to succor the pikemen, their grandfathers. When that war cloud blew over, the Loyal Sons of Erin Dhrim-an-Aran Hill Division, didn't know whether to feel satisfied or sorry.

Though the lad laboured sore on his father's land, times when crops and cattle called for hard work, yet had he plenty of opportunity for games — caman, duck, steal-the-caps, Barney-Barney-Buck-and-Doe, and a score more. But beyond and above all caman, the game of the country, game of all ages, wherein, at times, all boys and bearded men of two contending parishes lined up — the fieriest, fiercest, excitingest, beauti-fullest game on the globe — game that demanded man's foremost qualities, fleetness, courage, strength, and skill.

A loafing life is mostly thought a losing life, but to our lad it was a mortal gainful one, almost every heaven-sent idle day of his boyhood piling in his lap lashin's and leavin's of yellow gold. He loafed, in the slack periods, to his heart's delight. But loafing in its grand sense began at Hallow-day — when hay and corn were in the garden, the stacks of potatoes in the field-pit, and little more to be done till Candlemas Day came round. To get the best out of loafing the boy soon learned that it should be done while watching other men working sore. For, not only does the sight of someone slaving give edge to one's pleasure, but the very work and the watching of it are stimulants to story-telling. After school on leaden November days Jaimie was among the eloquent idlers — in the barn where the thresher was threshing, at the house where the thatcher was thatching, in the nailer's, the cooper's, the blacksmith's, the tinker's, the tailor's, the weaver's, or the shoemaker's. In gay bands he and his fellows deliciously roamed from one to another house of the busy ones, and found high entertainment in all. No biggest, gayest, busiest spot in the world offered to its idlers a vaster variety of pleasuring places that did Donegal, in its hundred hills and valleys. And surely none of all their high-priced pleasure palaces could offer such grand and continuous entertainment as was, night and day, in these houses presented free to all comers — with thanks and gratitude for the coming, thrown in. Only seldom again in his subsequent life, with its wide wanderings which brought him to gatherings of intellectual people and socially brilliant, did he get the high entertainment, mind-exaltment, soul-refreshment, which he absorbed from Stephen Williamson and his cronies in the mill-kiln; about John Burns's tailor-table or Briany MacDwyer's work-bench; in the joyful circle that hunkered on the earth-floor (for there was only one stool) around Shan O'Quigley the tinker, him at once narrating his adventures and plying his sothering iron.

Good as it was to go to the tailor's own house, and the shoemaker's, and sit and listen with the ramblers there, better still it was to follow these to the homes where they were brought to work. Aristocrats like Billy Griffin and other such *warm* farmers of the country-side would, at winter's beginning, command the tailor and shoemaker to their house for a week's work, ten days', two weeks' — that they might outfit the whole family, from the skin out, and from crown to sole. During all the engaging time that the tailor occupied the kitchen-table in Billy Griffin's, and the shoemaker the middle of the floor, it was high holiday for the country-side, man and boy; and if at any time of the day or night attendance at Billy's dropped below a score, one could easily conclude that there was something extraordinary entirely transpiring elsewhere. The debates there conducted, that reminiscences called up, the adventures narrated, the tales recited, during that most profitable pause in the country-side's year, would fill volumes which, for interest, education, and quality, might shame many a boasted encyclopaedia.

Roaming the hills, the woods and scrugs, the boy, temporarily escaping from one good world, discovered to himself a new and better one — one completely equipped, physically and spiritually, to fill up and round out the life of any lad. No mere dream life that! so crammed it was with knocks, cracks, scratches, bruises, blood, and broken bones. Real adventures and escapes too — some of which may be set down later. Times that he could slip the slave-chains, Jaimie made glorious bursts to the wild freedom of this other life, which stimulated and nurtured and developed him. The shadowy mysteries of the Marquis's woods, with their teeming wealth of bird and beast, enthralled him; while the stony *hauteur* of the hills and their loud silences bewitched him — sometimes to the verge of fear — of a dangerously beautiful fear that they were taking him away. Just as boys before him who from those hills to their homes never returned — but were taken by spirits remote, to immortality in magic lands beneath

41

the mountains.

His mother's fireside at night was a great, and loved, school for our lad — here well called his mother's fireside, because always that was her domain. At her own fireside, at night, Jaimie's mother loved to have, and strove to keep, her children round her. Though with children's waywardness they would roam to farther firesides, yet rarely found they finer entertainment than at hers. By the chimney-corner, in her own seat — the only chair with arms to it in the country-side she sat the night through, knitting, sewing, patching, darning — and at the same time with song and story held a restless group almost motionless — until the father, lifting the latch at bedtime, returned from his ramblings.[3] To her audience's grief, then, she would end her entertainment, and, drawing the beads from her pocket, or lifting them from the nail on the wall, announce that rosary time was come — with bed behind it.

NOTES

1   This brother of the boy had a romantic after-career. First, having passed the examination for Model School Assistant, and no vacancy occurring within the year, the Board of Education, because of the brillance of his answering, did the unprecedented, awarding him a First Class Teacher's certificate. Refusing then, to teach under a British Board, he emigrated to the United States, engaged in sundry adventurous pursuits and finally became a sailor. He sailed the world for eight years, in the U. S. Navy, where he was a great favourite with Rear-Admiral Baines. Quitting the Navy, he went to the Argentine, a country in which he knew no soul, and of whose language he knew no word, and was, within twenty-four months, both Professor of Mathematics and Professor of English Literature in the Argentine Normal Colleges. Three years later the Governor of Buenos Aires commissioned him as travelling tutor to, first one, and then the other, of two young men, his wards and nephews. Each of these young men (the Leloirs) he took on a two-year tour of the world, visiting and studying every country of the globe — four years touring in all. When he returned home with the second of them, he was made Manager of their great estancias on the Pampas. And, finally, he owned his own estancias — three. Besides a modest estate (Rossylongan) in Donegal. He organised in a virile and militant Irish Association, the many influential Irish of the Argentine — and introduced to the country, for the large colony of Irish-blooded ones there, Irish games and the Irish language.

2   What John L Sullivan was to America a long generation after, the unconquered Donnelly was to Ireland then. As did John L. in later years, Donnelly in his day met England's Prince of Wales, and gave him something to think about. Everyone knows, that when John L. was introduced to that royal gentleman, who greeted him, 'I'm glad to meet you, Mr Sullivan, I've often heard of you', John answered, 'Glad to meet yourself, Prince, I've often of you, too'. When Wales greeted our Donnelly and said, 'Mr Donnelly, I understand you're the best man in Ireland', the Irish champion replied, 'No, sir, I'm the worst man in Ireland: I'm only the best man in England'.

3   Rambling was a main feature of night life in Glen Ainey. Almost every man, and many boys, rambled on every night the winter round — ramble being term for the leisured night-visit to a neighbour's house, where, around a gay fire, the family and the rambler, or ramblers — sometimes there was one visitor, sometimes there were ten — sat and talked and listened from dayli'gone till rosary time. Rambling was done to neighbouring houses, homes within a mile's distance from the rambler's own, and was an every-night occurrence. When on

occasion, the rambler took it to his head to visit a house three miles or six from his own, that was raking. 'When I was rambling over there at Peter O'Cuinn's night before last, I heard such and such news.' But, 'On Sunday night was eigh'-days, I was raking above in Altidoo in Neddy Cassidy's, when I heard so and so.'' Our gasúr did not rake till later years, but through his childhood and early boyhood was an inveterate rambler. The Gaelic term for the pastime, céilidh, commonly used in many other localities, was not used in Glen Ainey.

CHAPTER EIGHT

Mountain Adventures

In roaming the mountains, Jaimie, for his years, had adventures a-plenty. But a few outstanding ones befell him there — some of them memorable — to him — and at least one blood-curdling.

Every year his father sent a heifer or two to the hills in the spring — to the Gasúr Mór's mountain, Sru-Aill. The Gasúr Mór[1] took many such beasts from the seaside for the summer grazing. He herded them on the hills till they were wanted for selling in the Harvest Fair, or for fattening on the lowlands — when he got five shillings a head for his grass and his services.

It was a thrill to the boy when he was sent to Sru-Aill, a couple of times over the summer, to find how a heifer was doing. He started the seven mile journey at break o'day; and at Sru-Aill the Gasúr Mór would advise him about where on the hills the heifer was likley to be. When the boy had climbed the hill and found the heifer, and seen that she was lively, eating well, her nose moist, with herself growing big and bony, he went rambling exploring, discovering the wonders of the hills and of their lakes lying next the sky — sometimes tramping as far over the hills, and through their maze, as to view inhabited valleys on the other side — the Big Glen of Glenties, the Reelan, the valley of the Cruachs, and even a glimpse of magic Glen Fionn. The Gasúr Mór, alarmed for the lad's hardihood, often warned him of the danger of getting lost, advised him to fix, watch, and never lose memory of landmarks. But young as he was Jaimie had a good mountain sense, chose and kept his landmarks like an old hand — and smiled inside of himself at the Gasúr Mór's caution.

Yet he smiled too soon. Once a quick fog came down on him along way from his base — first time he had ever been caught in a mountain mist. It was with the boy — as it would have been with many a wiser one after nearly two hours trying this way and that way, falling into and out of bog holes, and by miracle missing a precipice, he realized he was lost. Drenched to the skin by the cold wet fog, through which he could see only a few feet, he sat down in despair, on a rock. Whilst sitting was safer far than aimless wandering, still the fog-chill would quick and the way to his bones: and since maybe the mist wouldn't lift before dark came down, it might well be his blanket till morning. Morning that he might never live to see!

Hard and fast he began to pray. And his prayer was surely answered — for in a little time his ear caught a tinkle, tinkle, the sound of which sent the blood (that he had feared would freeze in him) trotting through his veins again. He got up, and, exploring a bit this way and a bit that, found, to his joy, a tiny stream. Falling and rising, he stumbled along by the stream's side — which, if his strength endured, must eventually lead him off the hill; and into an inhabited world again. He realized that the stream flowed, not toward his own, the Glen Ainey, side of the mountains, but toward Glen Dubh. — But, what matter?

In less than half-an-hour's break-neck following of the Heaven-sent rivulet, lo, the fog lifted as quickly as it had come down! And, climbing an eminence to look out for a landmark that should place him, behold, the whole landscape had changed! No peak of his acquaintance, no hill-shoulder that he knew, was in sight! He had often heard in the old stories, of the *ceo draoidheachta*, the druid mist, under cover of which evil things worked their ill-will, and now he knew that he had been through one! So unfamiliar was every hill that he felt he must, in the magic mist, have been carried from the hills of Donegal to those of Connaught.

Sore perplexed, he returned to his tinkling friend, and followed it down, down the mountain side, till at last, to his delight, he saw far below, and off to the right, a thatched hut with smoke from the chimney. Drawing on the hut, great was his amazement — bedazement rather — to behold, standing at its gable-end, the Gasúr Mór! He, too, had been whisked off to Connaught in the *ceo draoidheachta!* And, when he was led within the hut, there was the Gasur Mor's wife! After a few dumbfoundered moments he asked, 'Are you people here, too?' Roisin, looking at him with pain in her eyes, said to her husband, 'He's *away*.[2] He must have met the mist, and been taken in it.'

Again unable to speak for a while, he looked from the door to make certain — which he did — that he was in a strange country, among hills that he had never seen before. The Gasúr Mór and his wife, Roisin, and even their little cabin — which he now began to recognize, although it had not looked itself from the outside — were in this strange country, too.

Roisin, who kept repeating, 'He's *away*. He's *away*' — about the only words of Enghsh she knew — soothed and fed him, took off his wringing wet clothes and on the out-shot bed in the corner wrapped him up warmly. He soon fell into a sound sleep and did not awake until it was broad daylight in the morning. On getting up and going to the door to look forth, he found to his relief that the cabin, himself, the Gasúr Mór, and Roisin had been whisked back to their own proper country during the night. There, to the left, was the familiar Grey Mare's Tail, its raging white waters roaring down from the hill. The infant Ainey Water he saw scurrying the valley a hundred yards below, the Laodhai Mor rearing his bold, bald head into the skies right above the cottage, and great grey Cruach Ghom shutting out a deal of the sky, opposite.

45

A wonderful tale now had he to tell, at home, to wide-eyed comrades who had never been taken in a *ceo draoidheachta*.[3]

But a far more alarming adventure was his on Maon-a-Uis mountain — not afterward, but maybe a year earlier — when he was still more a child.

This time, too, he had lost himself on the mountain top — not, however, in a *ceo draoidheachta*, but by heedlessness. He had wandered long, and was getting fearsome of the dark overtaking him on the hills, when he got a guiding mark, and was soon hurrying down the familiar and unsure, steep face of Lachtai Ban. Night had begun to fall when he reached a cabin, where were two people, man and wife, both of whom spoke Gaelic only. The *gasúr*, coming from the shore-side whose people had unfortunately lost the language, managed to let them know that he had missed his way on the hill, had now too far to travel home, and needed a roof and a bed till morning. It was a very poor cabin, and they were very poor people without a bowl or a mug on their dresser — although there were a couple of plates there, and a few tin-pandies filled with milk. A pot of stirabout was boiling for supper ; and the woman added to it more meal — from an arc that stood by the wall-side near the fire. She stirred it in with a pot-stick that was a bit of bog-fir, which she likewise used as tongs before and after its pot-service. When the food came off the fire it was laid outside the door to stiffen in the breeze. And there the woman had to herd it — fighting off a hungry red dog, who, in spite of her, managed a couple of times to get his nose in the food. But at length she reached him such a whack of the pot-stick that he went howling over the fields, and didn't come again.

When the stirabout was stiff enough she brought it in, set the pot in front of the fire, and made a hole in its centre into which she poured a pandy of sweet-milk. Three hungry people seated themeslves on stools circling the pot, and the boy was given the spoon of the house, that he might dig a chunk from the side of the pot, dip it into the milk-lake in the middle, carry it to his mouth and then pass the implement to the *bean-a-tighe* (woman of the house) who, after using, passed it to her *fear-a-tighe* — who, in turn, passed it to the boy again. So did the spoon keep circling till three good appetites were satisfied, and the pot almost empty.

After supper the *fear-a-tighe* fetched in a large wap of straw and with it made for himself and his woman a shake-down in one corner — while Jaimie, for honour, was shown to the out-shot bed, off the other chimney corner.

To the child's puzzling, as he stood up to make ready for bed the *fear-a-tighe* felt his arms and then his legs with a grip that wasn't gentle; and said something to his wife, who answered him only with an angry grunt. The two of them set to argue, then; he insistent about something and she impatient — while the boy, in wonder, remained on middle of the

46

floor. The man fingered the boy's arms and legs again, and wanted the wife to come and do likewise ; but she snapped at him — and then he got angry, and she angrier still. The boy began to get as frightened as a rabbit in a rat's hole, and instead of undressing and going to bed, as both the man and woman were now pushing him to do, sat down on the bed's side. His fear, however, flew off him when the *bean-a-tighe*, noticing his nervousness, came and patted him, spoke soothingly, and helped him off with coat and britches. She put him in bed, then, and wrapped him up.

Through eyes half-closed he watched the two seat themselves by the fireside, and the man light his pipe — both of them silent. The argument looked to be done with. But, just as he thought he would fall asleep, up it flared again — only, now they wrangled in low voice. Yet it soon grew hot, the man now and then turning half round to point at the bed. Jaimie's fright grew again — till his heart began to thump as if it would smash its way out.

The *fear-a-tighe*, at last, jumped up from the fire with a snarl, strode to the dresser, and taking up a big knife that glimmered and glinted when the light of the fire fell on it, felt its edge — which seemingly was not satisfactory, for he went out of the door and started sharpening it on a stone. The lad in the bed began to shake, and his shaking grew till he believed it was making the bed rattle. What made things sorer to his heart was that the woman at the fireside, her back turned toward him, now seemed content to let her man work his evil will. She had taken the man's pipe from the bole where he had laid it, and was puffing it as carelessly as if the world was turning to please her.

Bravely making up his mind to act before it was too late, Jaimie slipped without sound from under the bed clothes, grabbed his coat in one hand and britches in the other, tiptoed to the door, out into the dark, and away with him — in the opposite way from whence came the sound of the sharpening of the murder-instrument. He went carefully till he got beyond the garden into a meadow field, where he took to his heels, in spite of the darkness, and or like a hare with the hounds after. His legs were whipped by the night air, and his shirt tails floated after him; several times he tripped and plowed his nose in the earth, but was up and off almost before he was down, taking the drains at a step and the ditches at a hop. The darkness grew thinner before many minutes, though, and the starlight — for there was no moon — gave him enough view to let him loose his proudest speed.

He had run a mile and crossed a river, wading and hopping from rock to rock, before he halted by the byre of a house whose light had drawn him. Here, modestly, he stepped within his britches before entering a Christian habitation. Lifting the latch, he walked into a cheery kitchen where a large family were chatting round a blazing turf-fire the sight of which was enough to put the heart back in a half-dead poor lad's frame again.

For some reason or other he didn't care to tell these people (who spoke both Gaelic and Beurla) that he had just fled with his life from a terrible murderer of little boys who lived farther up in the hills. He told them how he had lost his way on the mountain, but at last got off it, by good luck, before the too-black night had trapped him. Rejoicing with him for his escape from a cruel night among the rocks, they wanted to press on him every eatable in the house, but he wouldn't and couldn't take a bite. Then they bedded him in a wide bed, with three other boys bigger than himself — in one of two bedrooms that were in this comfortable house.

Little rocking Jaimie needed to put him in his sleep — but wasn't well into it till he was awakened again by a flood of talk that swelled in the kitchen. Among other voices, he could clearly hear the rough big voice of the man who had wanted to murder him. The villain had followed him, it was plain, and discovered his refuge. Yet, Jaimie wasn't the wee-est bit frightened now. He knew good people when he came in contact with them: and the people of this house were unquestionably good, and would see no harm come to him.

Fast and excited grew the talk in the kitchen — all in Gaelic. And then, strange to say, there was laughter — a whole lot of hearty laughter. Now, the room-door opened, and the *bean-a-tighe*, a woman of very kindly face, coming in with a rush-light, followed by one of her girls, drew to the bed and looked into the face of the lad, who, pretending to be asleep, watched like a hawk through nearly closed eye-lids. He saw, after a little, the woman smile as she looked at him — and then her daughter smile, too, and nudge her mother. Then both of them laughed low and crept out of the room.

The next thing the boy knew, the streaks of dawn were coming in of the room's wee window. And he was remembering last night !

Quietly he got up on his elbow and saw his bed fellows yet sleeping soundly. He listened: everyone in the house was still sleeping. Out of the bed he slipped, and into his clothes — easy enough not to startle a cockroach. Then tip-toeing out of the house, and striking a bee-line over the hills, he scampered for his home, five mile away.

Come home, Jaimie said nothing about his awful experience for some reason or other felt afraid to say anything about it — but went around, miserable, with the dread secret festering in his breast. He told his father and mother that he had lost his way on the hills, and, getting off them too late, had spent the night in a mountain house. But lo! on coming from school that day — with mind made up to unburden himself of the horrible secret that was breaking him — when he walked into the kitchen what did he behold there but the *fear-a-tighe* of the mountain murder-house!

As if that in itself wasn't enough, the man was offering meat for sale — meat! — a haunch of it, from a creel of the stuff standing on his father's table. Jaimie put out of him a scream that alarmed everybody — including, of course the villain. And what would you have of it, but the rascal, when he saw the boy, put out of him a cry of pretended pleasure, and ran toward him. But Jaimie, giving off from him wild screams, jumped behind his father, and yelled, 'Get the police! Get the police! He's a murderer of wee boys, and it's a leg of one of them he's trying to sell you. — Get the police! the police!'

Ignorant of Enghsh, the bad man looked fearfully puzzled. But determined to soothe the lad, he stepped toward him again in friendly way. The boy made a burst to the room, slammed the door, bolted it, and through a knot-hole yelled back into the kitchen, 'Get the police, father! the police! He has murdered another poor boy this morning!'

Now he heard the man, in great excitement, get off a rapid flood of Gaelic to his father, who was a Gaelic speaker. And in a couple of minutes he heard his father burst out laughing loud. And soon his mother was laughing also. Just like the kind people in his house of refuge had done when this butcherer of little boys had told them his excited story.

Our *gasúr* was less relieved than he was angered and mortified on learning that it was only flesh of a calf the man was selling out of his creel — a calf that, it seems, he had knocked down last evening shortly before the lad arrived at his house. The boy's arrival suggested to him the solution of a difficulty: he had wished to kill two calves and make one journey to the village with them and their hides — but his creel couldn't carry all. As he needed to get the price of the hides as well as the flesh, the coming of the boy was a godsend: *he* would carry the skins. His wife objected that the lad was too soft for the task. The *fear-a-tighe* knew otherwise; and proved it by feeling the lad's good muscles. When she wouldn't be convinced he would have his own way, anyhow, and would kill the second animal. But the lad's flight — which astounded both him and his wife — left him to come to town with one calf only.

To the boisterous enjoyment of the household — everyone of them, that is, except Jaimie — the father, who was of a mordant humour, finished the man's story for him — 'And at the heel o' the hunt you found the other calf here before you.'

NOTES

1 The Gasúr Mor was then beyond three-score-and-ten, but was still known only by his youthtime nickname.

2 Taken away by the fairies.

3 Later, he was to learn — what the Gasúr Mor and Roisin well knew — that his was a common enough experience of people who, getting lost in the mountain mist, had their senses left in confusion for a time after.

CHAPTER NINE

Confession

Because he was so active, and consequently frequent in sin, the boy's going to confession was a fearsome undertaking. The beforehand raking of his conscience to count his sins was like digging old potato ground and trying to count the uncountable worms. And, even after this racking of his soul it needed the strength of a horse and the gall of a goat, to go kneel to the holy priest, and exhibit him, bit by bit, his depravity.

The *gasúr's* first confession was to a very holy man indeed, Bishop Logue of Raphoe. For all this good Bishop was so holy and so eminent that, later, he was to become Primate of All Ireland, and then Cardinal, he was a singularly simple man. When he came on parochial visit to Glen Ainey, always he shouldered his part of whatever parish work was proceeding — praying, preaching, or confessing. On a confession day, he sat, like the humblest curate, in a gloomy corner of the chapel, from dawn to dark, listening to old, sighing, moaning, groaning women, and little gabbling children tell him their woeful tales: and, even though he was tireder than a turf-cutter at the day's end, he was gentler and patienter with the crowd of sinners who then tramped him down, than he had been at the day's starting.

The *gasúr* edged himself to the Bishop's knee, artfully, following big Eamonn Og, card-player, cockfighter, poteen-drinker. For more than a hour he had let chances go by, go by, to execute this bit of strategy: for though the Bishop would still be startled at the recount of the lad's sins, yet, with Eamonn Og's crimes agitating his mind, the shock to the good man's soul wouldn't be quite so severe.

Most of his sins were against the Marquis. And God, of course. The boy was eminently descriptive and detailed in the confessional. He had snared a rabbit that had one black ear — in the Marquis's little, dark wood — not the big wood by the shore side, the Bishop was warned. But, in the big wood he killed a pheasant one day, knocking it down with a stick. He had robbed pheasants' nests of more eggs than he could rightly mind. From the Plantin' he had stolen sloes, nuts, wild cherries — and a nest of young thrushes. But two of the thrushes turned out no good. He had said bad words — *faith, troth, bedad* — *goghedies*, too, sometimes. He told lies — one of them mortal, that a serpent, one day, came out of a pool in the Ainey Water, near the Steps, and, putting its tail in its mouth to make a hoop, whirled after him till he got shelter in Hudy Hegarty's. He had told ten different boys, ten different times that he had seen Manus

51

a-Haraghey's ghost at the Bearna Dearg — when he knew it was a whinbush he had, for a wee while only, mistaken for Manus. He had found and kept a penny handball — asking 'Is it yours?' only of boys who, he knew, did *not* own it; and refraining from asking boys who were in danger of owning it. One day he had promised to tell Johnnie Carrabin the story of Jack the Apprentice Thief if he fetched him down a young magpie from the nest atop of the rowantree over Anthony MacNeely's — and didn't tell him the story after he got the bird. A far harder sin to tell was a grave wrong he did the Marquis — six different times that he was herding outside that noble's wood, he jumped his cows through the hedge to feed themselves on the long grass growing waste there — while he went looking for pheasants' nests. But, by far the shockingest, he had to confess to breaking the Seven Deadly Sins — he had been guilty of the dreadful sin of gluttony. On the morning after the fresh, sweet, new oatmeal had come home from the mill, he had shamefully eaten five bowlfuls of the stirabout! This ultimate crime he told after that of stealing the penny ball and robbing the Marquis. It climaxed his transgressions against a long-patient Heaven: and so mortified was he at spreading such depravity before so holy a man, that he broke down and wept; and the good Bishop, laying on his shoulder the gentlest hand in the world, said such consoling words to him that his tears, instead of stopping, flowed faster. He never could have anticipated that a so-high-up holy man could be so tolerant — indulgent even — to an infamous criminal. When he went away from Dr. Logue's knee he thought the world was a brighter place far than he had believed it to be — and felt himself stepping so light, after dropping his bags of sin, that he was sure he could cross the Ainey Water without wetting his ankles. The happiness he got from that gentle man's consolation, and absolution, almost — God forgive him! — would tempt him to go and sin again; so as to recapture or prolong that same happiness once more.

Though his first confession was to the Bishop, and in the chapel, usually he attended the Stations.[1] When the Stations were about to begin, after the harvest, the boy used to hear the Dean —saintly and beloved old Dean Feely, may God rest him! —call them from the altar on Sundays. 'On the morrow, Monday, eigh'days,' the Dean would proclaim, 'the Stations will start at the upper end of the parish. On that day we'll sit in Shan a-Bourke's of Shanveen for Shanveen, Cron Chairan, and the upper end of Deisard. On Tuesday they'll be at Litirfad, in Master Mulhern's, for Litirfad, Loch-fin, and Camlarigan. On Wednesday we'll sit in Drimarone — two of us in the Widow O'Donal's and one in Long John Meehan's of Litirtraina, for Drimarone, Litirtraina, and the upper end of the Ruahs. Thursday we'll be in Sallachas in Neil Og's for Lower Sallachs and the near end of Litirmor. And on Friday in Ellen McCabe's of

Dhrimagra for Dhrimagra, Upper Sallachas and the other end of the Ruahs. We'll have no Stations Saturday — but Father Mick will hear in the Chapel, in the evening, them that cannot conveniently attend in their own townland. I want to say that when we're sitting in Litirfad there's a rascally bunch of poteen-makers and card players in that territory, every man of whom I want to see there without fail. I'm going to have something to say to them vags, that day, that will raise blisters on their conscience, or I'm not Dean of Raphoe. I've had my eye on these laddie-bucks for twelve months gone, and been keeping a blackthorn in pickle for them — and if there's a one of them fails to show himself at the Station he'll be finding myself and the blackthorn paying him a call at his own backstone: and before we leave him, we'll put impressions on him that he'll be a *lachy* time losing.'[2]

Our *gasúr* often went the rounds of the Stations with his particular patron, the grey-haired old curate, Father Mick. Early on the Station morning the *gasúr* would see the men, the women, and the children flocking over meadow, moor, and bog to the Station-house — all dressed in their best. Crowds would be seated in the kitchen, watching — and sniffing — the roasting and frying for the Station breakfast — and observing the women-helpers dashing this way and that, tripping one another up, and scolding the seated ones for crowding the house and getting in people's way. Outside, knots of men gathered here and there, around the house and on the ditches, discussing the doings of Parliament while waiting for the priests' coming. But, up and down the lane that led to the house, and in the garden and nearby fields, worried ones meandered, examining their conscience and meditating on their sins.

The white-haired Dean was the first to arrive. He had driven Forgiveness (tied into a rattle-trap car) to Billy Haughie's at the end of the high-road, nearly a mile off — where the car was up-ended and Forgiveness stabled. Then he had walked the meadows, and jumped the river, to reach the Station-house. Father Mick would come a little later: for though he started from home early enough, he was likely to be footing it over the hills, with his hound, in behopes to raise a hare on the way. If the luck was with him and a hare up, the large crowd who'd bring themselves and their sins to no knee but his, would have a longer wait than that morning. If he hadn't had any luck on the moor they'd get shrived sooner.

When the priests had put on their stoles, and seated themselves by the big turf fires in the two rooms, sinners gathered around the room-doors outside — the lucky one holding the door-handle being next to enter the priest's presence. Outside Father Mick's door — because the greater part of the parish wanted to kneel to him — there was keen competition for the latch-holder. No wonder the poor man had often to quit his penitent, and come to the cloor to rebuke them — 'There ye are, pushing and

53

heaving, like bears, or the Red Indians of Buffalo. And some of ye don't even know where ye are going — don't even know your catechism. — Big Paddy Mailye, you're the most unmannerly savage of them all. And the most ignorant. Will you tell me,' and Father Mick posed him a regular, and easy question out of the catechism — 'Can priests forgive sins?' The regular — and expected — reply is, 'Yes, they can, for they have received that power from our Lord' — but Paddy, unexpectedly interpreting the doctrine by the spirit rather than the letter, answers him, 'Yis, your Riverence, they can — at their dead aise.' Whilst Father Mick hastily closes himself into the room again, Big Paddy looks around proudly over the crowd, who have lowered their heads, and clapped hands to their mouths.

For some reason all the notorious ones of the parish picked Father Mick as their confessor — maybe because he was very human, and known to say *damn*, times he was provoked.[3] He would understand them better than the Dean, who, though rough-and-ready, was, still, above and beyond all transgression against Heaven. And, the parish reprobates who put their trust in Father Mick had their trust justified, for though, outside of the Confessional, he could be, when provoked, one of the wildest and most violent of men, in it he seldom raised his voice above a murmur. Indeed it was one of the wonders that went forever unexplained to Glen Ainey people how the very roughest, bluntest, wildest priest was here transformed into a meek, sweet, tolerant, patient man. — You'd be puzzled what it was at all, at all, that came over him the minute he put on him the stole to listen to men's crimes.

After Mass and Holy Communion came off the great breakfast, when the schoolmaster, and the other notables of the district sat down with the priests — while those whose confessions were still unheard walked and talked in the yard, in the garden, and the fields, until the confessors should be at leisure to sit again.

It was to the Stations, then, as was the custom, that the boy Jaimie oftenest went to confession. But of the few Saturday evenings that he confessed in the chapel, there's one that will always be with him an embarrassing memory.— Because, as a child, he had begun tagging himself on to Father Mick when he found that beloved man taking to the hills with his gun and hound — or taking to his jaunting-car to journey to the Chapel or the Dean or to some old soul in the mountains who was getting ready to go to a greener land than even Ireland — the *gasúr* had, in a way, become a tolerated intimate of the good man — and because of this intimacy the little lad would sooner proclaim his sins on a public street crowded with scorners than uncover them to his adored patron. But on one fatal Saturday evening that he had journeyed to Frosses Chapel, to make confession, he, unfortunately, found no priest sitting but his own

54

friend. He first thought of going home again unshriven; but as he found that Father Mick was hearing in one of the darkest spots in a dark chapel, he pٰـٟtted with himself that he'd delay an hour till the dusk of evening, coming down, should make it entirely safe for him to slide from one side, unseen, to the knee of a man who, anyhow, heard confessions with face turned away. At a favourable time, burying his face in his coat-collar, the boy slid into the penitent's place, and in a voice he was sure his own mother would't know, said, first, the *Confiteor* and then detailed a long list of grievous sins, made his Act of Contrition, got absolution and was oh! so gratefully escaping into the unknown again, when a whisper from the priest turned him to stone. — 'Jaimie, child, wait a minute! — Will you tell Neil McCue to harness the mare and put her in the shafts, and have her here at the chapel-gate in ten minutes? — Then, you wait yourself and have a seat home with me!'

The humiliated boy delivered his message all right to Neil McCue —but the instant he did so took to his heels, and to the hills for home, his soul crushed with mortification. For a month after, by executing several bits of brilliant strategy, he kept from meeting Father Mick: till at length, one day, by misfortune coming against him suddenly, the priest greeted him, 'Why, Jaimie, you're a sight for sore eyes! Is it sick you've been for these five weeks, that I haven't seen hilt or hair of you? I'm hearing there's a hare in Micky MacMullin's land in Glen Cuach, and am going there this evening, and want you with me.' Father Mick spoke in such casual tone that it set the boy speculating whether God provided, like a miracle, that priests should teetotally lose their memory the minute they left the Confessional.[4]

NOTES

1 Held twice a year, at the end of harvest and at Easter, the Stations were a legacy from the Penal Days, those centuries when, their churches having been taken from the people, the priest was a hunted man who said mass at mountain rock, and heard confession in a hidden glen, or in some remote cottage, gathering the people to him there. This Penal Days' custom of the priest going the rounds of his parish, to hear confessions in this district and that, was continued down through the boy's day. Only on special occasions were the confessions heard in the chapel — on some Saturday evenings for a handful of people only.

2 The coming of the Stations was a great thing to them whose house the priest honoured. In the grace days given after the Chapel announcements the house was cleaned and scrubbed and white-washed inside and out; the whitest linens came out of the chest where they had lain for twelve months; from east and west, where ever they could be found, were borrowed fancy tea-pots, choice chinaware, fine cutlery, to grace the house and honour the priest. On the day before the priest's coming, and on that morning, there was, in the house, boiling and broiling and frying and roasting — and all the neighbouring women helped her on whom the burden fell.

3   Father Mick greatly shocked the child, Jaimie, one time that the youngster was with him on a hunt. The hound had raised, and was beautifully coursing, a hare, when a mongrel of Neil a-Moohan's, wanting his share of the fun, jumped in front of, tripped, and tumbled the hound. 'May the old divil himself out of hell damn you for a graceless cur'! rapped out Father Mick. Then, remembering little Jaimie, by him, and seeing the child's astounded look, he hastened to explain, 'You see, Jaimie, I consider that calling on the divil to damn anything is next best to asking God to bless it. It's only just out of grudge to the half-wit cur that I don't go the whole way'.

4   After Father Mick had, in his later days, got a small parish of his own, Killymard, Dr. Logue the Bishop, coming to visit, preached for him. Father Mick, disrobing in the Sacristy, after saying Mass, overheard the Bishop on the altar launch forth on the solemn subject of Mortal Sin — which the good man, at each frequently recurring repetition always pronounced 'mortal seen'. Those in the Sacristy noticed the old priest get impatient at hearing the subject — and his impatience grow as the sermon progressed — till at length, unable to contain himself in silence, he began striding up and down the Sacristy, exclaiming, in disgusted mimicry — all to himself — Mortal seen! Mortal seen! Mortal seen! — What's the fellow blatherin' about mortal seen? Sure mortal seen never came nearer here than the New Row' (a by-street of Donegal town in the next parish). Then he added — still to himself — 'Your old father, Mickey Logue of Carrig-Art, came nearer mortal seen than anyone here — the day he drove old Leitrim to his doom'.

Father Mick would have said, and possibly did later say, the same to the Bishop himself. And, if he did, the gentle man, himself a quiet wit, enjoyed it.

The reference to (Lord) Leitrim calls for an explanation: When this odious tyrant was, in Donegal, cut off in his crimes by tenants driven to desperation, it was on one of Cardinal Logue's father's cars he was being driven — whilst the accompanying car of police-guards were being driven by Michael Logue, himself. Logue's horse developed a mysterious lameness that, nearing the fatal spot, delayed the guards till Lord Leitrim was despatched. The legend goes in Donegal that when Michael Logue's son was chosen bishop, his consecration was delayed till an Ecclesiastical Court made searching inquiry, and was able to exonerate his father from all suspicion of complicity in a supposed crime.

Once that Bishop Logue and a priest friend of his were visiting Father Mick's church, the Bishop's friend noted for his prolixity, was set up to address the congregation; Dr. Logue, meanwhile, walking up and down the Chapel yard reciting his Office. When, after a long time had passed, with yet no sign of the congregation dispersing, and that the Bishop saw the Sacristy door open and Father Mick, fiercely scowling and pulling the hard hat down on his head, emerge — evidently having to hasten forth on some delayed business — 'Isn't Father Jimmy done yet'? the Bishop apologetically inquired. 'Done'? Father Mick flung back at him — 'The man's done a hour ago, but the divil can't stop him'.

CHAPTER TEN

His Father

The boy's family, like most in Glen Ainey, owned half-a-dozen head of cattle and half-a-dozen acres, which by dint of hard work and much coaxing helped them to exist from harvest to harvest. But though Glen Ainey was poor in worldly wealth, it was rich in that something greater which develops in the souls of a people noble by nature — refinement, intelligence, spiritualty. And, though his own people were unwealthy even among the unwealthy, the boy recalls with gratification that the family stood among the foremost. That was by reason of two things — the father's pride which compelled the respect, and the mother's fineness which drew the admiration, of every soul from Cruach Ghorm to the sea. Even those who were far better off, and should be of higher standing — by the world's measure — looked up to his mother with deference, to his father with respect.

One quality which his father had a-plenty was lack of diplomacy. He was as blunt as the back of a scythe, and direct as a dart. Commonly he wasn't a talker; but when he spoke he had something to say — and said it without a wasted word. When he had nothing to say, he left it unsaid — in a country where talk was the order of both day and night. He liked gabble a long sight less than a cat likes milk, and would go acres out of his way to miss the gabblers — people who, having nothing to say, said it in seven-mile clips. When there came into his home of a night, to gossip, one of those women with tongue hung in the middle he was likely to rise up, snort, shake from his shoes the ashes of his own fireplace, and choose a more congenial place to pass the night till bedtime. When he was provoked he could, off-hand, saddle on the provoker a nickname that proved a sticking-plaster —or cut off his nose with a bit of caustic wit that he didn't intend as wit, at all. For his wit was for use only, not ornament. During the Franco-Prussian War, when Glen Ainey was terribly troubled for poor France, the friend of Ireland, and for France's army led by the valiant Irishman MacMahon, a gathered group of neighbours, discussing the fight in Dainey Gillespie the cooper's, were drowned out by a deluge of blatherskite from Dainey's gabbler wife — who laid down for them the pros and the cons of the situation, and forecast the future moves of the French army. The lad's father simply commented, 'Marshal MacMahon must be writin' to you, ma'am.' And, after the little silence that ensued, the men found themselves free to continue their discussion.

He had that sort of spirited pride which, while never making him feel himself any better than his good neighbours, always and instantly lifted him over anyone, of any rank, who'd dare look down on him, or his neighbours, or the common people — and with sizzling scorn he could wither the snob. But if, for any good reason, he didn't want to express his contempt in words, he would radiate a scorn that could burn the eye-brows off his victim. Withal he had in his nature, deep-down, a well of gentleness, thoughtfulness. He could walk ten mile and stand Donegal fair with his cow, from sunrise to sunset of a summer day, without eating, and then, for wife and children carry home in his pocket, untouched, a half-dozen fine apples he had bought for them in the market-place.

Though he rarely gave it voice, his patriotism was deep. Love of country was in his blood anyway — for his grandfather and grand-uncle, who founded the Donegal branch of the family, had, for their work with the United Irishmen, to give up, at the rebellion's collapse, everything they owned in Armagh away, and fly for refuge to the wilds of Donegal. In remote Glen Ainey they sheltered — his grandfather, Torloch, and his grand-uncle, Seumas.[1] And, in their new home, they and their descendants always considered it their duty to keep love of Ireland warm in men's hearts.

Taking life seriously, he looked with pity on one of his brothers, Thaidy — not only because he was handicapped by a handsome face and figure, but because he was a country dandy, a sport, and — still worse — a famed dancer, the choicest runner of a reel, and fanciest stepper in jig or horn-pipe, that the three parishes knew. Thaidy cultivated a lovely, long, silly, auburn beard, the ends of which, for both protection and pride, he looped and plaited in and out of the buttoned front of his flowered waistcoat. Our boy's father, never heeding the good lines of his own well-chiseled, if weather-beaten, face, despised the rare complexion and beautiful beard of the dandy — just as much as he did his nimbleness of foot. But while he spared sarcasm on his brother's beauty, considering it more the poor man's misfortune than his fault, of his dancing he would say, 'The Lord pity the creature whose heart is in his heels.' And high-humoured Thaidy of the twinkling eye, to whom life was a song, could heartily enjoy the rap, and lead the laugh at his own expense. And, proud as Thaidy was of his own heels, prouder still he was of his elder brother's fists.

For, in his younger days, the boy's father was a famous boxer. In Glen Ainey of good fighters he never met the man who could best him. Though he was short, he was well knit, of powerful muscle, set steadfast on his feet as the rock of Carn, and with the courage of a wild-cat. The very biggest went down before him — till he became famed as the best boxer between the mountain and the sea. Even in his graver years, when he grew to consider fighting a vanity that sensible men should forget, his skill with his fists never forsook him — nor his courage and hardihood — as the great, strong Dinny Haughie, the blacksmith, and a few other big, strong, young, husky ones learned to their cost, when, presuming that his prowess had gone with the years, they dared to provoke him. On one such occasion a big fellow of these, suddenly finding himself hitting the ground with his head, asked — when he could — 'What was it you had in your hand when you hit me?'

'My fist,' was the quick answer.

The prostrate man, after pausing a moment on his elbow, to consider the reply, said, 'Well, in the Lord's name, keep it there.' And he got up and went away.[2]

The hardy man made handsome use of the great endurance with which God had blessed him. Early and late he slaved with the spade, sore striving to wrest from stubborn hills a living for his family. And in pursuit of his purpose he had the deepest disdain for the rigors of Donegal's mountain climate. Cold, heat, rain, frost or snow, storm or shine, were alike to him — and none of them ever stayed his unresting hand. He never found work that was too hard for him — and the very hardest was never known to tire him.

The boy thought the strong, patient, lionest, dutiful man was the salt of the earth.

... And he was. Strong and undaunted, that man faced moral hardships harder far to bear than physical ones — both he and his prized wife. For he brought up to the full-and-plenty of a *warm* mountain home, and she, to the comfort and refinement of a lowland one, had to face, after marriage, sad reverse of fortune and its succeeding scrimping and skimping, straining and struggling — as multiplied around them the family that had to be fed and clad and kept respectable on some paltry acres of niggard soil. Ill-fortune, though, called forth, in both, their noted family pride, which so bravely buoyed them in the hardest struggles that neighbours came to say the lower fell their fortunes the higher they held their heads. Their heartbreaks — and many, many such they must have had — they would betray not even to their children. For their bravery and faith the good God rewarded them — through their children. They were to see the long-ebbing tide turn — and flow again — bestowing on them bounty in full and ample measure.

NOTES

1 Torloch there took to carpentry, and Seumas to weaving — and worked their way up from nothing to leading places in the parish. Some of Torloch's chairs are, after one hundred and forty years' rugged use, still doing stout service by some Glen Ainey firesides.

2   Here for a minute, to take a long jump ahead, it may be related that, after the gasúr had grown to manhood, sailed to fabled lands to push his fortune, and made his name known in those land, he found himself one day in the city of P————, in an out-of-the-way corner of Texas, where he was due to lecture at the College. A good old Irish priest, Father Barney Lee, turning up to welcome him, was showing him the sights of their city when they beheld coming their way, a man of generous proportions. 'Why', Father Barney cried, 'here comes Denis Meehan — and I do believe he's from Donegal, too'.

He stopped the man. — 'Is it from Donegal you are, Denis'?

'It is so, thank God'.

'Thank God'! clerked Father Barney — though it was from Leitrim himself hailed: — 'Then you're going to be delighted to meet the greatest Donegal man of them all, my friend here, So-and-So' giving the gasúr's name.

''Tis welcome ye are to P————', said Denis, shaking our lad's hand cordially enough.

'He's a gr-r-reat writer', said Father Barney, wanting from Denis more than ordinary heartiness for the high occasion.

'Oh, indeed'! remarked Denis, with the calm of who didn't know or care much about literary achievement.

'And a notorious lecturer', prodded Father Barney.

'Indeed! That's fine'.

'Known, read, and famous through every one of the forty-eight States, with Canada thrown in', Father Barney resolutely worked on.

'Ah! I'm glad to hear it', with a casualness that provoked, though it didn't yet discourage, Father Barney

'He's a man has an international reputation'.

'Good'! said Denis.

'He's come from the University at Austin where he was lecturing for the past week. And going to lecture at the College here to-night. And after that they are waiting for him at Baylor University, the morrow'.

'Glad to hear it '.

'He's lectured at Harvard and Yale, and the University of Arizona'.

'Isn't that wonderful'!

'He's made the name of Donegal known and noted the world over '.

'More power to him'!

The disgusted Father Barney turned to our lad, saying angrily, 'come on'!

But Denis put a hand on the lad's arm. — 'Wait a minute. — You say you come from Donegal. — Where in Donegal'?

'From Glen Ainey'.

'From Glen Ainey'! the man's eye flashed, and the laziness left his voice. 'Why that's my own Glen Ainey! — Where are you from, there'?

'From Knockagar'.

'Knockagar! Where did you live in Knockagar? and whose child are you, anyway'?

'Ours is the house that stands at the foot of the Old Brae, where the three roads meet. My father is Pat So-and-So'.

'What'! roared Denis with a roar that brought back Father Barney.

— 'What'! Denis seized the gasúr's hand in the grip of both his big ones — 'The son of Pat So-and So! the best boxed man that ever stepped in to shoe leather! Best man in all of Glen Ainey, and the County Donegal! It's a thousands welcomes ye are to P————! — Father Barney, will the two of ye come home with me till I let the wife and children see Pat So-and-So's son? Wait! Don't move from that spot till I buy a bottle of whiskey. My soul, this is a terrible day for P———— entirely'!

When the boy, returning later to Donegal, told his father of the encounter, the man couldn't completely hide his pleasure at hearing how the praise of his prowess was sounded in far-away Texas — though he made desperate effort not to show it.

CHAPTER ELEVEN

His Mother

To be sure every boy's mother is the greatest mother that ever was. The *gasúr's* mother was all that — and something besides.

A rare combination she was of sarcasm and sympathy, whimsy and deep feeling. Nothing short of a slave to home and family, she yet took heart-whole interest in all humanity that came her way —and much of it came her way, for that very reason. In the midst of scantiness she was a wealthy woman — inside. Backburdens of trials and troubles she wouldn't let herself bend under — but carried them with light heart and high head. Through the thousand hardships that march with struggling mountain people striving to raise a large family, Jaimie rarely remembers his mother without either a glint of fun in her eye or a stave of song on her lips.

A neat sarcasm she had — mighty handy for keeping in order a troublesome family. If you too bothersomely nagged her about something, that woman could strike you speechless with an old proverb, or crack on your head a joke that stunned like the blow of a stick — but was sorer far, because it left you no place to rub. Full of both whimseys and saws she was anyway, and kept them bright from constant use. To hurry Jaimie, sent on an errand, she would warn, 'Let you not be there till you're back' — and 'If you fall don't take time to rise again.' If he blunderingly came back without his errand, or botched it, he would be scored with, 'Send a goose to Dover, and there'll come another over.' Every time she found him too ready to fall in with the ways of each latest adviser, it was, 'Hagh! Billy Harran's wee dog, who went a bit of the way with everyone.' 'His mind's a kingdom to him' — she would unwittingly quote Shakespeare (or were Shakespeare and she only quoting the same old saw?) — this when he chose to be uncommunicative. 'There he goes to dig praties, in the bottom of the trunk!' many a time frightened the lad out of a new waistcoat or from under a new cap — when occasion didn't call for formal dress. On the other hand, 'Here she comes in her dizzy-bells!' terrorized the too-hurried daughter who showed up without tidying herself: and the Frenchman who first coined *déshabille* didn't give a word to the world half as true-sounding as it became in his mother's mouth. And many times when he thought he could, unseen, slip to school with hair uncombed, he was staggered by, 'There he goes, with his head in an uproar like the Fair o' Carney!' When, as often happened, one of her children on an urgent errand dilly-dallying, returned long late, he was sure to meet the grim greeting, 'The grand messenger you'd surely be to send for Death.'

61

Faith in, and reverence for, the traditions of her race were in the marrow of her bones; and to her children she gave that faith and on them impressed that reverence. On May Day they should strew the doorsteps and window-sills with the blest Mayflower that to all evil barred entrance from Baal-tinne to Baal-tinne. On Bridget's Eve she had her children cut the rushes and at fall of night bring them in with due ceremony and place them beneath the table on which the festive supper would be eaten — and showed them after supper how to plait from them the lovely Bridget-crosses which, when blest, should guard bed-head, door-head and byre till the Saint's ever came again. At bedtime on the even of All Souls' Day she led in the Long Rosary for the departed ones; and, on that mystic night when the souls of the near and dear ones, getting respite from purgatorial fires, revisited the home and the hearth where they had had their joys, she, before retiring, tidied the house for them, rearranged the rows of flowered delph on the sand-whited dresser, swept every nook and corner, built a cheery fire, wiped every stool and chair and set them in wide circle around the trigged hearth — for the seating of the silent ones who ere midnight would come trooping in and before cock crow take their departure again.

Scrupulously she observed the treaties of tradition — more eminent far, in her eyes, than those indited by lawyers on parchment. — As those long ago made with the now-dumb animals who, poor creatures, are at everybody's mercy. She brought up her family never to beat a cow with the *borach* — the heavy-looped, hard-knotted rope that bound the animal to its stake in the byre. Whilst she would never hesitate to punish the thief of a cat whom she found pushing the cover off the milk-bowl, the same cat could help itself to the most precious of pieces left uncovered, and then, unmolested, come sit on its tail along-side her on the hearth, and look up impudently at her, while provokingly licking its chaps.[1]

She taught her children never to presume future action without con-ditioning it, 'If God spares me.' She had a prayer to be breathed at kindling of a fire, another at its raking, and one at the giving to her brood of the blest candle-light. None ever quitted her house upon a journey without being sprinkled with the holy water, and blest in the name of Father, Son and Holy Ghost.

Although neatness was a passion with her, she never in all the years combed her hair on a Friday, but before retiring on the night before — for she, a Mary, remembered, and honoured by imitation, three Marys who, on a certain unforgettable Friday gave their disheveled hair no thought.

If Jaimie and the rest of the family hadn't absorbed fairy faith from the atmosphere their mother would have put it in them — for her faith in the Good People wasn't just static but missionary. She brought up her children to reverence all fairy haunts, the Mount, the raths, their playgrounds on many a Glen Ainey hilltop, their *sciog* bushes from which one mustn't break a twig, any more than they'd break a Commandment. She taught the youngsters always to pray, 'God bless you!' when anyone sneezed — the fairies having, for that instant, power over the victim.

Her children from her learned, no matter how hungry they'd be at quitting the table, never to finish their portions — to leave nor plate nor bowl lacking what she properly called the fairy bit — a modest offering which reassured the watching Good People that they were not forgotten by anyone in *her* house.

She was grateful for the fairies' constant kindness, and instilled her own gratitude in her children; giving many an account of their help to the distressed — and many another of their punishing people who earned it. Half-Scottish Bab McClay, for instance, who, scorning 'fairy super-stitions,' built his house on a fairy rath that all the world except himself reverenced — began to have his cattle die, his crops rot, his horse go lame, his wife turn against him, and the world itself begin revolving the wrong way. Until, his eyes opened through suffering, he threw down the house and built it on a spot that voices had indicated to him — thereafter, himself and a happy wife and family prospering as they had never prospered; till their well-doing was 'a parable for the parish.'

Jaimie's mother had twice heard the banshee cry — the — one that was attached to the Mulloy family, her family. And once she had herself seen the white-clad figure of the long black hair — in a tree by her father's house — raising her blood-curdling lament for one of the family about to leave the world.

But great as was his mother's interest in the ultra-human, human interest was with her greater still. Though she came — from Dhrimholme, beyond the Bay — a stranger to Glen Ainey, she soon came to know every man and woman from the hills to the sea, their relations and inter-relations — knew the name that Neil Partholan's wife owned before she took Neil; the boy to whom Nuala MacCahill gave the go-bye when she wedded old Neilis McGroarty and his forty-acre farm — likewise the girl whom, then, the deserted boy chose to console him; knew what fortune Manus a-Tolan forwent when he refused to be matched on Maura Kelly, and what fortune exactly — a pitiful one — he got with the girl he loved; knew the ludicious goast that Maura Kelly's father made at the matchmaking, and the odd omen that showed on the way to the wedding. All this by reason her humanity was keen, and her memory marvellous.

It was this same humanity of hers that drew to her door a constant stream of friends, acquaintances, and would-be acquaintances — all clamouring to confide to her the latest chapter, or maybe only paragraph, of their family history. These people just mortally hated to pass Mary Mulloy's[2] door without dropping in — and having dropped in, it was like talking to themselves when they unburdened to her everything that was on their minds and the minds of their family. The boy watched his mother, while they spoke, come and go at her work, still give them heart-whole attention — and send them away lightened of mind, brightened of heart, and right well pleased that they hadn't let hurry carry them 'past the road' without stopping. He knew some of these unburtheners who, after sitting and speaking for a solid hour, and only hearing from their hostess an odd word or question, would remark to companions, as they quitted her door, 'Well isn't that or not a wonderful woman? Did ever you know her likes?' Which always the companion never did.

His mother had particular interest in all *shuilers*. There was never wanderer or beggar, tinker or pedlar, crossed her threshold without finding themselves seated, and their story drawn from them. Ere they arose to walk the world again, she had got the history of themselves, their family, their friends, their enemies — and they had left with her, moreover, their griefs and their gaieties, troubles, trials, and prospects.

Seldom she left her house to go on any 'jaunt' (as she facetiously named every outing) — because home duty was too heavy. Only, one jaunt there was that she never in long years missed, the six-mile walk to and from early mass on Sundays. For that, she put on her lovely, old-time, flowered petticoat and linsey-woolsey skirt, and tied round her neck with big bow-knot her broad, white, sprigged tie, donned her flowered bonnet, and her paisley shawl (taken out of its careful folds in the trunk), and started her three-mile jog over the hills the bogs and the moors, to Frosses Chapel, driving royal tandem (as she called it) — one foot before the other. Both because it was notable to be in her company, and that her words were wisdom (with a colour of gaiety), to walk the way with her, there and home, was a prize for which the women, her neighbours, vied. And it was proud to them to tell, when they returned, 'We walked with Mary Mulloy.'

On Sunday aftenoon, first time in a week that she halted for breath, she did, always, one or other of three things : She sat straight (her only way) in her chair, shut her eyes, and slumbered for an hour, while peace, flowing in of door and window, wrapped her round and filled the house till she awoke: Or she mounted her spectacles and read one of two books — off which she had worn the backs and the corners and parts of many pages, and which she kept bound with a bit of tape when not in use — The Holy Bible and The Lily of Israel — books which, no matter how poor their appearance to blind eyes, for her never grew old nor lost their lustre. Or, if the afternoon was enticing, she wandered up the Mount, and, sitting on a rock-seat half-way to the top, would, for a solid hour gaze across the Bay to her own Dhrimholme, searching out the hills and the holms where she had played and herded in her childhood, and from which her heart had never departed.

When, in later days our lad, gone to a big town, brought home a shilling telescope he brought her joy — for it helped her to see, in far Dhrimholme, houses that had almost receded into dreamland, fields over which she had liltingly footed, and her uncle's hillside farm, with the tide washing its toes. She thought she could see bushes that she knew forty years ago, ditches she used to leap, gaps that she often flew through, and, plainly, the fairy rath that crowned Carrig Alt. Coming of the Mount, now, she would tell the family long-forgotten happenings and anecdotes which this bush or that cog-field or Nancg Tummany's white gable-end brought to her mind. Then she would start the Sunday supper, crooning to herself a snatch of some old ballad that she used to know in the far-away land and days she had just been happily revisiting —

> 'Heigh-ho! — I heard the dogs barking,
> Then I — went out for to see:
> And, oh — I saw a man coming,
> But ah, — he wasn't coming for me.'

She found no time to read on week-days — with a slight exception. — On the time that a borrowed *Derry Journal* was brought into the house she would always take ten minutes from her work — not to *read*, but *study*, the Births, Deaths and Marriages. Though these great events occurred in and around the far-off, big city of Derry, in families of social rank far, far above her own, of whom she had never before heard, and never would hear again, they were of tremendous interest. These bare dates, names, and places, she would pore over — and would want to read aloud to anyone, friend or stranger, who would listen, for such wonderful happenings must be of the same vast importance to everyone else in the world that they were to her.

Though she was of a charity as wide as the world, Jaimie's mother had a quick eye for both the ridiculous and the ludicrous in anyone — in everyone. Affectation, or anything approaching it, drew her devastating irony. As the boy's father was plagued by a too-nice brother, his mother was bothered a bit — but oftener amused — by a *precieuse* sister. Aunt Cassin, a nice maiden lady, was as correct as the Queen of Spain, only a wee bit higher-mannered and choicer-spoken. She had got her grand manners from an ancient aunt who reared her, the wife of a navy officer who had been a middy under the Englishman Nelson.[3] The exquisite Aunt Cassin was the keeper of the relics of the family from the far-away time they had been famous — the shawls, silks, jewels, and genealogy. Of the last she was naturally proudest, and on it descanted when opportunity offered, or did not offer. When, as sometimes happened, the poor lady went without breakfast and dinner so as to afford a supper, she didn't much mind, because always she had the proud family-tree to browse on — even if it was a good bit withered. Jaimie's sensible mother had nicknamed her The Viscountess. — 'Get on your drawing-room manners, now, children,' she would announce, after looking from the window — 'I see her ladyship, The Viscountess, coming to call.' [4]

When the lad's mother, who always faced the facts of life sanely, didn't shut off with a sarcasm Aunt Cassin's genealogical dissertations, she would say, 'Your Ladyship, it's what you *are* that matters, not what you might have been.' Then the aunt would shake a noisy, very ancient satin skirt that always frightened the cat, sniff the size of a small tin-pandy of air, and mutter something about ignorance being surely bliss to some. But, on one such occasion, when the noble aunt remarked that she should have known it was idle to put pearls before swine, her quick sister answered her, 'You let yourself off easy, my dear, calling it idle. — The one who'd put a pearl instead of a pratie before a pig, shouldn't be left loose.' Aunt Cassin, this time giving the rich skirt such a rustle that the dog fled from the house with a howl, arose, stalked across the floor, and out of the door — letting days pass without re-visiting one who considered it no mortal sin to treat noble lineage with levity. 'What better could you expect of me,' the mother pleaded, 'when I disgraced the noble lineage by marrying the grandson of a gallows- bird?' She was looking mischievously under her eye at the descendant of refugee Torloch — who smoked his pipe in the chimney-corner facing her. He, never in his life getting to know when this woman was serious and when frivolous, snorted and went on smoking. Then — for, once the mischief caught hold of the woman, there was no halting her — she looked down to our *gasúr*, sitting between her and the fire, and said, 'Who knows but maybe wee Jaimie here will some day captivate a born lady and make all of us nobility again?' The *gasúr*, who was taking his usual serious interest in the fireside argument, arose from his creepy-stool, swept over his mother's feet, and out of the house. It was too much of a joke to crack upon a poor wee boy in hand-me-downs several sizes too big for him, and he would never, never again enter a house in which he had been so wantonly insulted. A vow that he religiously kept till a late supper time.[5]

NOTES

1   His mother would tell the boy how the animals that now we call dumb could all of them speak once on a time; but abused their gift and were deprived of it. Once that the King of the World returned to his castle from a long journey, the animals whom he had left in charge while he was gone met him and poured in his ear such evil about his beautiful young wife that, in a passion, he slew her. When remorse came to him, he, enraged with the tattling creatures, called together all of them in the world and commanded that they should give up again the gift of which they had proved themselves undeserving. They refused, and there

followed a long and bloody war between them and mankind — ended at last by a compromise: — in exchange for certain privileges to each, they all agreed to resign their speech. Each animal claimed the best boon for its kind. As, the horse's compensation was that he should not be pushed against the hill, the cow claimed not only not to be eaten with the borach, but the privilege of being sung to when yielding her milk for the family. The cat for her part claimed and got three boons: vision in the dark, a noiseless tread, and the good-wife's forgetting.

2 In the boy's country, then, a married woman's maiden name often persisted into, and through, her married life — more especially if she had a distinctive personality. The boy knew some cases where even the children went by their brave mother's name, rather than that of a colourless father.

3 A drinking-glass of Nelson's (from The Victory) is still in possession of some member of the family — with many other heirlooms which Aunt Cassin had guarded as she did her soul.

4 They were descended, through their mother, from Sarah, Viscountess Ranelagh, whose worth, in the now-Irish side of the family, was that she was sister to the gallant Donegal man, General Richard Montgomery of American Revolutionary fame. The boy's mother and aunt were General Richard's grand-nieces by two removes. For Sarah, a great grand-daughter of Viscountess Sarah, fallen on evil times, and coming as guest-governess to the Brookes of Loch Eske Castle — Brookes who had grabbed the patrimony of The O'Donnell, Chieftain of Donegal — met, fell in love with, and married a brown-haired, broad-shouldered, tall, handsome, young Donegal farmer — thus to become grand-mother to our Mary Mulloy.

5 Two other sisters the woman had, Aunt Sarah and Aunt Anne, fully as remarkable as Aunt Cassin — only in different ways. Aunt Anne, a high-souled woman, was a philosopher-humourist with the sparkle of the quartz on Cruachan Airgid, and all the calm of the Loch of Carn. If the skies cracked and the moon dropped to her feet down the chimney, she would just remark, 'Well, sure I've been looking for a pot-lid, anyway'. Than Aunt Sarah the boy was never in his life again to meet a woman more impressively, and yet effortlessly, the great lady. The wife of an irascible — yet lovable — small shop-keeper in a cross-roads hamlet, that woman had a natural poise, composure, affability, and royal graciousnesss that would instantly pleasure and put at ease Queen Cleopatra if she happened to drop in for a penny spool — and send away the titular royalty examining her conscience, 'Now, why is it, anyhow, that I can't seem to find the way to be as true-queenly as that woman'?

CHAPTER TWELVE

The Mother's Entertaining

The boy remembers his mother best when she was most in her element — among her children by the fireside on the long winter nights. For when, with a 'God be thanked, that's another day in!' she subsided into her own straw-bottom chair in the chimney corner — with nothing more to do till morning except knit and sew and darn for eight people — it was the beginning of a great evening. Free of the day's cares, she plied her needle (for she never let her hands lie in her lap) and soliloquised on memories so captivating that no child would stir for fear of stopping her. She went on to tell funny stories, sing bits of songs and old ballads, take off quaint characters of her childhood days, recount strange experiences — ramble through a medley of rare entertainment, from candle-light to fire-raking. And as she rambled she smiled to herself a curious sort of inside, self-enjoying smile, that was well worth watching. As Jaimie was, later, to realize, that was what made the whole thing so extra delightful: in entertaining the family, she was first, foremost, and above all, entertaining herself.

Far different ballads she chanted from those that were common in Glen Ainey — old English ballads most of them, come down through the English side of her family from the time they had come into Ireland, centuries before — chief among them the many and long, delightful adventures of Robin Hood, Will Scarlet, and Little John — which she could sing for the length of the lee-long night.

Some of the stories she told her children by the fire were parables meant both to entertain and to instil in them principles good. A few samples —

When the hungry fox, unable to find better prey, would raid the wren's family, he found them on the barn floor, a father and eighteen children, threshing — and there was no telling father from child because of the almost equal thumb-size of all. Could he only know the father and pounce on him, the panic-stricken children would then be at his mercy; but if by mistake he pounced upon one of the young the father would get seventeen safely away. So, the sly fellow sang out, 'Good the old man's stroke!' Whereupon the foolish old fellow, lowering his flail and putting a hand on his side, with head held high, said proud-boastingly, 'Tis so, thank ye, but you should have seen my grandfather's.' Next instant the vain fellow's head was off, and the heads of his eighteen children quick followed it to the floor. — 'Don't be too quick to swallow every bit of idle praise, children —till you know well who's the praise-giver.'

In her own grandfather's day there was in the upper end of their parish, a miller who, when came the Dear Summer,[1] with meal scarce and corn not to be found, wouldn't let the fairies want howsoever he might hunger himself. As ever good miller, when his milling ends, always leaves some meal in the hopper for benefit of the Gentle People, he from the bottom of his near-empty last bag of meal took a mether of it and threw it in the hopper for the good purpose. Behold ye, on the next night after, and on the next, and the next night again, and every night for a week, he could hear the mill grinding and him in bed; and in the morning there would be bags of meal ground and filled for him. Out of respect for Them that he knew were working he didn't pry for a while; but one night, overcome by curiosity, he sat up and, after the mill began grinding at midnight, tiptoed to the mill-window and looked in. What he beheld was a leprechaun sitting on a high stool in middle of the mill floor acting as miller and directing the operations of a hundred little fellows who as fast as they could trot carried in on their backs and emptied into the corn-hopper little bags of corn-while the mill worked at full speed. Noticing that the little fellow was dressed in the raggedest dress that man or mortal ever beheld, the miller, out of gratitude, got next day the finest silk dress that money could buy and left it convenient for his benefactor. When at midnight the leprechaun found the beautiful dress, he quick threw off his old duds, stepped into the new, and fell in love with himself in the grand rig. After admiring himself to his heart's content, he cried, 'Tis a sore thing that such a hand-some prince as me should be doing dirty work in a mill!' —and strutted off with him. The workers, without a head, began neglecting their work, and soon stopped altogether. The mill ran out of corn, couldn't grind another grain, and the miller's luck was ended. — Her children never must let fine feathers (God look to her innocence!) turn their heads or decoy them from their duty. And the moral was double-barrelled: the children saw, now, why their wise mother didn't risk spoiling them with too many gay trappings!

There was a loch that she knew in the Laighey Barr mountains at whose bottom was imprisoned the last serpent in Ireland. It had escaped Patrick when that saint was driving out its fellows — so, when, thinking his work finished, the Saint found this fellow on Laighey Barr, he angrily ordered him also off to the sea. But the fellow was so stubborn, the Saint so tired, and the sea so far off, that Patrick, wearied from arguing with him, struck a bargain that he should go into Loch na Peiste (Loch of the Serpent), and remain at its bottom till 'the morrow.' The rejoicing snake agreed to what he, silly fellow, thought was a mighty light sentence. But the fellow is still at the loch's bottom — waiting for that ever-fleeing 'morrow.' In her young days all the children within miles of Loch na Peiste would, at break of day, hear the fellow, putting his head above the waters, cry out in mournful Gaelic, 'Is it the morrow yet? Is to-day to-morrow-? Is it the morrow yet? Is to-day to-morrow?' But no, the morrow was always twenty-four hours away. — Children should know, what the snake learnt in bitterness, that the morrow they would depend on never, never comes.

One parable, however, she had, a perennial delight to her children, but the application of which they never figured out —nor indeed ever lamented its loss. It was the story of Conal, Donal, Hudy and Taig. Let out from school one day to play, the four stole to the loch to bathe, and Hudy was drowned. The angry Master had the other three up before him. 'For what reason did you dare go to the loch to bathe?' he demanded of Conal. 'Sir,' Conal answered him, 'I didn't know how to swim and I was wishful to learn.' 'You, sir, dared go into the water without knowing how to swim! It's a miracle that we didn't have two drowned people today instead of one. I'll teach you! I'll tan your hide and teach you! — just as soon as I get rid of these two others. — Stand aside.'

Then of Donal he demanded, 'Why did you, sir, presume to go into the loch today to bathe?'' And Donal, profiting by what he had just heard, answered confidently, 'Because, sir, I knew how to swim, and so thought it no harm.' 'You already knew how to swim! Then, sir, you had no shadow of reason in the world for going into the water — except to tempt Providence. Sir, I'll whip you till I whip every inch of the hide off you! — Stand aside till I've time to attend to you.

'And now you, sir,' he said to Taig, 'what business had you going into the loch to bathe today?' And Taig answered, very clearly as he thought, 'Sir, I didn't know whether I could swim or could not swim, so I went into the loch to find out.' 'You didn't know whether you could swim or could not swim, and went into the loch to find out! You, sir, who don't know and want to find out, are the very fool at bottom of half of the world's tragedies. You, sir, are by far the worst reprobate of the three, and I'll *ludher* you as long as I'm able to stand over you! Let the three biggest boys in the school come up here and mount these three blaguards on their backs, till I introduce to them some wisdom through the medium of their hides.'

But most of her stories were of her own childhood-country, Laighey in Dhrimholme. And she had a way of story-telling that Jaimie never knew any other woman, and only one man, to possess — a way that could take hold of the littlest anecdote and make it a gripping tale. And at the same time her way bestowed on the story such perennial freshness that when she told it for the hundredth time (as musing persons will) it charmed the children even more than it did the first. Not that the woman *needed* to repeat herself just for sake of something to tell: for, never in a lifetime could she come to his end of all the sayings, doings, and happenings, the characters and customs of Dhrimholme in the time when, a lithe, blithe youngster, she had a free foot and a fellow for it, there.

Aside entirely from her infinite stock of lesser stories, it would need a mighty great book to hold her epics — of happenings dramatic, romantic, pathetic, or heart-breakingly funny, that fell in the same droll Dhrim-holme.[2] In her childhood — as well as now in her womanhood — her eye for character was keen as flint — and for the ridiculous, and the whimsical. The Dhrimholme neighbours of her childhood days, men and women long dead, she called up on this Glen Ainey hearth, and set walking again — with all their quirks and quips, oddities, sayings, and doings — and she showed all that befell themselves and their children — till *her* children (and maybe Jaimie especially) came to know them as if they had lived with them.

Jamie knew, as though he had neighboured them, the ghost-fearing Ned Haran and wife, who wouldn't cross the road to the cow-byre after dark, but at bed-time fothered their cattle by flinging them a wap of hay — from their own open door, through the byre-door beyond. If the cows could reach it that was good — but if they couldn't reach it, it wasn't altogether so well with the poor things.

There were the three very nice old bachelor MacGragh brothers who did, each in his turn, the housewife job, in a home that shone like the Silver Strand — who marched shoulder by shoulder to mass and market, wedding and wake, in like blue-broadcloth suits and overcoats, polite to everyone but over-familiar with none, 'the Three Wise Men of the Aist' — but who, despite their wisdom, met with disaster when they let the youngest, at the frisky age of nine-and-forty, try his hand with a wife. Unappreciating the boon of being trained by three masters, Rosie Throwers refused to be broken to their ways — but broke their furniture, and their heads, and, almost, their hearts — before they bought her off, and became bachelors again, and comparatively happy.

And Long Val Connolly, persistent night-rambler though timorous of the evil things that walk in the dark. Against these Val always carried with him two prayer-books, one in each side pocket. With one prayer-book he began his career — but since the fearful Candlemas night that the ghost walked with him from Mullinasole to Carrig Alt, always on the side that the prayer-book was not, and changing sides as often as Long Val changed the prayer-book — he carried two for efficiency.

And his mother's kind neighbours, the orchard-owning MacCaslans, who, good Methodists, never engaged in financial transaction on the Sabbath. The sinner (like his mother) who *would* buy apples on the sacred day, could walk past their open door into their orchard, pluck four fair-sized apples (the sinner's honour was implicitly relied on), and leave the penny at root of the tree, covered with a leaf to hide it from an always inquisitive Heaven. And on Monday morning the good people, undefiled,

71

would collect the lucre.[3]

Jaimie knew the edifying life, and beautiful death of her own uncle Brian Connolly, who kept, each in its proper place, every cobble on his lane and every straw on his roof — the tidiest worker and neatest cropper in the barony of Tyrugh — and at the same time justest and most upright man. The boy had by heart Father Tunney's words over the open grave, while he dropped tears on the coffin-lid, — 'There you lie, Brian Connolly, a man and a saint! — But ah, sure it's falsehood I'm speaking — for it isn't there you are at all, at all, but at God's knee this blessed minute. — Och, if only it was Father Tunney's luck to've slipped in of the Gate alongside you, Brian, the good God, seeing the company he was in, wouldn't have had the heart to shove him out again.'

And ah, the stories she told of that beloved *sagart*, Father Tunney himself — of his exiling, by a hard bishop, to a strange parish — where he died of a broken heart for Dhrimholme, for the people he loved and who to distraction loved him! — And of his homecoming again — in his coffin! On that woeful morning when, all the rest of the household having joined the sorrowing throng that went miles of the way to meet Father Tunney, she alone was left — a small slip of a girl. But at length she burst from the house, and, skipping hedges and ditches, on the near- cuts across Laighey Holme, reached the Old Bridge of Laighey just as the men carrying the coffin came in sight. But the wail which that instant went up to the skies from the mass of waiting women, made her leap off the road, and hide under the bridge-arches — where, with fingers in her ears, she crouched cowering till she was sure the funeral was a mile gone and the crying dead in the distance.

'The wail of the women of Laighey,' she would tell, 'is, this blessed night, in my ears, — and will be, I believe, the day that I'm dying! — But, children, reach me my beads. — It's long past rosary-time, and I should have the fire raked and me in bed: for the morrow's a new day — God spare each soul of us to see it!'

NOTES

1   Two years after Waterloo.

2   Little she knew and less she cared about writing of books, but if she had been born into a leisured, literary world, instead of a slaving one, that woman would have had a nation straining to listen. And the name of Mary Mulloy would be remembered.

3   And she would tell of these same good kind neighbours how sorely they deplored the fickleness in religion of one of their own people, Andy Gregory, who they lamented, wore the knees out of his britches converting, and the seat out of them back-sliding.

CHAPTER THIRTEEN

The Still-House

One other memorable mountain adventure of the boy's was his first visit — unpremeditated — to a still house.

In the Cruach Ghorm mountains poteen-stills were as plenty as the bad weather — and the peelers spent a deal of their time tramping the hills to find them. The lad was used seeing these gentlemen set off still-hunting several mornings of each week — in threes, one of them carrying a loaded gun, another a spear for searching bogs and du'g-hills for the buried treasure, and the third a gallon measure. But so well did the poteen-makers hide their work, and so alert were their sentries, who had horns for raising alarm, that it was rarely — maybe twice in twelve months — the boy saw the still-hunters bring home spoil. Then, one of them would be carrying a keg on his shoulder, another a worm, and the third an empty still. But more seldom did they succeed in bringing back prisoners — one or two bare- foot, wild-eyed fellows: for the poteen-maker was as fast as a fox, and had double as many tricks: the boy knew more than one of them who on occasion ran down hares and brought them home alive.

Our *gasúr's* introduction to whiskey-distilling happened on a day when he had gone on the mountain to look at four sheep which his father grazed with the Gasúr Mór. (One of these, a black-faced white sheep, was by a pleasant fiction supposed to be the boy's very own. There was never a time in his childhood that he wasn't 'owner' of both a sheep and a calf: from each of which, when sold, his revenue was one penny ! But he was at once reappointed owner of a new sheep and calf: so, though his pockets stayed light he was always a stock-master.) As was his custom on these rare mountain-trips, he went exploring, after he had inspected the live-stock and found everything as it should be. In a gully where tumbled a little stream, he was surprised to see a thin, blue smoke rising out of the ground, close by a spink's edge. As he had heard of volcanoes his first impulse was to take to his heels and get as far as he could from the coming eruption: yet, this blue smoke was so like turf-smoke, that he didn't spring away at once, but waited to study the puzzle. The question arose whether the Bad Man Below used turf for fuel. But it was quickly dismissed: in all his bog-days he had never heard of anyone seeing either That Man or his staff cutting turf and winning them. The fairies, he knew, burnt no turf — never had a fire. This was the curiousest thing he had ever known. Cautiously he crept near to investigate. And, behold, it was real turf-smoke — and coming from a hole in the ground less than six inches across.

He stepped closer — and had sudden strange feeling of the world going from under him! There was a crackling and a crash — and he was engulfed in the earth's bowels! Frightened and frightening yells went up — some of them his own, some from beings unseen — and he found himself sprawling in a heap of burst sods and broken sticks in a cavern, a big blazing turf-fire close by, and over it a great tin tub — one of the self-same stills that he had seen the peelers carry home after a seizure.

Soon he saw, from the earth above peering down at him, a very red face with a patch over one eye — and then another, a smaller face. And then, gleeking from the cavern's entrance, he beheld a frightening bushy-bearded countenance.

'In the divil's name who or what are ye?' was demanded by the patch-eyed one aloft.

'I didn't mean it. — I'm only a little boy that has four sheep grazin' with the Gasúr Mór.'

'Well bad luck be off ye, every day ye see the sun rise and every day ye don't!' said Bushy-beard, entering. 'I'd give me'davy the dam peelers had us.'

Patch-eye followed him in; and after that a little fellow of about twelve.

It was to a still-house our lad had so impolitely introduced himself. The two men — as Jaimie was to learn — were the most notorious poteen-makers in Glen Ainey. They were running a few kegs for a wedding that would be the next week — on the thither side of the mountain. The sods and broken sticks, that had come from the roof with the *gasúr*, they cleared away — while their lad piled fresh turf to the fire.

They let Jaimie seat himself on a sod, and watch their work. From the tip of the great worm the liquor was dripping into a tub, whence from time to time, bailing it with a tin-pandy, they funnelled it into one of three kegs that stood by. There were a tub and two tin-basins in a corner of the cavern, filled with liquid. It was First-shot, they told him, waiting its turn to go in the still for the second running. Patch-eye wanted to give him a taste of the real poteen, the Second Run, a sip in the bottom of the tin-pandy: but Bushy-beard angrily swore at him. 'The divil a morsel o' harm — but good — a hogshead of it would do the chile,' answered Patch-eye. 'If I had three-and-thirty childre instead of none, I'd make poteen the mother's milk to rear them on.' Yet he withdrew the poteen, and gave the lad an egg-shell of First-shot. With curiosity Jaimie tasted it, spat out the mouthful, and threw the remainder on the floor. 'Bad luck be off ye!' Patch-eye gently cursed him. He went on with something that Jaimie tried in vain to picture — 'Put a poteen-head on a youngster and you'll have a sober oul' man.' Bushy-beard swore at him again, and said, 'Be all signs, then, 'tis mortal little poteen must have gone down your throat when you were a snot-nose brat'.

All four of them, now, were seated in a circle on sods, watching the still. Patch-eye held for a while a tin-pandy under the drip, helped himself to a drink, and began singing a ballad — that Jaimie was often after to hear sung at raffles and weddings — Pat Shinaghan's Cow:

There's a man in Ardaghey both proper an' tall;
Och, he's wan Paddy Shinaghan, we do him call,
For he brews the cordial that does excel all —
Sure it bates all the doctors aroun, Dinnygal.

For if ye were gaspin' and ready to die,
The smell of it fastin' would lift your heart high;
So hoist it up farther, quite near to your nose —
A Glen Ainey man loves it whereever he goes!

We can't have a christenin' without it at all,
We drink and sing chours, shake hands and sing all.
Your health now, dear gossip, as I may you call!
Sure if this be's a ghost, that it may meet us all!

This, Paddy, me hearty—of late it has been —
With steam and hot water he brewed his poteen;
He left it in barrels, as I hear them say,
But his cow took a notion of drinkin' that day!

Wirrasthrue! when the cow, sure, the notion did take,
She first broke the borach and then pulled the stake,
Then drunk at the barrels till she drunk her fill —
They tell that she didn't leave much of the still!

But when she got drunk she begun to feel shame,
And she says, 'Paddy Shinaghan' — callin' him by name —
'I'm as dhrunk as a beggar, with juice o' the malt,
But Paddy, avourneen, it isn't my fault.'

Then she hiccuped, and staggered, and axed Pat to fight,
And threated that through him she'd let the daylight;
That his breed was all cowards she tould him to note,
And dared him to tramp on the tail of her coat.

Next day she woke up with a bad broken horn,
And begun for to curse the day she was born;
She cursed barley, and kilty, and poteen likewise,
And cursed all the still-tinkers inunder the skies.

75

She warned all good cows for to mind their fair name,
And to never taste liquor would fetch them to shame,
And she wispered to Paddy and sayed in his ear,
Sure you will not tell Una I went on the beer?

An' Paddy, ahaisge, if mercy you'll have,
I'll bring ye each year a fine heifer calf,
For I am right honest, though fond of a spree,
And sure, Paddy, mo bhuachail, you're as fond of't as me!'

And Paddy had mercy (we give him renown!);
But when Una did milk her, her milk was brown.
'Poor cow!' then says Una, 'tis your heart's blood ye give,
For ye won't see us wantin' milk while you do live.'

Now, we'll dhrink and be merry, and forgive the cow;
Here's a health to bould Shinaghan, wither or how!
Let us pray may he niver lose head, worm, or still
On that sanctified place they call Keelogs Hill.

Here's a health to meself, an God save Ireland's King!
Sure it's me makes the valleys of Keelogs to ring,
It's me makes the valleys and taverns to roar —
But without a drop whiskey I can sing no more.

Whilst their little boy dutifully tended the fire, which was big, and burned like whins in March, and Buslay- beard and Patch-eye took their ease on their sods, watching the drip from the worm into the tub, they told stories that were mighty interesting.

Jaimie wanted to know if they weren't afraid of the peelers. Patch-eye laughed heartily at this, and said, 'Every peeler is born with one eye blind and the other unable to see what it looks at. I can hie the poteen into the town and sell it under their nose.'

'You take it in at night, do you?'

'In blazin' day-light — hid in the heart of a cart of turf most times.' Giving another laugh, a very hearty one, he began reciting an escape of his father, and his turning the tables on the peelers. — That man had a ten-gallon keg of poteen, it seems, in a cart of turf he was dragging to the town with his grey pony — both turf and keg for Manus O'Dougherty, the publican. On the way, he met the news that his secret was slipped to the police-sergeant's wife; and the sergeant was now on the lookout for himself and the cart. His father was a rascal who loved danger because he could always fool it: so, instead of turning his horse's head and pushing

76

for home he waited till Hughie Mulrainey came along with an honest load of turf and bribed Hughie to swap carts and cartloads with him. Hooking his grey pony into Hughie's cart, he continued his journey— travelling ahead of Hughie and the poteen. And at the town's edge there was the sergeant and his men, waiting. The sergeant said, 'Being bad in need of a cart of turf, I'll buy this one of yours.'

'Sorry I can't sell it to you,' said Patch-eye's father. 'Manus O'Dougherty hasn't a clod to warm his wife, and sent word to me to hurry him this cart-load before his family fruz. — I'll bring you a good load thi' morrow'.'

'I'm out of turf, myself,' said the sergeant. 'I must have this load, or we'll all be found froze to death in the mornin'."

'I wouldn't part this load to a man but Manus, for less than ten shillin's,' said Patch-eye's father. 'But I'll fetch you a bigger in the mornin' for three shillin's.'

The sergeant pulled out of his pocket ten shillings and put them into the other's pocket. 'There's your own price for you.— The load's now mine.' Grabbing the grey pony by the head the sergeant led him to the barracks, with the other peelers marching alongside, and Patch-eye's father trailing them, his head between his legs, *maryach!* as if someone stole his scon. But behold ye, when the turf was unloaded in the barrack yards, and nothing in the cart but turf, and plenty of them,'twas the sergeant was looking the down man. Patch-eye's father, with ten white shillings jingling in his pocket, drove off, whistling The Wind that Shakes the Barley. Manus O'Dougherty had meanwhile got his keg, and hid it where no peeler's eye would ever light on it.

Shaking with laughter over his father's cleverness, Patch-eye caught some more of the poteen-drip and drank a toast that one of them might never meet up with either peeler or divil. Such a capital story-teller was he that for hours our lad forgot he ought, ere this, to have his toes turned to home — till he was surprised by the sound of a horn on the hill. While he was only surprised the other three were startled; and jumped to their feet at a bound. Again the horn sounded — and the three dived for the exit. But Patch-eye called over-shoulder to Jaimie, 'Now, *gasúr*, it's run for our life, and the divil take the hindmost!'

Our lad went out, climbed the spink above the still-house, and spied around him. The hill had swallowed the three who ran. Neither up nor down the winding gully through which the stream tumbled — nor anywhere in hill or valley — could he see a human being. But after a while far above him on the mountain side, he beheld four peelers jumping, running, tearing toward him, break neck. The *gasúr* was stuck to the spot till they arrived by him. 'Take care of him,' called the leader, one with three stripes on his sleeve. And while the others dived into the broken still-house, one of the policemen grabbed him by the shoulder, and gave him a shake that Jaimie thought loosened the nails on his toes. 'Where's the other scoundrels, you rammed wee rascal?' he yelled, fit to blow the roof off Jaimie's head.

But the *gasúr* couldn't answer him, if he would: he was speechless.

The three who had leapt into the still-house, rushed out again, almost as quickly, and bounded to various high points to search with their eyes the hill. But they got no sign of the fugitives. They gathered round Jaimie questioning and threatening him. But he could only cry and say that he had fallen into the still-house, and knew nothing. The man who had all this time held him by the shoulder professed to smell whiskey off the boy's breath. 'You dam drunken wee liar,' he said, giving him another awful shake, 'I'll bate the brains and shake the soul-case out o' you, if you don't tell us who they are and where they've gone to!'

No matter what they did the boy could only cry more and say he knew nothing. They threatened that he would hang like a dead rabbit if he didn't give information — but though it frightened the lad out of his skin it did them no good.

After they had measured, and emptied out, most of the liquor, one of the men shouldered a keg of it, another took the worm, and a third lifted the empty still, while he with stripes on his sleeve took charge of poor Jaimie — and all set out. They were police, not from the lad's side of the hills, but the opposite, the Glen Mor, end. So, instead of down the hills toward home, it was up the mountain and crossing away from home, that the heart-broken boy found himself going. As he toiled his way over the hills, in midst of his captors, Jaimie kept wondering, wondering if they would really hang him. But he very much doubted that they dare go so far. Transportation to Van Dieman's Land was probably the worst they could do to him. He wondered would he ever again see Glen Ainey, and his sorrowing father and mother.

As they came down the mountain's other side, and reached inhabited country, people ran from hill-cottages to see at closer range the sad procession of heartily-hated peelers and their spoil — and, oh, their one little prisoner! From hillocks and knowes on either side of the peelers' path both men and women jibed and joked the peelers, praising loud the dauntless bravery of four big, tall, stout, strapping fellows who were able to take captive one wee, bare-foot, torn-trousered, weeping *gasúr* 'More power to yous, brave fellows!' one called. 'Yous have captured Molly Maguire at last.' And another, 'Thanks be, boys, all o' ye'll get the stripes for this exthraor'nary victory!' 'If it was me had the devlin' of the stripes,' called a third, 'it isn't on their arms I'd lay them.' 'How many of ye did the *gasúr* kill, sergeant, afore ye overcome him?' cried another. And another, 'Faith, Watherloo'ill be miserable mention, after this.'

But to Jaimie they called so heartily their encouragement and admiration that, soon, from depths of despair he was rising to realize he was a hero! He wiped away his tears — for no hero would cry — lifted up his head, pushed out his little chest, and strode boldly forward in the centre of his great big captors.

He began calling to mind other heroes of Irish history who had won honour and glory, and had songs and recitations made about them. They had been hunted like him, and sometimes the very best of them captured and jailed. Some of them were martyred, too — Red Hugh, and Robert Emmet, Lord Edward and the rest — names that would never, never be forgotten. He was mightily comforted. A scrap of ballad he had often heard sung, about a brave Ribbon leader arrested a generation before, came and went in his mind — and he strode to the tune of it —

> They marched him off to Liffar Jail without no more delay,
> 'And the traitment that they gave him was sevair upon the way.'

The boy who had been in tears and begging for his release, now came to scorn his captors — and to scorn their jails, too, and their Convict Ships — even their gallowses. Forgetting, for a while, home, father and mother, he took on a glow of pride. It grew to be a great hour for Jaimie, the very greatest his young life had yet known!

When they reached the Glen Barracks and held consultation with their comrades there, the conclusion was come to that, as he had from the first protested, the lad only happened into the still- house, and didn't know the distillers. And as they would make themselves a bigger laughing stock putting it further, they must let the *gasúr* go. Somehow or other, now, their decision disappointed the lad. Reluctant, he had to let go his grasp on Glory.

He was a long, long way from home by road; and they couldn't and wouldn't undertake the journeg with him over the hills again — even if he was able for it — which he wasn't. They kept him that night. In the morning, when a car that they had been expecting came west through the glen, from Bally-mo-Feadh, they had to pay from their pockets ten shillings to the driver to take charge of the lad to Glenties and from there send him out on the first car crossing the mountains back to Glen Ainey.

This meant for the *gasúr* the greatest ride of all his life — more than twenty Irish miles, through half of the known world, on a jaunting-car! Over the mountains it was blowing bitter sleet and snow, yet was he the happiest man who was ever soaked to the skin crossing Binban. It was midnight before he reached his home — late, but still all too early for a *gasúr* who was wishing such enchanting journey would last for a year and a day.

But, worse than the beautiful ride's too-quick ending was his father's dread threat — after he had listened to Jaimie's story — 'Your mountain towering will have to end, young buck- o, since you must always search out and drag home with you every disaster that ever hid in the Cruach Ghorm hills.'

So They Said And Felt And Saw

Aquaint and simple world, full of a beauty all its own, was that whereunto the lad was born.

All his life he regretted that his lot had not been cast in the Gaelteacht, the Gaelic-speaking territory, amongst the purley Gaelic people. Instead, his was the borderland of Gaelteacht and Galltacht — here, because of the infiltration of English and Scottish Planter descendants, the language had become English. — Still, in Gaelic idiom and a plentiful scattering of Gaelic words and phrases, this border people eked out the paucity of the *Beurla* to express their feelings.

Especially by the multitudinous soft terms of endearment — *a theagair* (O Treasure), *a mhilis* (0 Sweetness), *a phaiste* (O Child), *a ghradh* (O Love), *a chuisle geal mo chroidhe* (0 White Pulse of my Heart), and a score of others, with which, as with diamonds to a tiara, did this fond people still brighten and beautify their converse. And though, as one entered a house here, he might salute in Beurla, 'God bless all here!' the return greeting was still '*Sé do bheatha!*' (May He be thy life) — *Agus cead fáilte romhat*' (And a hundred welcomes before thee). But if he was a long-looked for friend, whose coming brought to the hearts of the household more than ordinary joy, it was '*Céad mile failte romhat*' (A hundred thousand welcomes before thee). And the parting prayer he carried with him when he left was in Gaelic, 'To God we commend thee,' 'May God send you safe,' or 'May the road rise with you.'

So Gaelic was still the spirit that the most incidental reference to the dead, invariably demanded a parenthetic prayer — 'May the heavens be his bed,' 'May God rest his soul,' — 'We hope he's with God.' With prayer the mother ended the nightly fire-raking and accompanied the morning's unearthing of 'the fire's seed.' The lighting of the candle at night brought, 'May God give us the light of Heaven.' The Christmas candle was still lighted and placed in the window-pane to shine in the night and guide wanderers, who, like Two of old, might be seeking where to lay a weary head. In Glen Ainey, then, the joy or sorrow of each was the joy or sorrow of all. In their work neighbour helped neighbour, and everyone helped the widow and orphans.

When death visited the district, all field labour was suspended till after the burial. The beggar treated with reverence, welcome, and hospitality, was always referred to as 'a poor man looking for his share' — always *his* share, never yours; for not only did they realise that the few possessions of those who did possess, were only held in trust — but also that any ragged comer to their door might be Christ himself in *shuiler* guise — come to find for himself if people still remembered.

Every passing caller took part, as matter of course in whatsoever was proceeding under the roof. If eating, he sat down to the meal; churning, he took his *brash*; if the rosary was chanting, he dropped to his knees the moment he entered, joined the chorus answering the decade, and when it reached his turn, led in his own decade.

The prophecies of their own great Donegal saint, Colm Cille (Dove of the Church),[1] were on everyone's tongue, and their fulfilment hopefully and eagerly awaited — especially that part which foretold for his children the dawning of freedom's day after Eire's long, long night of suffering. Indeed, the first of the signs that were to precede that glorious event ('The seed,' said Colm, 'shall wither beneath the sod and the crops be in mourning'), behold all men had witnessed in the great potato blight! and during the Crimean war the second sign, when phenomenal prosperity gilded the land for a while ('The cow shall bring the full of her horn of money'). Succeeding signs all men awaited, and the old expected ere they died: the black pig that was to run through Barnish Mór Gap from mouth and nostrils belching fire and smoke[2] — the three black *cuts* (assessments) that were to be levied on the land and lifted with steel hands — the harvest that would never be reaped because Ireland, through her echoing hills, should send a call for fighting men that none dare disobey. True, before freedom was achieved a certain corn-mill in Donegal, run by a miller with two thumbs on one hand, would turn three times with human blood — yet oh! how eagerly those devoted old men questioned all *shuilers* and strollers whether in their travels they had heard of the miller's appearing!

The old-time feasts were honoured, and festivals, pagan and Christian, still celebrated. On May Day, Baal-tinne, the Druid New Year, the houses were decked with May-flowers and protecting lines of them laid along every doorstep and window-sill. On Mid-summer night, bonfire night, devoted in ancient Ireland to the Druid's sun-god, huge fires leaped on every hill-top, and crowds sang, danced and made merry around, whilst torches taken from the sacred fire circled each home, its cattle-sheds and field crops, thus, for twelve month to come, averting from them all evil things.

The eve of *Samhain* (Hallow-eve) was one of the great social festivals of the year. Then there was St. Bridget's eve in February with its plaiting of the rush crosses which in her name adorned and blessed the homes for the year to come. Lammas Day, first day of August, the day of the ancient god Lugh, was still one of the year's great landmarks. But, crowning all, was Christmas — of which the eve, not the day, was the time of feast and merriment.

Moreover, several festivals had their double date and honour : for, even after some centuries of the new calendar, people still observed and feasted upon Old Hallow eve, Old Christmas eve, Old New Year's Eve — in each case eleven days later. In the farmer's calendar, Old May Day (12th May), Old Hallow Day (12th November), and Old Lammas (12th of August), were the reckoning days — not their newer substitutes. For crop, cattle, weather reckoning, always these were used. The Lammas floods were looked for at Old Lammas. Old May-day began the farmer's year; and if he was one of the fortunate ones who could afford hired help, the half-year hiring terms began, never on May 1st and November 1st, but always on Old May-day, and Old Hallow-day.

In our *gasúr's* country, the herbs of the field were, as they should be, cures for all ills. No district was there without at least one woman wise in *yarribs*, who advised and compounded for the few who were troubled with complaints — and always gave gratis of her wisdom and her work. When the wise one was called, six, seven, ten miles, to a patient, the honour done her more than compensated for the trouble. Special cures for special complaints, the rose, the whittle, the heart-fever, cancer, rabies, were secrets handed from father to eldest son in certain families. And these cures were unfailing. In both christian and beast fairy doctors cured the mysterious ills induced by fairy power — such as heart-fever in one, and elf-shot in the other. There was in the territory a medical doctor who drew his salary and did little else; for few were ever sick enough to need him. Except of course, when they came to die; and then he was no good. For when it came a man's time to die, he just naturally stretched him out and said good-bye. A doctor has called to witness his slipping off, only by a few who were vain.

The boy's district of Glen finey, like every other district in Donegal — and indeed, in Ireland — was passing rich in tradition and legend. In his child days there wasn't a bird in the bush, nor an animal running on four legs but had its own story. There was hardly a bush whereon a tale did not hang, nor rock on the hillside. Every loch and every *cnoc* had its own story — tragic, poetic, romantic, dramatic — every cave, and every cairn. So, 'twas no wonder that story, story, story, filled the minds of the youth every day, and their homes every night of the year. In the Atlantic, just off the headlands which the boy could see from his own hill, lay that land of enchantment, Hy- Breasil — under the ocean, just where sea and sky met — rising up, however, and revealing itself, on rare occasions to a favoured few. Even in the lad's childhood it revealed itself to three far-drifted fishermen. The Blessed Land was to be won for Ireland — its spells to be lifted and itself recovered in its blissful reality — by a hero yet unborn, but every year expected — a saviour eagerly awaited.[3]

Heaven still rewarded virtue in the boy's country and visited punishment on evil-doers. Instances occurred in every generation, every decade. The boy himself saw the all-powerful family of the MacCullochs wrecked, 'melt like the snow off the ditch.' Everyone knew why, even if the wild fowl had not proclaimed it. They were a Planter family living in a purely Irish locality, and though they had acres *go leor*, and houses and barns crammed with full and plenty, they coveted and got the landlord to transfer to them the one little field of the Widow Meehan. On a spring day, later, when the MacCullochs were cutting turf in the Litirtraina bog, many families turf-cutting around them saw and heard a strange bird circling above the guilty ones, screaming, '*Eric! Eric!*' — which (in free translation) signifies 'Vengeance! Vengeance!' In the years immediately following, their cattle died, their crops failed, their barn burned down, one of them broke his leg, one was found dead in bed, one of them was impaled on a pitchfork when sliding off a haycock, poverty overtook them, one went to Australia, one to Canada — and in the next generation a once great family was only a legend in Glen Ainey — remembered because of a bird's cry.

The blessed fairies, to be sure, were all around. People were still seeing them in the *gasúr's* day. Everyone heard their music, and saw the fairy lights — on the Mount, by the Battery, on the moor between the two lochs — where they still danced and made merry during the long summer twilights and the moonlight nights. People were still being taken by them — just for a merry prank — ridden around all night, and set down unharmed by their own gable-end at break o' day. The boy knew several who had got the fairy ride — one of them Robin Porter of the Glibe — whisked all the way up to Connaught and over the tops of Cruach Padraic and Neiphin.

Lovely children were occasionally carried off by them, and fairy beings substituted. There was, for instance, the case of the strange child in Manus Mór Mac Fadyeen's cradle which everyone knew was a changeling — but of which they only got final proof the day that Doalty MacLafferty the piper left his pipes in Manus Mór's whilst he went to the hayfield where were all of the family — except It in the cradle. The pipe-music that soon began floating over the fields, the strangest and most enchanting anyone had ever listened to, drew them — as well as every worker in every field for a mile around — step by step — back to the house: and when people peeped in they beheld the 'child' in the cradle hugging the pipes like a veteran, and putting from them music that would make the hills lean to listen. When It found It was discovered, It vanished, with the pipes, and Manus Mór had an empty cradle for which he was grateful to God — thereafter.

Everyone respected and regarded the good people highly. No one interfered with their *sciog* bushes, and there was no man so sinful as to set spade or plow to the fairy rath, their pleasant green knowe on the hillside, their habitation and playground. A couple of generations before our boy's day, they had been more in evidence, had had more intercourse with human beings, and endless were the stories still told by the old people, around the fireside of the fairy happenings in their young days.

The boy himself, as a child, knew old Máire Manachan who in her young days — when she was called the Star of Glen Ainey — encountered a fairy lover on the Alt Mór one beautiful May day. She didn't at first know that he was a fairy lover — till, as God sent it, before she let him kiss her, Father Phil, out hunting, came up with his hound Bran, and the fairy young man fled. But the particular thing which fascinated Jaimie, about Máire's adventure, was the item — which often he heard her tell: The handsome young stranger gave her to look through an emerald ring that he took off his finger — letting her get one glimpse of the fairyland he wanted to take her to, where she beheld the fairy *caman-men* playing *caman* (hurling)[4] in a green vale —'And och!' Máire would ecstatically exclaim, 'no sight on earth was ever grand to me after that!'

Thank God, evil spirits did not flourish in Donegal. One was known, but rarely did he blight the country. He was the *púca*. Two generations before the boy's day he had materialized in the Glen — in Kilian. It was a dread time for the people that winter of 1829-30, when from the first full moon in November to the eve of the following St. Patrick's day, the *púca's* howlings, nightly, froze the marrow in men's bones. During all that fearful winter few there were in Glen Ainey who dared stir abroad after nightfall. A very few had seen him — or it — a formless mass that lumbered toward them down the road. God and His Blessed Mother saved these men — saved their lives, that is. Their health was wrecked — or their mind. The end of the Púca Kilian (as he was and is known) was as sudden and strange as his coming. It was on St. Patrick's eve of 1836 that night caught Neilis Doherty returning from the hilltop bog with a creel of turf on his back. He met the Púca. Yet so sure was Neilis' faith in a protecting God that he did not throw down his creel and run. He braved the evil thing — challenged and conversed with him. Yet what was said, what passed between them, no mortal other than Neilis himself ever knew. But the Púca that night took his departure from Kilian and Glen Ainey — and was never after met or heard in the parish of Inver.

When Neilis returned home from the encounter — the creel of turf still on his back — he laid down his load and took to his bed — without saying anything — and never arose again. Within twelve months he was dead — and the secret of what passed between the Thing and himself died with him. But, after a lapse of a hundred years the Púca Kilian is still a dread memory in the Glen.

It is wrong to say that the Púca was the only evil thing which appeared

85

in the boy's country. The devil himself was known to have appeared —
usually to someone who had done, or was about to do, wrong. He appeared
to such person on a night-journey, and travelled with him step for step.
He appeared to inveterate card- players — or to men returning from a
card-bout where there had been cheating and swearing, hot argument and
bad blood. There was one particularly strange play of the devil with the
card- players, a hundred years before the boy's day — in the neighbouring
parish of the Oileigh — not only strange in itself but with a still stranger
outcome.

There were in the Oileigh, then, half a dozen hard and hardened men
who were notorious drinkers and card-players, wasting their time and their
substance by both. The priest denounced them from the altar and they
were sort of outcast. In a *shebeen* half-way between the mountains and
the sea they played and drank and spent their money. The devil came to
see them one Hallow night, and with them struck a bargain. He promised
them all the happiness and pleasure the heart of man could wish — money
in their pockets always, all the drink and all the card-playing the worst of
them desired; they should lead a life of highest pleasure, with full and
plenty and overflow everything — for seven years — till All Souls' Night
at the seventh year's end. But on that night they should come for their
final card- playing and drinking-bout in this *shebeen* of their choice, when
it was to be his right to take with him the last man of them who crossed
the threshold going out of the *shebeen* at midnight. To this six-to-one
gamble — for such a royal stake — they gladly agreed. For seven years,
then, a pleasurable life they surely led — money, cards, drink without end:
and no shade or sorrow bloomed their souls till came the critical night.
Honouring their bargain then, they assembled in their favourite *shebeen*
for their last great bout: but as midnight neared they grew fidgety and
throughout their carousing most of them couldn't help casting glances
toward the door where the dread drama must soon be played. There was
among them one man, Torloch Gillespie, loudest-swearing, hardest drinking fellow of the lot, but a man of wild daring — one whom they looked
to as a leader: and Torloch, when it came midnight, said to them, 'Fellows,
I know what is in all your minds — No one of you wants to be the last
going out of here. Every man of you is willing in his heart to murder
another, in order to get out ahead of him. Now, we have been comrades
for long years; we have had our pleasures together, and plenty of them,
and good ; and I'd be loath to see ill-feeling and treachery show now: so
to prevent it I'll myself undertake to be the last man out. — Open the door,
Conal O'Donnell,' he said to one man of them as the clock began striking
midnight — 'Open it wide, and walk out with ye, one by one, calm and
with your heads up as good men should. I'll bring up the rear.'

Conal O'Donnell opened wide the door, letting a white full moon flood

86

the floor. One by one, calmly, steadily, they marched out — and saw, each of them as he stepped over the threshold, the Old Boy crouching by the left door — jamb, outside, readied for his grab. When five had passed, and Torloch was putting out his foot, the Fellow reached for him. But — 'You're a poor rackoner,' laughed Torloch at him — 'Can't you see another man still behind' — jerking his thumb over-shoulder to where his shadow crept after. For a moment deceived, as much by Torloch's manner as by his shadow, the Fellow, allowing Torloch to pass, grabbed — the shadow! But so mad he was for Torloch's making an idiot of him, that he held on the shadow — and carried it off to hell with him!

The evil society broke up. The men reformed and came to their duty. But, from that night forward people shivered as Torloch Gillespie passed them by — for, no matter moonshine or sunshine, till the day of his death the man never again cast a shadow.

NOTES

1 To non-Irish people better known as Columba — he who, when exiled from his beloved Donegal (in penance for a wrong he had done) founded, in the sixth century, in Iona of the Hebrides, one of the many great Irish schools of that day. — It may be noted that besides being beloved saint, teacher, poet, and prophet, Colm was a humourist. His great friend St. Mochua, back in Ireland, lived a hermit in the wilderness devoting himself to the service of God — his wordly wealth just a cock, a mouse, and a fly. The cock called him to prayer at certain hours in the night. The mouse scratched his ear if sleep deafened him to the call of the cock. The fly served him as a pointer, on his psalter — creeping along the page under each line and each word of the line that he chanted: and when his chanting was, for other business interrupted, the fly paused on the next word till he came again. When the cock, the mouse and the fly at length died on Mochua, he wrote mournfully to Colm, in Iona, seeking sympathy. And Colm replied to him: 'Brother, thou must accept in humble spirit the affliction that has been sent upon thee. For thou shouldst have known that worry will always follow in in the wake of wealth'. Many are the tales still told of the great Colm, in Glen Ainey, where oft he had walked.

2 When, recently, the old men saw the first train come through Barnes Mór they at once recognised the black pig of the prophecy — and knew the Dawn was nearing.

3 Tir-na'n-Og — the Land of Perpetual Youth — was another name for Hy-Breasil. So real was it to the Irish people, and so circumstantially were its wonders related abroad by the Irish scholars and saints of the middle ages who then wandered over every country in Europe teaching and preaching, that it came to be marked on ancient continental maps and charts. In a Dutch chart of the sixteenth century this writer has himself seen it set down — at a distance of about fifty miles from the west coast of Ireland. So vivid and so circumstantial were the accounts of it current at home that it was believed in even by the hard-headed Scottish planters whom James 1 loosed upon Ulster, to grab everything in sight. With good Scottish proclivity they then wanted also, everything out of sight. The Leslie family (of which Sir Shane Leslie, gifted man of letters, is today the best known representative) petitioned for, and secured a parchmented grant of, Hy-Breasil from the Scottish James. In The Story of the Irish Race (by this writer) is set down copy of a letter written more than a hundred years ago by a friend of the Leslies in Donegal to a representative of the family in London,

announcing the final discovery and locating of their island paradise by a captain sailing out of Killybegs — and enjoining the Leslies to make haste to establish their claim in the proper quarter.

4   THE LOVE-TALKER

I met the Love-Talker one eve in the glen,
He was handsomer than any of our handsome young men,
His eyes were blacker than the sloe, his voice sweeter far
Than the crooning of old Kevin's pipes beyond in Coolnagar.

I was bound for the milking with a heart fair and free —
My grief! my grief! that hour drained the life from me:
I thought him human lover, though his lips on mine were cold
And the breath of death blew keen on me within his hold.

I know not what way he came — no shadow fell behind,
But all the sighing rushes swayed beneath a fairy wind,
The thrush ceased its singing, a mist crept about,
We two clung together with the world shut out.

Beyond the ghostly mist I could hear my cattle low —
The little cow from Ballina, white as driven snow,
The dun cow from Kerry, the roan from Inisheer —
O, pitful their calling and his whispers in my ear!

His eyes were a fire, his words were a snare;
I cried my mother's name — but no help was there;
I made the blessed Sign: then he gave a dreary moan,
A wisp of cloud went floating by, and I stood alone.

Running ever thro' my head is an old-time rune —
'Who meets the Love-Talker must weave her shroud soon', —
My mother's face is furrowed by the salt tears that fall;
But the kind eyes of my father are the saddest sight of all.

I have spun the fleecy lint and now my wheel is still —
The linen length is woven for my shroud fine and chill.
I shall stretch me on the bed where a happy maid I lay—
Pray for the soul of Máire Og at dawing of the day.

Ethna Carbery in The Four Winds of Erinn

CHAPTER FIFTEEN

Reading

In that day the *gasúr* had two loves, Ireland and reading. When these
ran together, as in national ballads, his happiness was higher than Errigal
hill. If there's any happiness higher still, it was his when he was de-
claiming to his comrades at the herding, the latest, warm Irish ballad he
had learnt—

> *'When comes the day all hearts to weigh,*
> *If staunch they be or vile,*
> *Shall we forget the scared debt*
> *We owe our mothers isle?*
> *My native heath is brown beneath,*
> *My native waters blue,*
> *But crimson red o'er both shall spread*
> *Ere I am false to you,*
> > *Dear Land—*
> *Ere I am false to you.*
> *'My boyish ear still clung to hear*
> *Or Erin's pride of yore,*
> *Ere Saxon foot had dared pollute*
> *Her independent shore;*
> *Of chiefs long dead who rose to head*
> *Some gallant patriot few—*
> *Till all my aim on earth became*
> *To strike one blow for you,*
> > *Dear Land—*
> *To strike one blow for you.'[1]*

Ballads were easier to get than books, a great deal. They were the
everyday reading of Donegal. Few men ever thought of leaving a fair
without a new ballad in their pocket. He wasn't fit for a fair who thought
otherwise. And it only cost a halfpenny from the ballad-singer. The old
stand-byes you bought in a broad-sheet of twelve for a penny, at the
Stannins — and plenty of stirring, real Irish, ones were mixed in them.
The street-ballads were the boy's first literature, and first love — and they
never lost their place in his heart. Over and above their own intrinsic
beauty — and all of them, including the drowning, murder, and hanging
ones, were beautiful to him — they had big value for bribing boys to help

him gather *diarcan*. When a stroke of good fortune put the first penny his way, it went into a broad-sheet. And by the light of the turf-blaze, as he stretched on the hearth, was every song on the sheet, good and bad, got by heart. Out of the sheet of twelve then he made two sheets of six — which, under the school-desks, he sold at a penny apiece to mountain-boys: and that meant for himself two more broad-sheets.

Books, of course, the boy craved; but in Glen Ainey they were few and far to find. John Burns, the tailor, had to be sure, several books, some of them still whole, others well melted from a long life's reading and only kept from dissolution by a cross tying of web-selvage. But his books John watched like a fox, barricading them on the work-bench, between him and the window. As a great favour he once in a while let the boy — sitting on side of the work bench, right under his own eye — read pages of them.

Pleased with the youngster's great liking for books, John said to him, 'Maybe when you grow big you'll want to make up a book yourself. — Greater wonders have happened. — Then climb the Mount here' — his cabin was on the Mount-side — 'and look aist and waist, over the seven counties; and, startin' at Nephin in Mayo, the farthest — away peak on the southwest, come the ring around till ye reach Sliabh Laig, over the ocean at the other end — and if you only tell a thousand part of all the extromary things that befell between the two ends ye'll make a gr-r-reat book.' The dazzling possibility lured, even if it almost dumbfounded the boy.[2]

Joe Baxter, who, in throng seasons, was sometimes hired for a day by the boy's father, had, like the boy, a craving for the content of books: but as he didn't know B from the bull's foot he would bring his book, when he got one, to the boy to read out to him — preferably in the boy's own chimney-corner. But when comers and goers made there too much dis-traction, Joe dragged the boy, with the book to a quiet place under a boortree bush in the next field. With all the nerves of his body he would hearken to the boy's reading, lapping up every last syllable and listening for hours without himself letting out one sound. When the reading was finished Joe would sigh and say grace 'Thanks be to both God and you, Jaimie.'

Aunt Cassin would sometimes reward the boy for service done by letting him read for half-an-hour out of one or other of the prized volumes in Lieutenant Walsh's locked sea-chest. The grandest of these — the grandest in the world — was a big, well-worn volume of Duffy's Hibernian Magazine for 'the Year of Our Lord 1853' — with the most magnificent stories and poems that were ever penned! And all about Ireland! But ah, always when his delight in a piece was just reaching the bursting point, Aunt Cassin, considering him now more than repaid for the very little bit of work he had done, would withdraw the book and put it back in its coffin again.

But, one deplorably sad disappointment beyond all others his aunt gave him. — Once, sending him a long errand, she lifted him to Heaven by promise of an hour at a book that, she said, she had never let anyone read before—a book he felt certain sure would be even rarer — if rarer was in the world — than Duffy's Hibernian Magazine. But what did she do, after he had gone the message in double-quick time and was back breathless? She took out of the locker, and — a stone to a starving man — put before an innocent poor boy, Lieutenant Walsh's three — quarter-finished manuscript book on Logarithms!

And another sad disappointment. — The boy can never forget one sad December day that he had to carry a message three miles — and for his Aunt Cassin, too, more by the same token — to Landlord St. Clair's Big House in Bun-na Gleann. As the letter called for an answer, St. Clair's lady left the lad standing in a drafty, damp, flagged hall, while she took long time to consider the latter and indite her reply — but the boy minded little the cold passage, or the time she took, even if it was to Tibb's Eve — because he had found lying in a window, a wonderful book about a ship-captain by the name of Cook, who was searching for savages in the Pacific Ocean. So deep-buried was the boy, in the narrative, that when Lady St. Clair called to him from her room-door he didn't hear anything except somebody calling some other body, far off. Suddenly he found the book snatched from his hands, closed with a snap and flung back in its window with a bang — while the good lady told him, 'Here. Take this letter, little fellow, and begone!' But — he's certain sure the great lady never knew that she had snatched the bite from the lips of a man dying of hunger.[3]

For books the boy screenged the country-side. Sometimes John Burns and Briany MacDwyer, the shoemaker, out of self-interest — for either of them would give his eye, if he had only one, for a book — gave Jaimie rumour that they heard of a book coming into Meena-Cran-óg or other distant townland, sending him a-scamper, over hill and dale, to run the rumour down — and if possible bring back the prize, for reading by their work-bench. Sometimes from the lads who came to school from all airts he heard of a Come-home Yankee having brought a book with him — to his home in the next parish, or at the back of the mountain — which sent the boy scurrying to the faraway home of the returned one. When from any of these expeditions he brought back with him the loan of a book, or even part of a sore-worn one, he was filled with joy: and joy-filled for him was that night, and many a night after, while, stretched on his stomach on the hearth, he drank deep by the flickering turf-blaze. Sometimes, when his father had a good stock of fir-spails seasoning in the chimney, the boy would take seat on a creepy-stool in the corner, and read like a king by spaillight. — Only, his father would sometimes raise a ruction if he caught the *gasúr* wasting his valuable torches.

Two or three great Scripturians[4] were in the parish, who boasted the ownership of a book or books — and our lad often lit upon their homes in search of hidden treasure. But these were mortal jealous of their treasures, and the knowledge in them — knowledge that gave them the high place they properly held in the world's eyes — so, naturally, they too often discovered that their prized books had been lent, lost, stolen, or else so well hidden that they couldn't get their hands on them, when the boy came a-borrowing. But, indeed, it's to be feared that he made himself something of a nuisance, descending on their homes often and at all hours. Paddy Sweeny, greatest Scripturian of them all, and the boy's own grand-uncle, too, by marriage — Paddy was so afraid of the boy getting hands on his yellowed (turf smoked) volumes, and was so pestered by him, that he trained his grand- children to raise the alarm every time they'd behold the *gasúr* louping down the back of Dhrimkeelan hill. And he'd reward the child-informant with three dhraws of his old black pipe.[5]

Paddy, undoubtedly, had that biting, wonderful book, without which no Scripturian of them all could hold his own at a wake, Cobbett's *History of the Protestant Reformation*; but the *gasúr*, greatly as he coveted it, could never get it. 'Troth, yes, child,' Paddy would acknowledge, 'I have Cobbett — and the like of him, again, isn't to be found between two covers. — But that natarnal rascal and humbug, Shan a-Griffin of Tullyfin' — Shan was a rival Scripturian — 'came here, rakin', last Chewsday-was-a-week and got his paws on it — where it was by inadvartance left exposed — and, whither or why, he'd have to have the loan of it. He s'ore his solemn oath it would come home to me in three days, but hilt or hair of it I haven't seen since. — Purshuant to the vagabone!' When Jaimie, next evening, burst in on Shan a-Griffin in Tullyfin to borrow the borrowed Cobbett, bitter was his disappointment to learn from the outraged man, 'He's a liar, Paddy Sweeny — a natarnal utorious liar! He never was anything else, and never will be anything else till the day he hears the clods hoppin' on his coffin! And you're welcome to tell him that same from me, too. — he oul' desperaado wouldn't lend that book to his own father if it was to get him out of Hell. — As often as there's hairs in his whiskers he's promised me the loan of it; and every time I go for it, it's been borrowed by Neil Jaimsy, or it's at the shoemaker's gettin' a stitch in it, or it's in hell or any other handy place that keeps it off me.' And when, next evening, the boy tramped hill and bog again to Paddy's (for he lived in middle of the great bog of Mullin-a-Chorraigh) to inform him that Slian a-Griffin said he hadn't borrowed the book, Paddy would say, 'And you'd take that oul' blaguard's word before mine, would you ? If the divil is the father of liars — and he is — Shan a-Griffin is the grandfather. — If he didn't borrow Cobbett, though I'm sartain sure he did, then oul' Shan O'Cravsey from the uplands of Altidoo' — another Scripturian — 'must ha' made unlawful love to it the day, five weeks ago, that he came here under pretence of getting from the wife a cure for the heart-burn — which, he made out, was conshumin' him. — May the divil conshume him! for he's a manoeuverin' two — faced pilgrim, that you need an eye in the back of your head for, while he's in the same townland with a book.'

Uncle Paddy was the man that the poet surely had in mind when he talked about people a little more than kin. To his pain, the *gasúr* heard of his own uncle's actually warning people against him — If ye have anything that's in black ink on white paper, slip it six foot under the sod every time you detect that young buck-o in the same square mile with your house.' One would think people actually got pleasure from putting barricades in the way of ambitious budding genius.

As mentioned before, the boy benefitted on fair-days from spells of reading in the chap-books on Paddy MacBrearty's Stannins, where, in winter, he'd stand till his feet froze or till Paddy ordered 'Come now, avic-o, begone with ye! The divil a salary does the gover'ment pay Paddy to run a free library; and you've got plenty for nothin'. Come again when you sell a pig or pick a pocket and there'll be a welcome and twenty afore you.' But also some of his reading he did through a shop window where on Fridays was shown, until sold, a copy of the Dublin weekly story-paper, Young Ireland. Its front-page always feasted him with the first five hundred words of Chapter Forty-seven of a story that must have been glorious out-and-out to them that could turn the page. On the lower half-page the story was — on the upper half was a beautiful picture of the boy and the girl of the story roaming the Shannon banks; or the Irish Chieftain running his sword out- and-in, through the iron waistcoat of the English Knight. Mouth- watering, Jaimie used to watch a moneyed man, a school-monitor from four miles away (who drew a salary of thirty shillings a year), go in and pay his penny for the paper, while he passed remarks about the weather and the like. Then, with the paper sticking out of his coat-pocket, he would start for home, whistling The Ladies o' Carrick, just as if he wasn't one bit excited.

While real books like Cobbett, or Keating's History of Ireland, or The Seven Champions of Christendom, got, as they should, the greatest reverence, the name of storybook wasn't in too-good oder in Glen Ainey; but, far, far worse the kind of very sinful story-book — which, thank God, no one in Glen Ainey had yet come across — called a novel. Once, Aunt Sarah, back from a visit to Glasgow, sent word to the boy that she had a book with her which must be a prize, because everyone in Glasgow was reading and speaking about it: she wanted Jaimie to come and read it, on nights, at her fireside.Mighty little grass grew under the boy's heels till he was in his Aunt's and had the book in his trembling hands. It was called 'Kidnapped,' and was composed by somebody called Stevenson. But alas, his heart which had been up in the roof's rafters, plopped down into his shoes, when he read on the third line of the title page-

'A NOVEL'!

Bravely Jaimie closed the book, and walked away from it — and from his Aunt's — back to his lonely home.

In those years the boy reasoned out for himself that the why reading of novels was sinful was because they were made up out of some man's head — things that never happened — just lies. Story-books weren't much sinful — if, indeed, they were sinful at all. Of course there was nothing in them beneficial to anyone's soul — but they weren't lies. The ones whose title- page said, Founded on Fact, were not of course real truth, out-and-out, entirely — but very, very near it. Those that did not say Founded on Fact, were plain, common fact — in every sentence and syllable downright true records of real happenings.

(The real fact story-books always made the *gasúr* marvel for the exactitude with which ten pages of a conversation were recorded — and that in a day when only one in a thousand knew shorthand. It was plain, though, that the man who made the book must have been a shorthander and a good one; and by a lucky accident he happeened to be under the sofa, or something, when the hero and the heroine were making their beautiful speeches to each other. But, what puzzled Jaimie, entirely, and made him rack his poor-brain, was how the man was able to take down, even to the very exclamation point, what the heroine said all to herself, when she went to her boudoir — just after the hero had told her he loved her and she had promised to give him his answer to- morrow. Jaimie must have wrastled with this contrairy puzzle for three years — till light dawned, and he saw that the man, before he even wrote the title-page, called a conference of all the characters, and got from their own lips the real, true, genuine, exact facts, words — and thoughts — from the time the whole thing began until they were married in the paragraph before the last. To be sure there bobbed up the question of possible poor memories in one or another of the parties — but he's a mean man who'll let himself be too much of a skeptic.)

The boy read with pleasure, and learned, the history of the whole world — from the Creation till the Franco-Prussian War — in the twelve terribly interesting back pages of his Geography. Still greater was his delight to read, by snatches and gulps, — while seated on corner of John Burns's work-bench — Keating's History of Ireland — from the Flood to the Siege of Limerick — which book planted in his young breast something that was never to leave it again. A gloomy satisfaction he got from reading, over and over, one hundred and sixty-four yellowed and ragged pages which remained of a book called, he thinks, The Man of Feeling — come to him somewhere out of the unknown. He found glory, joy, and magic glimpses into a new world, in two books lent him by an American youth who spent a summer with grandparents in Donegal — one of these, tremendously exciting, was called The Green Mountain Boys, the other The Black Eagle. This latter moved and enthralled him: it was a story that followed the fortunes of General Lee in his gallant fight for the land he loved.

But though he got delight *go leor* from every book of the few that came to bless his life in those days, from none of them all did he get such lifting joy as from Shandy Maguire. And Shandy was his very own and bought with his very first shilling. On one glorious bright day — maybe it was a cloudy and rainy and miserable day to people who judged things only by their outsides — a day after a winter fair, he picked out of the mud a shilling that had been washed bare by the cold rains. As scrupulously honest as was everyone in Glen Ainey, the boy went up and down the hills enquiring if any unfortunate man had lost a shilling in the fair — a painful duty. But with happy ending, for he failed to find an owner. His bothersome conscience being satisfied, he had no difficulty deciding how his first shilling should be invested. The book of greatest renown in Donegal, then, was this same Shandy Maguire, of Donegal's own Barnish Mór Gap — a great story and wonderful, of which everybody had heard, and which all the old men who could read had read. The boy had seen the book on the Stannins; had read half-pages of it, times that Paddy MacBrearty's back and turned — It was always bought by Yankees who come home with money from the States — and who then brought it away to America with them.[6]

As Jaimie skipped the hills to Donegal to make himself master of the coveted book, like the flying hero in the old stories he felt the sparks from his heels light the skies behind him, and saw the sparks from his toes strike the skies ahead — all the way to Clabber Lane in Donegal town, and Paddy MacBrearty's — got Paddy to unpack the trunkful of precious merchandise which he had ready for the fair of Dunloe — till the book was reached, at the very bottom. Home with the treasure he hied, only touching the tops of the highest hills on the way back. He hadn't told at home of the silver fortune he had found — and dare not tell now how he had wasted it — for wasted is the very word that hard-hearted people would have used. Out of the garden-wall behind his father's house he pulled a big stone, pushed the book well in, and put the stone back again. For days after, whenever he could steal half-an-hour without risk, he was crouched at the back of the stoney wall, reveling in the most enthralling tale that ever went between book-covers — entrancing, romantic, and in every second or third chapter so heart-breakingly funny that, to avoid drawing on himself disaster, he often had to drop the book and clap both hands, hard, on his mouth — the whole body of him shaking like a *bog-quagh*, from the agony of inside laughter. Sometimes he had to roll on the ground and kick at the sky to ease his distressed insides. Often, however, at many of the most thrilling moments of Shandy's wonderful story the family's calling and bawling for the boy would compel the snatching from his very lips the cup of joy. He would shove Shandy into his secret place, and the stone after — and then, casually strolling from aback of the wall, reappear to his puzzling family from nowhere.

The ten times ten thousand nervous minutes which the lad stole with Shandy at the back of that stone-wall were fearfully joyous ones. *How* joyous he will never be able to tell. And anyway it could only be realized by passionate book-lovers to whom — like him — books came with the frequence of comets.

NOTES

1 Such fervid ballads in such fervid days planted in the boys breast the seeds that later sprang to songs of his own — as,

FOR IRELAND

A fierce flame burned, at boy-hood's dawn, within my tender breast,
Impassioned love my soul consumed for Motherland opprest.
Her glories gilt my waking hours, her woes my dreams o'ercast;
And the love that fed my soul's first fire, please God, shall light the last.

There's not a little bell that blows in Ireland's dewy glens,
There's not a sagan waves a spear above her many fens,
There's not a tiny blade of grass on all her thousand hills
But, this fond breast, with tender love to over-flowing, fills.

O, Ireland, for your holy sake I'll joyful bear all pain.
To your high cause I consecrate my heart, my hand, my brain.
If life and strife avail me not to save that soul one sigh,
Then, crowning joy, in your proud name would one unworthy die.

2 John was to figure large in four of the boy's books — when finally he came to be a book-writer. Then John read about himself with delight and pride — and after, would eagerly inquire, 'Will I get into your next book, Jaimie dear'?

3 The boy wouldn't like to leave the impression that the Lady St. Clair was either cruel or hard — only, for the moment, unthinking. For one in her station she was true neighbourly to the poor people around her — and would quickly help any of them who suffered from physical hunger.

It may be added that, long years after, when she found the gasúr's writings begin to appear in magazines she took occasion to meet him — for the first time in her life as she thought! She had her coachman pull up, on the Doorin road one day, and hail the boy to her. She heartily congratulated him, expressing real pride and pleased surprised to find what she called 'genuine worth' coming out of — 'glen Ainey' she said, but meant Nazareth. The boy smiled inside of himself for the greater surprise he could give her if he would — only, he feared she mightn't be a philosopher like himself, and so feel embarrassed. He even resisted a mischievous temptation, when she said, 'It's strange that I never met you before — ' and contented himself with paying the compliment (to both herself and himself) of an old Irish proverb — 'People often meet, but the mountains seldom'.

4   Men who could dilate upon, and argue at wakes, the Sacred Scriptures, Irish history, or any other learned subject.

5   In his old age Paddy, pulling at this venerable pipe, seated in his straw-chair in the chimney-corner, spent his days and nights either reading or holding forth to the audience of neighbours that sat at his feet — on history, the Scriptures, Martin Luther's (admitted) truck with the devil, Dan O'Connell's Speeches, or other deep subject.

6   In later life the boy was able to secure a copy of it in America — from a family whose parents, coming from Ireland, had brought the book into exile with them. It was written by a brillant and scholarly Donegal priest, Father John Boyce, who, in his Massachusetts parish wrote also 'The Spae- wife', and 'Mary Lee,or the Yankee in Ireland'. All three of his books had, deservedly, great popularity.

CHAPTER SIXTEEN

Characters

Though when he was a young child he thought there could be no place in the whole world as rich in original characters as his mother's Dhrimholme, our was to find that his own Glen Ainey was richer still. Two things that started off his mind on the way it went, were— the wealth of folk-lore that lay around him every way he turned, and the throng of originals that he found himself moving amidst.

Of the proudest men that the boy ever knew, two were tinkers, one a thatcher, and one a rag-man — all of them proud with a pride inborn. Erewin O'Rafferty, travelling tinker, tall, broad, bold of eye, noble of mien, walked a prince with head in the stars; and, without himself looking down upon anybody, drew everybody to look up to him. The other proud tinker — not a wander like Erewin, but with wife and children living in the full of your hand of a hut — was Sam O'Quigley, six-foot three in shoe-leather, square-shouldered, straight as a mountain-ash, splendidly stepped out in silver-buttoned knee-britches and grey leggins, carrying the respect of all who knew him, and compelling the respect of all who merely met him — and with sons and daughters brought up to be as proud as himself. James MacGuire, in his long black coat, mild of eye and of manner, fine of mind, philosophic of soul, soft-spoken as any genuine gentleman should, and possessed of a quiet power that made itself felt where ever he went, was far-and-away the most dignified thatcher that our lad ever saw shouldering straw and briars up a ladder.

Then, Tam MacGarvey, politest of men, of accent exquisite and manners charming, was a Chief of old come back to the world to shoulder a rag-bag round the town-lands. When Tam entered a house the *bean-an-tighe* knew at once that no common man had come in — and when he left, that a born and bred gentleman had gone out. He accepted her contribution of rags with a graciousness that put her under everlasting obligation — and when he rewarded her with the usual row of pins, it was a prince bestowing royal bounty on a favoured subject. As a gentleman Tam disdained all coarseness: when he was very greatly shocked his profanest was, 'Well, I'm ondamned!' Provocations that the rude man would with, 'May the divil take you!', Tam would turn aside with, 'May God accept you!' In extraordinary situations where the common christian, provoked, would rap out, 'Go to' — (a certain unworthy place), Tam's severest curse was, 'Go to Heaven, madam!' — the most impatient expression that ever escaped his lips. As he tripped the hills, rag-bag on back, he trilled a gay love-song or whistled a tune that held the larks listening. You knew, the minute you saw and heard Tam MacGarvey, that he was the one millionaire in Donegal.

Tam put into his children such pride that, when, in a famine year, free biscuits were bestowed on school-children, the rag-man's son was the solitary one who, drawing in his empty stomach and drawing himself up, turned the charity away with a polite, 'Not for me, I thank you.'

But the most polite of all men that the boy ever knew — of all beggarmen, especially — was Jimmy the Thrasher, who, with his wife, Ellen, and six children tagging at his heels — each one of them, big and small, shouldering an alms-bag — laid seventy square miles of country under tribute. When he'd return again to Glen Ainey from a begging sortie up the Tyrone way, Jimmy would announce , 'Meself and Fair Eleanor, and the young masters and missesses have been vacationin' at our shootin' -box in the Barnish Mór mountains. I hope, ma'am, you received, in due good ordher; the leg o' venison I transmitted you, her Ladyship's own shootin'?' — And, himself and his retinue coming from roaming and gathering through Connaught, he'd modestly inform his first patron, 'We were enjoyin' a short visit of a couple o' months with our dear cousin, Lord Clan Ricard, who was outrageous entirely for our laivin' him so soon. But I remarked to him, we couldn't afford to slight our other noble friends by extendin' to him ondue partiality. — Madam, have ye a few cold praties from dinner, that ye'd kindly sarve up on your silver sarvice to her Ladyship and the young gentry? Since 'twill be too late for our own luncheon when we reach the Castle today, I telegrammed the head-butler not to expect us before our usual seven o'clock dinnertime. I notified him to have my bawth ready, and lay out her Ladyship's lavendar evenin' gown. — Thanky ma'am', with a gracious curstsey. — 'And now, Fair Eleanor,' with another curtsey extending an arm to his wife. 'may I lead you to a seat at my right hand? And you, young Lordships and Ladyships, proceed to scramble for creepy-stools.'

Indeed, the wanderers who sought other men's roofs for their sheltering, and never knew where their next meal was coming from, our *gasúr* usually found the most humoursome. Owen O'Boyle, travelling tinker, with wife and seven children in his wake, was the most care-free gentleman that came in and out of Glen Ainey. Owen had one weakness — a drop o' drink. But he got small joy from the indulgence — for when the whiskey would make him happy, Sally, a grand scold, would, as like as not, turn his happiness to misery. 'Twas no wonder that when she was laid down with a small stomach trouble, and that someone, taking her ailing seriously, solicitously asked Owen, 'Do ye think she will die?' Owen should answer, with a sigh and head-shake, 'Troth, I'm afeared she'll not.'

And indeed Sally's removal should, in ways be a realief. Once, she

99

went to the Dean, with loud scolding complaint on Owen and his weakness. 'And,' she said, 'that Owen and the drink should stick together, isn't for want of advisin' on my part.'

'No', said the dry Dean, 'I've often myself heard you advisin' him — a mile up the road.' The Dean added, 'I don't think you take the right way of Owen.'

'What other way, I'd like for to know, would you handle a man who's as contrairy as Dan Andy's puckin'-goat?'

'You know,' the Dean answered her, 'the Scriptures tell us to return good for evil, and thus heap coals of fire on our enemy's head. — Why don't you try that plan for once?'

Said Sally, 'I never tried the coals — but I tried scaldin' water and 'twas no use.'

When, eventually, Sally departed the world, leaving a large charge of children on poor Owen's hands, and that, feeling he should make haste to put a new mother over them, he soon led Sarah Creighton to the Dean seeking the marriage ceremony, the Dean remonstrated, 'But, Owen, Sally's only six weeks dead.' 'And,' the practical Owen answered him, 'sure, in six weeks isn't she as dead as ever she'll be?'

Jaimie liked, and liked to listen to, bushy-bearded, curly-haired, carefree Pat MacGroarty, the thatcher, who, most every day thatching some roof by the roadside, always with song whiled his working-hours away. Sleeting, storming, raining, or freezing, Pat minded neither wind, weather, not anything else in the world except three things — his work, his song, and the passers-by. But neither his song not his salutations halted his work one instant. He bunched and dressed and laid the straw, and then pegged, pegged, pegged the scollops that would bind it to the roof, unceasing. And, because the hammering home of scollops with one's bare fists calls for appropriate gymnastics of the mouth, both Pat's song and salutations were often left hanging mid-sentence till the scollop was home. —

'*As I roved out one evening clear* — (Ay, Mrs. Manachan, it is a brave day, troth) — *all in the month of May*

Down by you flowery garden — (Peg, peg, peg) — *as I carelessly did* — (peg, peg) — *stray.*

I overheard a fair maid — (How's all your care Roddy? Well and hearty I hope?) — *in sorrow to complain*

All for her — (Peg, peg, peg, peg) — *absent lover, and Johnnie* — (Peg, peg) — *was his name.*

I boldly stepped up to her — (I see you're as well again as you ever were, Mrs. McGonigle, and gettin' as fat as a fool) — *and put her in surprise* — (Peg, peg.) —

I owe she did — (Peg, peg, peg) — *not know me, I bring* — (Yes, Molshie,

glory be to God! it's a great mornin' entirely) — *being in disguise.*
I said — (How's every bone in your body, Mary?) — *my pretty fair maid,*
my joy and heart's delight.
How far do you mean to — (Peg, peg, peg) — *wander this dark and*
lonesome night.
Kind sir, the road to — (Peg, peg) — *Claudy, will you be pleased to show.*
And pity my distress for there I mean — (That's a brave baste you're
drivin' Padraic, good luck to you and it) — *I mean to go,*
In search of a faithless young man and Johnnie — (Peg. peg) — *is his*
name.
And on the banks of Claudy — (God bliss ye Marg'et, your heels are as
light as your heart) — *I'm told he does remain.*

Glen Ainey had its own ballad-seller — an *amadáin* (Half-wit), Paddy
MacCalliog, with a beard like a thornbush, the face of a philosopher, and
a stride that was two yards long and taken with a lean and a lurch. He often
got Jaimie to read him the ballads, while he tried to learn them — which
never could. Paddy tramped to every fair, selling the songs which he could
never sing. Murder ballads and ballads of hangings were his glory — and
he lived from day to day, always in hopes to hear of another 'good
murdher' — in any blessed corner of the three Kingdoms. And when
Paddy had got and sold the murder ballad, he knew no peace of mind till
someone — anyone — was on trial for it. Then, as the time was drawing
on Ardara fair-day — a particularly fine ballad-selling district — Paddy,
entirely unbothered by the evidence for or against, would be praying, 'God
send they hang him for the fair of Ardara.'

But no half-wit of them all interested the *gasúr* more than Myles
Tunney. He was tall and gaunt, with a pompous manner, and dressed in a
cast-off uniform. Whether it was priest, parson, policeman or soldier's
uniform, Myles didn't mind — so long as it was a uniform. He wore all
four of them in turn. Although he lived by them and on them, he despised
common people who were without a distinguishing garb. He, and his silly
sister, Marget Tunney, were the children — the cursed children, everyone
agreed — of a turn-coat father, one of the very few who traded their
religion for the land with which a proselytising Protestant landlord would
bribe them. The country ballad of Myles's father's change of religion
said—

> *'He sold his God for sake of bog,*
> *And went to Tullyfinn.'*

So heartily did Myles react from his father's recreancy that nothing
maddened him more than the nickname the bad boys gave him, 'Orange

Mylie' — for which he would stone them from Formaol to Frosses. And a splendid stone-slinger he was. The Frosses Boys, notorious rascals of the parish, were his worst tormentors: so, no wonder 'twas that when, on a night in Phil Divver's, Heaven being the subject of discussion among assembled neighbours, and Myles being asked for his idea of the blessed place, he should answer. 'I dunno what Heaven's like, but I know what I'd like it to be like — a hole in the wall with meself in it, a heap o' stones by me, and the Frosses boys filin' past, durin' etarnity.'

But, once, he was willing to give up his dream-heaven and take on its competing establishment. That was on a time that the Dean had refused him a sadly-worn yet sorely-needed pair of breeches and chased him for his life. Highly indignant Myles hot-footed it to Minister Carr, who had spiritual charge of Doorin's good religious Planter people, and, after a raging denunciation and repudiation of Dean Freely, flopped on his knees, blessed himself firecely in preparation and implored, 'An' now, Minister Carr please make a good Prodesan o' me that I may go to hell with yourself an' the rest o' your damned Doorin scoundrels.'

It was in Phil Divver's of Frosses, that, asking for a dinner on an August day, and being told to help in the hay-field and earn his dinner, he replied to Shiela, 'Madam, an emp'y bag can't stand.' And, when, seeing the logic of the thing, Shiela gave him a good, large dinner, and then ordered, 'Now, go and help hard at the hay till night,' Myles answered, 'Madam, a full bag can't bend.[1]

But the one character of all Glen Ainey characters whom our lad best loved, and in his memory cherishes, was the fiddler and wit, Donal a-Thoorish — him of the impudent, gathered, grinning face, and short, stout, stooped figure — in long, greenish coat that sheltered the fiddle as well as the figure. Famed far and wide for his music as well as his wit, without Donal, no christening, no wedding, no raffle or spree, had a soul to it, or was worth shoe-leather tramping to. From the ridge of the mountain to the rim of the sea, Donal was courted and his fiddle coveted — while his wit was cheered or feared, as the case might be.

Wedding time was Donal's merriest time. And that was, of course, chiefly during the weeks before Lent, when the coming of a prohibitive period always put a hurry on the boys. To christenings he was called at all times. But his professional year began with the beginning of winter — when the long nights shouted for raffles and plenty of them, dances, and sprees. He saw to it that the dances kept going every week of the winter. At the season's beginning he gave out that he would hold a dance on Tuesday night next in Ownie Dorrian's of Derraherk. When word went to Ownie of the honour to be done his house, he threw out of his big kitchen everything movable that couldn't or shouldn't be sat upon. The country-side came, cramming and jamming his house on the happy Tuesday, and footing it to the fiddler's fiddling till nigh morning. At midnight the boys passed the fiddler's hat, into which every guest put a penny or silver thrupenny — or, if he was a come-home Yankee, a shilling, to prove that he had brought a fortune back with him. Accepting the eight or ten or sixteen shillings collected, Donal would then call the next dance — 'on' Neddy Shinaghan of Fanaghan Barr, next Sunday night. At Neddy's he would announce the dance to follow — calling it on some other fortunate fellow who owned a big kitchen in other corner of the parish. So he carried his entertainments round the country and the season, from winter's start till its finish. The honoured man on whom the dance was called was never consulted beforehand — only overheard the good news as it passed from mouth to mouth among the merry ones.

Donal was an old man in our lad's earliest days, his large family raised and scattered; but in his far-away young days, before the family came to him, the days when the Univarsal Spelling-book — 'the Universal' — with its moral lessons, was the standard reader in all schools, he had in Mullin-a-Chory a poor hut that was a contrast to the *warm* houses (well-provendered and well-furnished) of the more comfortable farmers. When his little hut, one night, went afire and the gathered neighbours offered him sympathy, while they and he gazed at a conflagration too far gone to stop, Donal, a philosopher always, answered them, 'Gentlemen, for once in my life I can boast the warmest house in Glen Ainey.' For a couple of years after that — till he took a wife — himself and his fiddle were housed in this home and that, the country round, with whomsoever it pleased him to honour; and when, at the Chapel-gate on a Sunday the good Dean asked, 'Where are yourself and the fiddle stopping now, Donal?' the fiddler answered him, 'Your riverence, we have more stops than a Universal.

And on their way home together from a wedding, once, the Dean, riding Forgiveness, asked Donal, who plodded with fiddle under-coat, how much he had made that night. 'The sorra so much. Just thirty shillins.' 'Hagh!' carped the Dean. 'Thirty shillings for a fiddler, and for the poor priest sixteen-and-thruppence!' (amount of the marriage then). 'Yes,' remarked Donal with a sigh, 'your poor old father, Heaven forgive him, might well ha' give you a better trade.'

The Dean was another of the parish originals looked up to by the lad. Like many of the priests of those times — lately emerged from the Penal Days — the Dean had been schooled in one of the dozen Continental Universities whereto intending priests were from Ireland smuggled. He as a learned Latinist and theologian, and saint besides, yet rough-and-ready as though he had never in life lost sight of his father's turf-stack. The flock whch he kept in order with tongue and stick worshipped the ground he walked on. For years the home of himself and his dog and his books was one damp, small-windowed room in the Widow Meighan's by the Ainey's banks — and his chapel had been the Scalan (a three-walled thatched shed, which just shielded the altar and him from the elements — while the con- gregation knelt on the heather without).[2] When at last he got a curate to help him in his large parish and that they must have a roof of their own, he commanded James Griffin, the mason, to build him a parochial house. 'Plaise, your reverence, give me the plan and specifications,' demanded James. The Dean took him by the shoulder to somebody's near-by meadow-field — 'Go in there with you, and dig a foundation a dozen or fifteen steps one way and half a dozen the other: put four walls on it, not forgetting to leave proper openings for two doors and some windows; give me within it three rooms and a kitchen, and clap a roof on it, well-thatched. If your work's well done I'll make the parish pay you a hundred pound. If it's ill-done it would be well for you to find beforehand the shortest road out of Glen Ainey.'

When the Dean asked William Pogle to make him a pair of shoes, and that William drew out his foot-rule to make measure, the Dean snapped, 'To the devil with you and your measure! — There's my foot. Give a good look to it — and make me a sizable shoe for it, such that when I want, I can put in my hand and scratch my toe.'

The boy well remembers the Dean's turn-out when he went a journey. He had a mare that had served him faithfully from beyond the memory of that generation, and grown old with himself. She was nicknamed For- giveness. And when he tied her into his old rusty, rattly, rickety, jaunting- car with bits of leather, hay- rope, straw-rope and twine, she bore him over the landscape at a breath-taking speed of two miles an hour. Though, in justice to Forgiveness be it said, when the Dean was on a life or death errand to some old soul in the hills who, thinking of going to Heaven, needed strength for the journey, Forgiveness thought little of covering three and even four miles in that time. Then the conveyance behind her could be heard coming long before it was seen, and heard going for a good while after it had disappeared.

With the Dean, Donal a-Thoorish sometimes had his troubles. And, *vice versa*. Once the Dean forbade dances — off the altar on Sunday — because he had heard that drink was introduced at some of them. Next morning, as the priest breakfasted, Donal, with his fiddle, marched in, followed by his wife and eight children — and announced, 'As your riverence has taken away my means of supportin' the hen and her *eilean*' (flock of chickens), 'I'm supposin' you mean, from now on, to take charge' them yourself. — There they are, and may God bliss and prosper you and them!' Then the fiddler retired, closing the door after him. The Dean gazed from one to the other of the nine beings who were settling themselves around the room, rushed after Donal, and begged of him to come back, take away his family, and go on with his dances.

Yet the good man imposed on Donal two conditions — one, that there should be no drink allowed at any dance — the other, that he must not hold dances on Sunday.

Donal observed the conditions faithfully — for almost two months. He thought, then, that he would risk a Sunday-night dance in Condy O'Donnell's, in the remote mountain, where the Dean would not be likely to hear of it.

But the Dean did hear of it — in plenty of time and kept the secret to himself till it came time for action. On the dance-night he and his good blackthorn were nearing Condy's when the fun was in full swing: the music and the laughter met him half-a-mile down the hill. Ere he crossed the threshold, the house was nigh jammed with merry-makers, gaily footing it to Donal's fiddle — but within one minute after he appeared it was empty — except for himself and the fiddler. The dancers had gone out by doors and windows even, it is said, some by the chimney. The Dean, with his stick, had helped them all he could. The fiddler, a cool villain always, just sat his seat in the chimney-corner, fiddle on knee. With blackthorn vengefully shaking in his fist, the Dean strode across the floor to the mortal offender, who, affecting that he was about to be asked for a tune, got fiddle and bow into position. 'Sirrah!' thundered the Dean, 'Do you know the third commandment?' (In our Catholic catechism 'Remember thou keep holy the Sabbath day'). Taking on a puzzled look, and holding his bow still suspended, the rascal, putting wit above reverence, answered, 'not by that name, your riverence. — Would you whistle a bar of it?'[3] The Dean's stick flashed up! and then down again! — on the fiddle, luckily. And next instant all the king's houses and all the king's men couldn't put the ten hundred powered pieces of Donal's fiddle together again. But grateful he was, on reflection, that it wasn't his skull the Dean chose to him his stick upon.

Of the hundred and one stories still told of the beloved Dean around the firesides of Glen Ainey, there is one which the boy heard a thousand times — a story the literal truth of which he would hesitate to vouch for — but which is still told and enjoyed because it so well fits the man's rough-and-ready nature: Cock Tuesday, the eve of Lent, was then the great day of the year for marriages. As, after twelve o'clock on that night, no marriage would be celebrated for forty days, it was not uncommon for six or eight couples to present themselves for marriage that day. This particular story relates that on a certain Cock Tuesday the Dean was called away in the forenoon to sick call, and from thence had to journey on business to Donegal town; and after spending there some hours, was drawn to other sick-calls in various corners of the parish. Meantime, marrying pairs had been assembling at his house, till, when night fell, half a dozen couples were there waiting; and as the night wore on and the Dean not yet arrived, candidates for happiness kept accumulating, and impatience increasing. As the fatal hour of midnight approached, no less than twelve couples were in ferment. And they were in sad plight indeed, when, with the kitchen clock pointing to five minutes of midnight, the Dean walked in! And faced what should have been a dumbfounding problem! But the story goes that the good Dean, always equal to an emergency, ordered the twenty-four matrimonial aspirants on their knees, higgledy-piggledy, *tre na ceile*, bestowed on them, in bulk, the marriage blessing, and then commanded, 'Now, boys and girls, get up and sort yourselves.'

Here have been barely hinted at a few samples of the crowds of originals that peopled rare Glen Ainey in the days when our boy was a *buachaillín*.

NOTES

1   In Myles's early days when all Catholics paid their priest a five-shilling stipened at Christmas, and by England's motherly laws were compelled to pay the Protestant minister tithes of their crops in harvest, the Protestant Rector, Sandy Montgomery, and the parish priest, Dean Feely, riding together to Donegal one day, and meeting with Myles on the road, posed him, 'Which of the two, Myles, would you like best to be — minister or priest'? ''Tis too late for me to larn to be either, now', answered the half-wit. 'But if ever I raise a son, plaise God I'll have him a minister in the harvest time and a priest at Christmas'.

2   During the Penal centuries when a price was on the priest's head, Mass was celebrated at a rock in a hidden glen, while sentries watched from the hill-tops for coming of the soldiers. After Catholic Emancipation (in 1829) little scalans as described were erected for the shielding of priests and alter. Some of these were still in use in the boy's early days — one in his own parish.

3   Often the Irish dance tunes have different names in different localities, and when the fiddler doesn't recognise by name a tune that is asked for, the asker will whistle a bit of the air for his recognising.

CHAPTER SEVENTEEN

The Shanachies

That our *gasúr* should be filled to the finger-ends with the old, old stories, and a teller of them, isn't to be wondered at; for the folk tales filled a large place in his life — a large part in all young lives in Glen Ainey.

There wasn't a hillside or a glen in those days where he didn't find and frequent a good shanachie — a story-teller who had inherited the thousand tales of imagination and enchantment wherewith it was his nightly pleasure to charm the country-side. As well as our lad all the youth of the country-side collected to the shanachie's cabin when the winter night was falling, and formed a circle round the blazing turf-fire — the only light in the house — whose leaping flame gilded a score of bright faces, danced up and down the white-washed walls and across the rafters above, whilst the old shanachie, on his creepy-stool in the chimney-corner, held them spell-bound with entrancing tale after entrancing tale till long after the time that all good boys should be at home and in bed.

Before he was ten the boy knew, and could himself tell, like any shanachie of them, a full hundred of the old tales — the same that were to found his life's work. The greater part of these he got at the firesides — but many, too, he learnt in Glen Cuach school. For the boys from the hills, and the glens carried every day to school with them, and there traded, the best tales they had heard the night before. Oftentimes, when the Master was happy at seeing half-a-dozen raggedy heads together — our *gasúr's* pretty sure to be in the center — puzzling, he thought, over a purty sore problem in *al-jay-bra*, grammar, or other useless subject, the rascals were really trading old folk tales.

Four shanachies there were who meant most to our lad. And the first of them was Marg'et O'Gorman, a girl who, in his childhood days, when there were five or six tow-heads to be herded in his mother's house, came from Mullin-a-Chorraigh to help — at twelve shillings a quarter with bed and board. Jaimie's mother's musings by the fireside at night were now often suspended, to let Marg'et entrance the circle with one of her wonder-tales. Each night she had a new tale, for there seemed no end to her store. That girl, coming in from the wild mountains knew everything in the whole world — everything, that is, that was worth knowing — everything in fact except reading, writing and sums (only useful for torturing wee children who had never harmed nobody). She had knowledge of everything that the birds said, and the fowls and the animals. In Gaelic they spoke. When the marauding pig was being chased out of the garden, even a deaf man — after Marg'et had explained it to you — could hear and realize what it cried as it skeltered away from the rod, 'Ni mise! Ni mise! — It wasn't me! It wasn't me!' And when the hungry turkey came complaining to the back door, the boy himself distinctly heard and understood (when Marg'et told him the Gaelic that it angrily gobbled out of itself), '*Nachfhuil an bean-a'-tighe istigh? Nachfhuil an bean-a'-tighe istigh?* — Isn't the good wife within? Isn't the good wife within?' And when the hen cackled so loudly after laying, what it was always saying in Gaelic was 'Gug-gug-gug-gug-gaigerly! Gug-gug-gug- gaigerly ! — There isn't a stitch to my back or a tack to my feet from laying eggs for you! Gug-gug-gug-gug-gaigerly! — There isn't a stitch to my back or a tack to my feet from laying eggs for you.' — There wasn't one of the farm-yard inhabitants whose plaint he didn't know, under that wonderful girl's tutelage. Our lad wished and wished that he could be whisked off to the country (a mile-and-a-half away) that Marg'et came from, a country that he saw filled with such marvellous tales as The Well 0' the World's End, The Widow Woman's Three Sons, The Giant of Bang-Beggars' Hall, The Snow the Crow and the Blood, and The Princess of the Garden of Eden. They were the first of the real, old folk-tales he had heard — he couldn't have been more than three years of age, then — and they were to him and his brothers and sisters real happenings of a real wonder-world that existed somewhere outside of, but right next to, their own. It was the first time he realized what enchantment truly was. He wished and wondered, and wished again, that his mother could only pay Marg'et twelve shillings a quarter forever. But she couldn't — though Marg'et was heartily willing that the good fortune should befall her. So, after she had for nearly two years enriched his mother's house and the lives of all in it — with riches that would seldom be reached and never surpassed in their lives again — she, rare young shanachie, to her weeping regret and theirs, took her departure for America. In announcing her going, she used the words which so often she had used in her tales — words that had always started the boy's dreams — said she was 'going off to push her fortune.' And though in the fabled land she went to she was to meet with romantic fortune far and away beyond her rainbow hopes, she carried away with her, and there lost, greater, richer, fortune far.[1]

When the child Jaimie had become a man, at the age of six, and was fit to go rambling at night, the shanachie of all others to whose white cottage and red fireside he oftenest returned, and there longest sat, was Owen O'Cuinn. He and his wife, Shiela Grianna, owned a little one-roomed cabin in which they reared seven brave boys and girls; and had a pony and cart for jogging to fairs, long miles around — to sell apples, gooseberries, and *dilisc*. Owen was, in ways, the rarest shanachie our lad ever listened to. He had his art to perfection: for he told them with honey

— and flowed just as smooth, for he told them with a rhythm that was in itself entrancing to his wide-eyed audience. He used, in his telling, all the quirks and quips and magic phrases, and studded it with all the beautiful rhythmic *ranns*, that were the wealth of the ancient shanachies.[2]

Owen's story might begin — 'Once upon a time when pigs were swine, when turkeys chewed tobacco, and pigeons built their nests in old men's beards — when every road in Ireland was paved with lovely pan-cakes, and little pigs with a knife and a fork stuck in the back of each, ran up and down the roads, crying, 'Come eat me! Come eat me!' — a long, long time ago, this was, and a happy time, too — and in that long-ago time there was a King of Ireland who had three sons' — and the great tale of The King of Ireland's Three Sons was off to a gorgeous start.

When the hero on his wonderful steed rides the far journey to the eastern world, or gallops for home just one leap ahead of his pursuer, Owen had his speed so swift, and leaps so long, that he only touched the tops of the highest hills in his passage, whilst the sparks from the steed's toes struck the stars ahead, and the clatter and sparks from his heels deafened and deluged all the world behind: he overtakes the wind before, and the wind behind cannot overtake him; over high hills, low hills, sheep-walks, and bull-runs, he rides away and away where you wouldn't know day from night, or night from day, where the cock never crew, the wind never blew, and yesterday falls a month behind the morrow.

Owen was a true successor to the olden bards, with all their knack, and all their art for enchanting their audience, and carrying it hoof and head, to magic realms where were castles of shining silver and glowing gold, each with a window for every day of the year, inhabited by mighty giants, noble kings, beautiful princesses, undaunted heroes, masters of magic, and steeds of swiftness. Or, it was a land of humour where the hero, Jack from Ireland, tricked, out-manoeuvered, fooled, bamboozled, and frightened to death, the greatest giants and the powerfullest champions that world knew, making them, in fear of his threatened prowess, shiver till they shook loose the nails on their toes. Owen's stories were good, but the telling of them was still better. He was a shanachie whose death (at ninety-five) the boy never could understand — for surely Heaven must have meant him to be immortal. But Heaven, it seems, yearned after his stories, too.

Owen was very human, though, in one point — his gift of sleep. Without the faintest, first sign, in middle of a story — in middle of a sentence — he was liable to halt, and instantly slip off, for a little while of forget, into the magic lands of which he told. Seated on his stool in the chimney-corner, a bit bent toward the blaze, his elbows resting on his knees, and his hands hanging limp to the heat, the sleep-cloak just slipped itself over the shanachie. If one didn't look at his eyes or hear his breathing, he was only a man meditating. The music and the magic of the old stories had possessed them of his soul!

No one spoke or stirred, when Owen slept. His audience held the same breathless stillness that had wrapped them for so far in the story. Sometimes three minutes went by, sometimes twice three, sometimes ten minutes, ere the shanachie's eyes unclosed — the only motion — and, without a missed or wasted word, he completed his broken sentence, and on with the story.[3]

Another of the boy's masters in folk-lore was the Bacach Rua (red beggarman) — a big, tall, stout, strapping, able fellow who, having taken begging as his profession, wandered wide over the barony laying all human-kind under tribute. He carried half a dozen bags tied round his neck and slung from his waist — for the various alms he would get at the various houses he visited. He got meal at one house that he put in one bag, potatoes at another house for another bag, and so on. With all his bags flying in the wind behind him, he made a picture when he strode the hills, twirling his blackthorn stick in his fist, and whistling against the lark in the sky — the lightest-hearted thing, he, above the horizon. When night fell on him, he mounted a knowe and looked over the country-side to see what house was sending up the biggest smoke — where, to be sure, would be boiling the biggest pot for the biggest supper. Upon that house he drew, and, lifting the latch, walked in with a hearty, 'God save all here!' He laid down his staff in one corner, shed his bags in another, and sat him down in the family circle, making himself at home for the night. He never insulted the hospitality of the house by asking permission to lodge there. Everyone knew that half of their roof and half of everything under the roof belonged to the houseless and the homeless, the wanderer and stranger — above all, to God's poor. The fact that he entered as night was falling, and that he laid down his staff and shed his bags, and sat down in the fireside circle, was announcement enough that he was honouring the house with his presence for a night. He sat, of course, to sup with the family, and when supper was over, made himself for a while head of house, ordering all on their knees for the nightly rosary. This was commonly the mother's prerogative — but when the Bacach Rua came, because he was the greatest prayer of the country-side he took over from the *bean-a-tighe* her duty. And mighty welcome to the youngsters that was: for, to prove his praying powers he strung out the rosary to twice its usual length, and tacked to the tail of it trimmings without end — calling for prayers for everyone who was sick in the parish and for everyone who was well, for everyone who had gone abroad to America and for everyone who had remained at home. — For everyone he could think of and everyone he could not think of, the Bacach Rua asked for prayers, till ere he had finished — as our lad often knew to his woe — all the children in the house had their backs aching and their knees cracking.

But when he did finish they knew they were going to be well repaid: since, now the great story-telling would begin. Taking his seat in the opposite chimney corner from the *fear-a-tighe* (man of the house), and accepting the pipe that the *fear-a-tighe* filled and lighted and proffered to him across the fire, the Bacach crossed his legs, pulled at the pipe fiercely for a while, and then began a great night's story-telling.

But he had a bigger audience now. For, all the youth of the neighbourhood would be thronging in and filling the floor and lining the walls. Because, always the word swept the hills, like moor afire, that the Bacach Rua had arrived at Condy Dorrian's — and all the hills knew there would be a great story-telling at Condy's tonight. So, the youngsters trooped here — only, taking care to come in when they were sure the Bacach's rosary was finished — filled the cabin from door-step to back- stone, and listened, spell-bound, to the Bacach's stories from then till nigh midnight.

The Bacach Rua told The Three Princesses of Connaught, The Giant of the Golden Castle, The Hound the Hawk and the Filly, Mac Ri na h'Eireann (The King of Ireland's Son), The Mistress of Magic, The Bee the Mouse the Harp and the Bum Clock, The Queen of the Lonely Isles, The Steed o' Bells, The Sword of Light — and a hundred more, every new one of them lovelier than the last.

But, by far the most remarkable of the shanachies at whose feet Jaimie sat, was Shan O'Hegarty of Meenawanna, the richest-souled, keenest-minded, unschooled man that the *gasúr* ever met. Shan's memory for the old tales was a well so deep that our boy never saw the bottom of it. His, too, were mostly the mighty kind, the old classic stories — of Fionn and his gallant Fian, Cuchullin, Conal Cearnach, and the Craobh Ruadh[4] — grand bardic epics that might well make Homer green to hear.

And some of Shan's were stories yet unheard by scholars deep in ancient Gaelic lore. When he recited his stories and chanted his poems (the poems of Oisin) to a kitchenful the very mouse in the wall would hold its squeak.Some of them he said in the Gaelic of a thousand years ago, and some in the tongue of to-day. Even the Beurla of this poor mountain man — when he consthered his tale into that language for the boy's benefit — was a wonder to listen to — so wide and deep and discriminating his command of it. On the hardest Gaelic in the old stories, and the finest beauties in the poems, he could enlighten a Lord Chancellor. When the boy, in later days, after he had come to know what literature was, said to Shan his wonder at the greatness and number of his tales, and his power of telling them, the shanachie shook his head, and answered, 'Ach, I'm no story-teller! You should have heard my poor father, Andhra, God rest him! — When that man was dying, the last word he gave us was, 'Ah, children, I'm willing and ready to die, but I only wish the Lord would let me leave my head with ye.'[5]

Our lad learned stories, too, from many a story-telling bout staged at wakes for the pleasanter passing of the long night — when some of the famous shanachies of the countryside there encountered one another, each of them not only willing but wishful to prove his title to front place. When the longest wake-night didn't leave latitude enough for each shanachie to prove his power and show the range of his stories, the finish of the bout might have to wait till another old neighbour or two died and gave the champions a chance to carry the contest to a satisfying decision. The Fianna of the old stories always divided the night into three parts (gauged by the three thirds of a big log put on the fire at dayli'gone) — a third for feasting, a third for story-telling and a third for sleep — but shanachies of Glen Ainey in our *gasúr's* day, grudging waste of time, often broke with tradition and gave the three thirds of the night to the one thing that was worth while.

The longest and loveliest story the boy knew he got at a wake story-telling. It was the Adventures of the King of Ireland's Thirteen Sons, told by Paudeen O'Hegarty, between night and morning, at the wake of Tomas Rua O'Donnell of Tully-na-ha. There Paudeen, telling the tale, told also how he got it. In his younger days when he, with many another stout fellow went to Scotland and England to win the harvest and bring back the pounds that would pay the landlord, he learnt the story from a Connaughtman in whose company he had travelled home from England. The night that the Donegal men and Connaughtmen reached the parting of their ways, a day's walk west of Dublin, they spent together in a barn; and, knowing they must seperate in the morning — the Donegal men to go north, and the Connaught men west — refusing God's good night to throw away in sleep, they used it in story-telling. Then Paudeen heard — and had away with him by heart — The King of Ireland's Thirteen Sons.

But, one of the delightfullest nights of his life the *gasúr* spent at a six-hour story-telling under the stars, on Cruach-an-Airgid. A company of mountain men, journeying to a fair, a festival, or a court of law in a far town, would, when night ovetook them in the hills, often shelter under a spink (precipice) and pass the night reciting the old hero-tales. The *gasúr*, once, travelled with a band of Glen Eask men, coming home over the Cruach Ghorm mountains from a Gaelic *féis* in Glen Fionn, and the harvest night falling on them near the mountain-top, they camped inunder a sheltering spink of Cruach-an-Airgid, and started the night with Tuathal O'Slavin reciting the epic of Diarmuid and Gráinne — whose mountain bed they weren't more than a mile from. After Tuathal each, in turn, told his own tale — till the ring of day formed in the east, and came light to carry them home. It was maybe the greatest night the lonely Cruach ever knew.[6]

112

1 Long, long, long years later, and a few years after the good fairies had translatef to America the gasúr — or the young man who had been the gasúr — he one day came on a news despatch going the rounds of the newspapers of that wide land — about a great lady who had died in Philadelphia, leaving — 'as a token of affection and esteem for two of the grandest and most faithful of women' — to her maids, Margaret O'Gorman, and Mary her sister, their weight in silver, together with a house (her own house) little less than a castle — 'to enable them to live in a style befitting such worthy women'. The Philadelphia North American, learning that the boy (whose name had then become known in that land) had, as a child, sat at Margaret O'Gorman's knee, requested from him her story — and under great caption, spread it, with pictures, over a full page — and syndicated the same to sixty Sunday papers of the land.

Going to see Margaret, in her grand house, Jaimie asked her to tell him, again, one of her stories that he had partly forgotten. 'Ach', she said, 'sure they all eloped out o' my head a life-time ago — for no one here would bother listenin' to the likes o' them'. Alas!

More than a dozen of her tales the boy had, however, saved — and some of them recorded in his book, Donegal Fairy Stories.

When he informed Margaret that The North American had commissioned him to write an article about her she violently objected. 'Why should they put me in their paper? Sure I never done anything I would be ashamed of!'

2 Reviewers have dwelt upon the rhythm in the lad's writings: From the old Shanachies he caught it, if it is there.

3 Owen, when he sat by his fire without anytime to talk to, would, at any he wished, just droop his eye lids and slip into sleep — as a man might pass into another room — and would slumber sweet for one hour, two hours, or fifteen minutes, as he desired. When, over-night, he travelled the mountains to Dunloe fair, seated on top of his apple-creels, whip and reins in hands, his eyes closed as he cleared his own Knockagar at nightfall, opened at midnight in Glenties village (in the heart of the hills) where the mare needed baiting, closed once more out of Glenties, and opened when the pony — which always knew its business, even, it was said the dates of the fairs it was due to go to — drew up on Dunloe street at eight in the morning. Owen was one of the very wealthiest of the many very wealthy men that the boy had the good fortune to know in those days — his soul filled with the peace of the old tales, the peace of the stars, God's peace.

To Owen's memory and that of another wonderful one Shan O'Hegarty, one of the boy's folktale books, The Donegal Wonder Book, is dedicated.

4 The Fian and the Craobh Ruadh were famed military bodies that flourished in Ireland in the first few centuries of the Christian era.

5 Andhra O' Hegarty, a poor mountain man, could speak Latin. Shan recollected the days, in his childhood, when many a Donegal mountain man did so. During the dark centuries when the schools were suppressed in Ireland, and a price of five pounds put on the heads of both schoolmaster and priest (who were sought out with bloodhounds), Latin was still taught by the hunted schoolmaster to his classes at the back of a hedge, or in a cave in the hills. Shan told the boy how, as a child, going with his father to attend the priest's dinner at the Station-house in the mountains, he listened to the priest and the guests — sheepmen and small farmers of the hills — carry on the dinner discourse in Latin. Details about this wonderful phase of Irish in the hills, and the dreadful Penal Laws which crushed the land for centuries — only revoked, through the might of the great Dan O'Connell, in 1829 — may be found in this author's Story of the Irish Race.

Shan O'Hegarty told the boy that 'the Scotch poet, Campell' came as far as the village of Glenties collecting old Gaelic tales, sent for his father and got many from him. Shan may have made a mistake here. About the same time that the poet Thomas Campbell flourished, there flourished also the Scotch 'folk- lorist Campbell — who left his monument in four grand volumes of 'West Highland Folk-tales'. Since all of the Scottish Highland Gaelic tales are, of course, the ancient tales, it would only be natural that some peculiarly Donegal tales, like that of O'Donnell and the Deer of Assaroe should be found among them — yet it is more than possible that the folk-lorist Campbell came to Donegal to compare and amend and supplement his Irish tales of the West Highlands — and that the O'Donnell tale in his collection, as well as others, were obtained from Andhra O'Hagarty in Donegal's West Highlands.

6   Before quitting the subject of folk-lore it is of interest to note that many of the imaginative tales which the boy heard from Glen Ainey shanachies around the turf-fires were the same that were brought into Ireland from the East twenty-five hundred years before, by their Milesian forefathers — and, accordingly, are paralleled by tales still told in Turkey, Arabia, Persia. When our boy became a writer, voyaged to America, and started publishing some of the old Irish folktales in magazines there, a panic was created in two editorial offices (McClure's and Harper's) as letters came in from orientalists, telling that the stories which they were putting forth as old Irish folk-tales by this adventurer from Ireland, were well-known Persian, Turkish, Arabic tales! When — long after this matter was settled — our lad's telling of that lovely old Irish tale, the Well of the World's End, appeared in an American magazine, he was written to by a German engineer on a Turkish ship lying at San Francisco, asking where or how he got the tale. The letter said 'A Turkish merchant in Constantinople told me The Well of the World's End — the same as yours in its chief features — twenty-five years ago, and it has been my favourite tale ever since: whenever I return home, my wife and daughtres always ask me to tell it: so you can imagine my astonishment at reading it to-day and finding it set down as an Irish tale. Between my Turkish tale and your Irish one, the difference is mainly in details. As, for instance, where you make mention of western birds, trees, and animals, in my tale there are eastern birds, trees, and animals. And it is a Sultan's beautiful daughter who falls ill in my tale, where in yours it is the King of Ireland's daughter.

At the boy's request his correspondent typed out for him his tale — which our lad has filed away, and which shows the most striking similarity to his own.

In The Well of the World's end, is healing for all ills and sorrows. But hard is the Well to reach — if not impossible. In the old folk-tales myriad champions set out to journey to it — but from the perils that beset their path few of them ever return.

> *Beyond the four seas of Eire, beyond the sunset's rim,*
> *It lies, half-forgot, in a valley deep and dim,*
> *Like a star of fire from the skies' gold tire,*
> *And whose drinks the nine drops shall win his heart's desire —*
> > *At the Well o' the World's End.*
>
> *What go ye seeking, seeking, seeking,*
> *O girl white-bosomed, O girl fair and young?*
> *'I seek the Well-water, the cool Well- water,*
> *That my love may have love for me ever on his tongue'.*
>
> *What go ye seeking, seeking, seeking,*
> *O lad of the dreaming eyes, slender lad and tall?*
> *'I seek the Well-water, the cool Well-water,*
> *That the cailín I love best may love me best of all'.*
>
> *What go ye seeking, seeking, seeking,*
> *O mother with the little babe folded in your arm?*
> *'I seek the Well-water, the cool Well- water,*
> *That nine drops on his lip may shield my child from harm'.*
>
> *What go ye seeking, seeking, seeking,*
> *O grey head, long weary of the vigil that ye keep?*
> *'I seek the Well-water, the cool Well-water,*
> *That nigh it I may rest awhile, and fall asleep'.*

From Ethna Carbery's Four Winds of Eirinn.

CHAPTER EIGHTEEN

Hospitality in the Hills

Whenever the boy went among the mountains, on duty bound or rambling, he must sit and eat in every cottage. Even the eggs and butter that they dare not eat themselves — that must be saved for the inevitable rent — were pressed upon him. Nothing within the four walls that he could possilily want must be withheld from a visitor. Aside from the fact that the spirit of hospitalty was born in them, the poverty to which they had been for ages condemned begot the habit of pressing a stranger to eat and eat more, lest he, too well aware of their poverty, might be wishing to spare them. As it became the custom of a host to press, it became the custom of a guest to resist and eat sparingly — lest eating to satisfaction abroad should sow suspicion of hunger at home.

When you ate abroad — as when giving a day's work to a neighbour — and some luxury was surely pressed on you — an egg, or bit of bacon, for instance — then, although you might plentifully patronise the potatoes, both your caution and your innate manners required your going gingerly on the rarity. Always when his mother was pressing a workman at dinner, 'Eat more of that bacon, Dinny, I tell you. — It's good,' the boy would hear the reply, 'Ach, the divil thank you, I'd do, ma'am, for bacon when there's plenty of good praties on the table' — in large manner that Dinny Brogan thought would conceal his real feelings. But once he recollects Hughie Dougherty, the notorious trickster of the countryside, sitting to a tattics-and-bacon dinner with fellow workmen, taking such advantage of their sparing of the bacon that the boy's mother, for sake of his more modest fellows, hinted, 'Hughie, man, them's good-eating 'tatties. — Try more of them.' And the callous fellow dumbfounded her with the reply, 'Ach, the divil thank you, I'd do, ma'am, for praties, with plenty of good bacon on the table.'

Sometimes a mountain guest resisted pressure to eat, from lack of confidence in his own table manners. Supersensitive about his lack of gentility and refinement at a strange board, it was much easier to suffer the pangs of hunger than show signs of ignorance. The boy's shanachie, Shan O'Hegarty, told him how, when the first cups and saucers came into Donegal his father brought a pair of them home from Glenties to treat the priest coming on Stations; but, a few days after, a mountain man searching for strayed sheep dropped into their house and was in the usual way made to sit down to tea. As a matter of pride it was served him in the strange cup sitting on its saucer — a puzzling contraption to him. Trying hard not to show either surprise or perplexity, he hoisted to his mouth the entire machine, hands holding fimly the saucer-base, and struggled to drink from it: but found it a painful, and deluging experiment. The family were pained for their visitor's pain, and grieved that they dare not allay it. It would be too rude entirely and hurtful to presume to instruct their visitor in its manipulation — implying that he and his family and forbears had not been reared from the cradle on the new invention.

For the homeless and the wanderer every hut in the mountains was a hotel — a hotel with no charges. In the old ballad about the fellow who, in olden days, voyaged to England and roamed that foreign country, the greatest wonder — almost unbelievable — in his account of the Sassanach land was that this uncivilized people actually asked him to pay for the bite he put in his mouth and the bed he slept on![1]

Our mountains were filled with wanderers — the simple, the eccentric, the beggar, the tinker, the fiddler, the piper, sthreelers, sthrollers, and *shuilers* without end; and to have one or some of these baiting and bedding in your house was the common and expected thing.

The harmless demented even. When the boy remembers the nightly vigils in his father's house of poor Ellen Griffin of Dhrim-na- herca. Ellen was jolly and cracksome despite her affliction — and a welcome was put before her every time she came to their house (or any house) on one of her periodic sojourns. She jested for the children, making them merry whilst she stayed — only, every five minutes she would have to rise from her seat, and, coming crouched to the hearth, gaze up the wide chimney to the sky that was looking down at her. She never told them what she was watching or seeking. The only drawback to the pleasure of Ellen's visit was that, as she never slept or lay down but sat on a creepy-stool by the fire from night till morning — feeding a strong fire all the time — and keeping ward up the chimney the night through — the father and mother were during the three or four, or seven or eight, days of Ellen's stay, always expecting to wake up in the morning and find Ellen, themselves, their children, and their home, one wee heap of ashes.

Half of your roof and half of everything under the roof belonged to the houseless and homeless — and they claimed their own without ceremony. When night fell upon a wanderer he put up at the first house handy. He might push forward next morning; but if weather was unpropitious and quarters comfortable, he took his leisure there. Even if he was ill-tempered and hard to please — undesirable, and making himself a nuisance — one could commit the crime of suggesting to a visitor to move. The great Connaught fiddler and great drinker of more than a hundred years ago, Raftery, despite the high honour in which he was held for his genius, often made himself a nuisance in the home of his visitation. But one witty woman bested him. When he wouldn't go, and they couldn't tell him to go but yet not stand him longer, this clever one asked him to oblige her by twisting a hay-rope — which she, seated in the chimney corner gave out from a bundle at her feet. Manipulating the twister, Raftery worked his way down the floor — backing, backing, backing as the rope lengthened — until he had backed himself out of the door — whereupon the good woman jumped up, slammed the door — against a bitter east wind — and barred it. Raftery had left the house of his own accord. The reputation of the family was saved. And its peace.[2]

The fiddler and piper not only baited and bedded overnight in what house they chose, but, around the winter, made use of any house to hold their dances — for musicians had the privilege, when they chose, of 'calling a dance on you' — which was oftentimes literally correct. But it was an honour as well as a pleasure to entertain the wandering musicians. They made the night merry while they were with you, and when, in the morning they pushed forward, they graciously accepted your thanks for their kindness.

The tinkers were visitors not so welcome — not only because they were rude, uncultivated fellows, with very crude and very large families, who never hesitated about imposing themselves and their long tail in your little home and their drove of asses on your few bare fields — and had elaborate hesitation about leaving you again. The boy knew a clan of them, once, at winter's beginning to select his uncle Taig's home for their headquarters — residence and workshop — and to quit it again when the spring sun shone out on a bright St. Patrick's morning — a very bright morning for their host and family. It is true that his uncle did not benefit much from his cows that winter, because his grass and his hay were needed for the tinker's many asses, but his house was kept warmer and more comfortable than it had been for many winters gone — since the large-hearted fellows were much less sparing on his turfstack than he had been used to be himself. They usually cultivated musical art as well as tinkering — were fiddlers and fifers and pipers — so that the house they honoured was made lively throughout the long winter. They were generous fellows, and invited the countryside for three miles round to crowd your kitchen night after night, and dance to their piping till dawn. Wheresoever they stayed, therefore, it was a very happy winter indeed for all the countryside — with the insignificant exception of their host and his household.

The most constant guest in the mountain cottage, and one of the most welcome, was the *bacach*, the wandering beggar. For 'God's poor,' above all, there was always bite and sup, and a warm shake-down in the chimney corner. The *bacach* came when he would, stayed while he liked, and went when he pleased. The heart-sympathy of the people was always with those who had nothing of their own, and no roof-tree. It was a comfort, too, to have the beggars come, because they had with them not merely the

117

complete news of the countryside, but of the world. Frequently, too, the wandering *bacach* was a story-teller and good about it, and like the musician, he too made the household happy for a long night around the blazing turf-fire. Almost always he was a generous fellow who without grumble or grunt put up with your poor fare and hard bed. Once in a while, though, a man was condemned to entertain a grumbler who resented straw for a shake-down, preferred sweet meadow-hay, and was insulted at not getting cream to his stirabout — or for getting bacon that was too fat or too lean, a little underdone or a taste overdone. But when he came that way again — if he consented to honour again a host dishonourable — he got the delicacies he craved, even if his entertainer had to traverse three hills and three hollows to borrow or beg them.

On the other hand some *shuilers* were so indulgent toward their entertainers' shortcomings that our lad knew several who, leniently overlooking their host's many lacks, settled them in a man's house for years — in a couple of cases, for life. But unfortunately, these who from leniency gave one house a monopoly of their patronage, acquired, by the by, a little habit of exactingness that was rather trying to their entertainers. Some few went still further, graduating into arbiters and directors of the house, and of the family, its comings and goings, ventures, decisions, and relations — made themselves absolute monarchs of their little domain. Outstanding among such instances familiar to our lad was that of Newcome Pat. Newcome Pat he was called the day that he first dawned on the district, and still was Newcome Pat the day, twenty-five years later, that they pulled the green quilt over him. He dropped into Long John Haig's of Glen Ainey before our boy was born — and was the accepted Dictator in Long John's home when our lad first knew him. Like many another *shuiler* no one knew who he was — except that he had come from Connaught — 'from Mayo, God help me!' He had fancied this Glen Ainey country because he found the people 'kindly' — the honorary distinction he bestowed upon people easily imposed on. When he came he distributed his favours — his boarding and bedding — among several homes, but at length finding the home of Long John most to his fancy, warm and comfortable, and about it an air of more than ordinary respectability, he settled himself there. At first he only took it as a headquarters wherefrom to make short exploratory expeditions into outlying districts; but always after an absence of a few days returning to Long John's to roost. He made himself at home there — gradually — but at length very much at home. It is true that, then, he would sometimes lend his presence in the work-field — when there was 'a throng' on, as in the early spring, and the harvest — but his attendance in the fields was more to direct and advise from his seat on the ditch, and to urge hard workers to work still harder. Yet indeed he wouldn't have hesitated, but been heartily glad, to add the mere manual to the wonderful verbal help he vouchsafed, but for a *maigrim* had in his head. This *maigrim*, which rendered it inadvisable to do any exerting, served him during all the years that he favoured Long John's household with his presence. After he had been seven years in Glen Ainey, a rumour developed that he had a wife and little farm above in Connaught — both whom and which he had left: and when some daring one at length confronted him with the rumour, he admitted it was so, but as the wife wasn't good to him, and he was a man of paice, he consithered it was wiser for the two of them to keep to diffierent hemisphairs. The *shuiler* who brought the rumour from Connaught, and who professed to know the circumstances, said, that looking after a farm, was, with Pat, too much like work; and work and he didn't rightly get along together. Three times, indeed, during the years of his sojourn in Glen Ainey, Newcome Pat girded him and went back to Connaught — experimentally, it would seem. But the experiments were never crowned with success. In six weeks or two months he would be back in Glen Ainey again. Always, on arriving, and easing himself into the straw-bottomed chair that he had made his own in Long John's chimney-corner, he would say with a sigh, 'Thanks be to God, 'tis good to be home again!' — which was not music in the ears of Long John's wife. Yet she resigned herself to him, and seldom complained. Once, however, when he was gone on one of these visits she expressed the hope that he might take a liking to Connaught again; and a neighbour-woman who was listening, said outragedly, 'Why, in the Lord's name, when he goes out and away don't you keep him out?' 'To do that,' said Long John's Nelly, 'we'd have to build up both the doors and the windows.' 'Well,' replied her indignant adviser, 'if I was in your place, and afflicted with that plaster, I *would* build them up.' 'But ach then,' said the poor woman resignedly, 'he'd come down the chimney.' And she was right.

After a while Newcome Pat discovered there was a deal of pleasure to be derived from breakfasting in bed — and he proceeded to establish the custom — for himself. From under the blankets of his outshot bed — to one side of the kitchen fire — he would direct the toasting of his bread in the morning, and the broiling for him of a bit of bacon on the tongs. Yet, because Nelly had a large family to feed, and multifarious household duties besides, he was patient with her beyond words on the occasional time that she let the toast blacken or the bacon burn. But if it was one of the idle children, doing the toasting, who neglected his duty, Newcome Pat was as likely as not to crack him over the skull with the oak stick which he kept handy by his bed-head for such and like purpose. When necessity required that the family should go out to their work before it pleased their honour-guest to awake and eat, one or other came back from time to time to find if he was yet awake, and if it was his pleasure to have breakfast served.

So far did Newcome Pat, at length, take to himself direction of the house, its activities, and the whole family, that he began matching off the eldest daughter, Ellen, upon a man whom he favoured but the family did not like. Yet the father and mother dared not oppose the wishes of a benefactor who was bestowing all his time and attention on them; and it was only Ellen's bold courage and spunk that saved her, just in the nick of time, from being married off on a fellow whom she neither loved, liked, nor wanted.

When at length Pat died — not of his faithful *maigrim*, but of a pleurisy — Long John's family grieved as if they had lost one of their own, and gave him a grand wake and a beautiful burial. Either they never knew, or else forgot, his rightful name — for Newcome Pat was the name Jaimie-boy read off the coffin the day that the lamented gentleman was slipped under the sod. Moreover, Jaimie recalls that the coffin-plate did not have on it (as was usually required) the inmate's age. He had been as particular as a woman about keeping his age to himself — and when he was dead they disputed about it. One told Shandy Maguire, the carpenter, that he ought to put on the coffin, 'Aged 84,' another warned him to put 'Aged 79,' and a third, something between. Shandy, who said he would part with his one good eye before he'd tell a lie on a man going into the grave, settled the matter, and satisfied his conscience, by printing on the plate:

'AGED CONSIDERABLY'

In Heaven he was undoubthely named again Newcome Pat. And it is to be hoped that he found in his new quarters a hospitality approximating the hospitality of Glen Ainey.

NOTES

1 Remarkable as now are our people for hospitality — and generosity, they were still more so the farther we go back into history. Of Guaire the Hospitable, a Connaught king of about twelve hundred years ago, a typical story:

Once, being beaten in battle by King Diarmuid, Guaire, in token of submission, had to kneel in front of the victor and take in his teeth the point of the victors sword. When he was in this humiliating position, Diarmuid, to test whether Guaire's famed generosity was sincere or ostentatious, had, first, one of his Druids ask of Guaire a gift in honour of learning (wherefor a giver won lasting renown in ancient Ireland) — which request the humiliated Guaire let pass without heed: and then a leper ask an alms for God's sake — to whom Guaire, with teeth still closed upon the sword point, gave the gold brooch from his mantle. At the secret instigation of the king, one of his people forced the brooch from the leper, who at once complained of his loss to the kneeling one. Guaire immediately unlinked the golden girdle that bound his waist, and reached it to the leper. This gift was instantly also taken from the poor man, when, with sore complaint he begged a third time of Guaire. Realising the poor man's distress, and knowing that he had nothing more to give, Guaire's tears ran from his eyes in a stream.

'Arise, Guaire', said Diarmuid, 'and do homage only to God'!

2   Twelve centuries before, in the same West Country occurred a historic parellel. Then the great poet of that day, Senchan, visiting the court of the Connaught king, Guaire the Hospitable, with attendant poets, students, servants, wives, dogs, and horses, treated his over-powered host to a year and a day of his party's joyous company! And, since under no conceivable circumstances could any host, much less a royal one, ask a poet to move on, this visitation might only have ended when Guaire was eaten into poverty, had not the king's brother, the holy hermit, Marbhan, been blessed with the inspiration to put geasa (an honour obligation which no poet could refuse or shirk) on Senchan and his company to go eastward upon a literary mission — in search of the lost Tain, which, tradition said, had been 'carried east over the sea with the Cuilmen — ' which promised to take years, if not eternity, for fulfilment.

Senchan's parting ode to Guaire must have sounded in that king's ears one of the sweetest by poet ever spoken — if we except the alarming last stanza:

'We depart from thee, O stainless Guaire!
   We leave with thee our blessing;
   A year, a quarter, and a month,
   Have we sojourned with thee, O high-king!

'Three times fifty poets, — good and smooth, —
   Three times fifty students in the poetic art,
   Each with his servant and dog;
   They were all fed in the one great house.

'Each man had his separate meal;
   Each man had his separate bed;
   We never arose at early morning,
   With contentions without calming.

'I declare to thee, O god!
   Who canst the promise verify,
   That should we return to our own land,
   We shall visit thee again, O Guaire, though now we depart'.

CHAPTER NINETEEN

Into the Lone World

The lad was advancing in years — and in learning likewise. He was now fourteen, and had been for three or four years dallying in the highest class. He kept the distinction of being the worst writer in school, and was, for this, by the Master held up as a bad example — and, because of this deficiency, he had barely managed to scrape through his successive examinations. 'If that lad could write good,' the Master would say, 'only half as well as he writes bad, he'd be a genius entirely.'[1]

But he had come to be a notorious mathematician. In geometry, in advanced algebra, in higher arithmetic few problems daunted, and none defeated him. Mathematics was bread and butter to Jaimie. It was the Master's boast — and there was nothing, then, that made the boy vainer — that, in forty-five years teaching, the *gasúr* was one of two memorable mathematicians in whose reflected glory he was proud to shine.

The Master had two 'Keys' for the higher arithmetic — one a slim, printed book, the other a thick, written copybook. When a scholar asked the Master's aid at solving an extra-knotty problem he would take the matter under advisement, and, at home that night, closet himself with the two Keys! Next day the puzzled one was usually shown that the solution was easy. But when, as sometimes happened, the problem wasn't to be found in either of the Keys, the Master would confess that it puzzled even himself, and put it to our *gasúr*. — 'Now, Jaimie, you think yourself the divil and all of a smart fellow — just try your teeth on this one.' The lad might worry fifteen minutes over it, or three hours, or three days and three nights — but, to the Master's joy, he never failed to solve it. And then his proud preceptor would announce, 'I don't care who hears it, but I'll say there's more in that *buachaillín's* head than a comb could take out!'

It wasn't that the lad had application. No. In both mind and body he had about the steadiness of a flea. But like the flea, when he chose for a little time to apply himself he was mighty quick at absorbing. And like the flea, too, he could only go on by jumps.

Anyhow, when he was in the higher classes application wasn't easy; for, he was then class-fellow to the worst bunch of vagabonds that, maybe, Glen Ainey ever knew. They chewed tobacco, played hard-knuckles under the desk, games on the slate when they should be doing sums, told uproarious tales of the tricks they had played on innocent people along the way to school, plotted orchard-robbing, stealing beans, going raking at night where they should find the best outlet for mischief. Every one of them, too, was a noted boxer. They fought all comers, and when there were no comers they fought one another. They were unanimously and enthusiastically again' education. It was a tyranny that spoiled life's purpose; and they were siginally successful in their resistance to tyranny.

One thing, hovever, they learned in school — and loved to learn — was, stories. The worst of the boys, Liam Griffin, was the best of the story-tellers — better even than our *gasúr* — which is saying much. The only time that these rascals were out of mischief was when their heads were huddled together, listening to another of Liam Griffin's wonderful tales.[2]

After school our boy was now doing more and harder labour in his father's fields. He had begun to think of the future — and wonder whether he would join the boys going with their little bundles to the hiring-market at Pettigo, or — if Heaven smiled and shook him the fine pound passage-money from the skies — sail to the land of gold with the troops of other lads who were flocking there. But, one day that kindliest of old Head Inspector of Schools, John Mulloy, visiting Glen Cuach, was, by the good Master, apprised of the *great* mathematician and scholar which his school concealed and was asked if he knew any way to save the lad from a life of hard labour. 'Wouldn't he make a schoolmaster?' queried John Mulloy. 'A great one — but his people can't afford to send him to the Dublin Training School.' 'But there are Model Schools where he can teach and train, and get thirty shillings for his first year's work and thirty shillings a quarter the second year.'

It was a glorious prospect! But, alas, the smallest age for a pupil-teacher in a Model School was sixteen, and the boy wasn't yet fifteen. 'Never mind,' the kind man encouraged the little fellow. 'Keep on, and you'll outgrow the deficiency. — I'll not forget you when you come of age.'

The Head Inspector was as good as his word. When the lad was two months past sixteen, his joy was unbounded to get a letter — the first letter of his life! — telling him that he was appointed pupil-teacher in Iniskillen Model School (in the next county, Fermanagh), where he should present himself in two weeks' time.

Proudly, for days the lad went around with a modest inch of the letter sticking out of his coat-pocket. When it was read to the neighbours assembled round John Burns's board it created amazement and amuse-ment — in addition to joy, of course. It was its list of worldly endowments necessary to the profession of pupil-teacher that stirred the neighbours' emotions. That he should be expected to have two suits of clothes, while unusual, wasn't dumbfounding. But when, in addition, an overcoat was called for, the audience did not know whether to laugh or cry. And when, finally, there was read out 'Three collars,' followed by 'A pair of slippers,' and the absurdity crowned by 'Three nightshirts,' there was no longer any doubt that the document was a purely hilarious one. John Burns remarked, 'Faith, the Prime Minister must thing the Prince O'Donnells are still living in Donegal.' The established dry wit, Dinis MacCue, said, 'Nobbut they're under the belief the boy's name's Rothschild.' Conal a-Friel, however, expressed the sober opinion — which seemed to all of them to be the real explanation — 'The Govern'ment, havin' little else to do, just likes to hear themselves talkin'.'

The lad's father, since the lad was going to leave him, acceded to the less fantastic of the Government's demands. Yet, the little carpet-bag — a thing of beauty in bright yellow, red, blue, and green checks — purchased to send the boy into the world in style, was still, after being 'packed,' in a sorry state of collapse. It was a very green, very small[3] and very innocent little lad who carried the deflated carpet-bag over his shoulder, away from his mother's door, that March morning that he set out to fight the wide world. As the mail-car that should bring him the first leg of the journey — from Donegal to Belashanny — would start at eight, six o'clock — dead of night — found his ringing on the road, his father with him for the tram to Donegal. Each of them in turn carried the carpet-bag — a good plan, for it consoled both of them with the fancy that there was something in it to carry. Over and above the amount of his fare which his father gave him — the boy had in his pocket two-and-fippence. Aunt Cassin, aristocrat, had bestowed a shilling on him (God bless her! for her fast-dwindling pile of shillings were then few). His Aunt Sarah, not only the most gracious but the greatest-hearted woman who ever walked the world, had pulled open, on its running string, her homemade black linen purse, and taking it by its two lower corners, shaken it empty upon her table for him. Eleven pennies it was that tumbled out. An uncle, a sailor-man who for forty years roamed the seven seas, and was generous to him always, had given him a sixpenny bit. Did he need more, his mother, thought she had not too much to spare, would have given what she could, but not — as she remarked when he had counted out his two-and- fippence — he had lashin's and leavin's. Besides, she consoled him, there was nothing that ruined young people faster than too much money for sporting and spending — examples whereof she had all her life seen around her. As she said this, the innocent Jaimie thought — but wasn't quite sure that the twinkle which always was in the woman's eye looked even twinklier.

The fourteen-mile ride from Donegal to Belashanny, on the jaunting-car of Larry-Come-Lately who carried the mail, was a wonderful one. Strange houses, strange fields, strange hills, new scenes, villages he had been all his life hearing about, but never hoped to see, came to him, a glorious procession. New countries, and, finally — grand climax! — a city! — a big city, of thousands of inhabitants, fabled Belashanny! One

124

of the supreme moments of his long life was when, at half past twelve o'clock on that winter morning, the mail-car topping a hill on the way, there burst on the boy's enchanted vision, and momentarily stopped his breath, the glancing, glimmering, shimmering domes, spires, turrets and towers, of a city of gold! It was just like the gorgeousness of the old folk-tales! Had he had no joy before in life, the splendour of that moment, which never again he could forget, amply repaid him for the sixteen years' servitude that had been life hitherto!

When, soon, he was driving through the heart of the big city, his wonder was further fed by the grandeur of the shops, the height of the houses, the awesomeness of the towers, the multiplicity of the streets.[4]

When Larry's mail-car put down himself and his gay carpet-bag at the post-office, he hurried to the railway station a quarter-mile away, as he had then only two-and-a half hours to catch the train. He did not go looking for anything to eat: it would not be wise, because the train might come in ahead of time, and, not finding him there, go on again without him; besides, two-and-fippence, big as it may sound, was, in his sober view, not any too much pocket-money to keep him till the July vacation. And, anyhow, the inordinate excitement left him little appetite.

He had never seen a train before, and couldn't have apprehended the chill that struck his soul, when, with the drear winter dusk dropping, the great, big, black, snorting brute, putting out of it fire and smoke, and shaking Belashanny and Heaven, rolled, rattled and thundered into the Station. He suddenly got such awful feeling of both weeness and lone-someness that he wished and wished he was sitting by a whinbush on Dhrim-an-Aran hill. But black night came down — over the earth outside and his soul within — with the train whisking him through the lone world, to far Iniskillen, at fifteen mile an hour. The heavy homesickness was now on him — which he had often heard the boys and girls tell about, who had hired themselves away from Glen Ainey.

In Iniskillen's bustling station he looked around him for guidance — and a raggedy, lame, lumbering, big slob of a fellow — whose name he afterwards knew as Joe Knock-it-out — came up offering to take his bag and himself wherever he wanted to go, for a sixpenny. Sixpence would be a terrific drain on his resources, but the lost lad agreed — except that he barred the bag from the contract. It was maybe too much trust already, giving himself to the big fellow's charge. 'You go first and show me the way to the Model School. Me and the bag will follow you.' 'Come on then!' Though Jaimie — recalling a story in Duffy's Hibernian Magazine about a traveller who was decoyed and murdered for his money — had misgivings, the fellow sure enough led him safely to the door of the School residence. A maid, hearing that he was a new pupil-teacher, directed him up a long hall, to a door at the end, which she said was the Study door, whither he should go.

Setting down his precious carpet-bag in the tiled hall outside the Study door, the *gasúr* knocked, and went timidly into a big room flooded with gaslight. (He had heard great things about gas, but never could have thought it was so bright.) Seven big fellows, with open books on the desks before them, were taking instruction — from a slim, tall, handsome, young man who turned out to be the Assistant Teacher. He greeted the lad in most kindly way, seated him at an idle desk beside himself and did his friendly best to make feel at home a bewildered stranger who was never going to feel at home anywhere, any more. But the kindness of that very handsome, very smartly-dressed, tall young man, was balm to an exile's paining soul.

Master Andrew Geddes — that was his name — announced at last that study time was ended, said Good night to his students, and a very nice Good night to the newcomer. But the instant he opened the Study door and strode out, there was, first a stumble, then 'My God!' and a crash. He had tripped on the *buachaillín's* carpet- bag — which squatted fair and square for that special purpose — and was shot, sprawling on his stomach, down the hall.

It was an embarrassing beginning of the new life for Jaimie. But, after seeing Master Geddes helped to his feet, his hat and pocket-money gathered and given to him, and his clothes beaten and brushed down by half-a-dozen pairs of hands, and he speeded on his way, still more embarrassing it became for the *gasúr* when he lifted the offending bag and carried it into the great light of the study. For there, the gaiety of its checks, combined with its notorious lack of *embonpoint*, too forcibly compelled the boys' admiration, and close inspection. The situation was aggravated when they noted that the lad's tie — first tie that ever adorned him — was of a smart, bright-red-and-blue check pattern, matching the bag. One of the more inquisitive of them examined the bag round and over to discover from what part of it the tie had been abstracted. But their merriment was quite frank when, after retiring to the dormitory an hour later, the boy exhihited attractive carpet-slippers of the same dazzling pattern.

Except for their involuntary amusement over the *buachaillín's* three prize possessions, they were lenient toward the stranger, kindly and good about instructing him what to do, on this, his first night ever from home.

Yet was the boy, on that first night, to distinguish himself more meritoriously. And likewise, alas, to draw on himself dire punishment. Each boy of eight pupil-teachers had for his room a cubicle, with partitions that reached three-quarters way to the ceiling: and, though not so intended, the vacancy above was incitement to general conversation after the boys had bedded. Knowing that he was among folk nearly all of whom, by religious race,[5] and up-bringing, were outlanders to him, our lad was delighted to find one boy, in the cubicle opposite his own, begin (after bedding) to recite aloud the stirring national ballad — which he himself had often declaimed on the herding hill — The Eve of Fontenoy —

'By our campfires rose a murmur at the dawning of the day,
And the tread of many footsteps spoke the advent of the fray.
And as we took our places few and hurried were our words
While some were tightening horse-girths and some were
girding swords.'

But he hadn't finished the first stanza till there came a bellow from the other end of the dormitory ! 'Shut up, you dam Fenian!' In a minute the Battle of Aughrim was on, except that the arguments were arguments and not cannon balls — but they were every bit as hot and fast. It was five staunch anti-Irishmen against 'the Fenian.' To our *gasúr's* pride, Frank Scanlan against all five fought his corner like the terrier he was. And when, at last, after smothering the Fenian with ammunition manufactured from ridiculous 'history,' the enemy seemed to the *gasúr* to be going to gobble Frank, he, forgetting such silly things as homesickness, lonesomeness, and insignificance, sprang to the aid of Ireland's hard-pressed champion. The anti-Irish men, at first a bit dumbfounded by the impudence of the newcome child, in short time fell from dumbfoundment to confoundment, before the pikes and guns, powder, shot, and red-hot cannon-balls, crushing arguments from real history, flung in their face by the child with the funny carpet-bag and fittings. 'By gad!' one of them gasped at length. And they subsided to meditation — and sleep.

The boy, too, went to sleep — little knowing the height and depth of the crime he had committed. It was not the offence of Irishism — for, as he was to discover, these boys, though they could fight like a flock of badgers upon Irish-English questions, were, back of it all, good-humouredly tolerant of one another's views. His high offence lay in a new-come Junior lifting his voice and pushing his view when his Seniors were speaking.

In the afternoon of next day, while peacefully studying at his desk alongside one of the biggest and strongest of the vanquished ones, the lad suddenly found another of the big fellows bind with a cord his ankle to the ankle of his neighbour. Then the big husky neighbour, John Irvine, arose casually, and saying, 'I'm thinking I'll take a bit of a walk to myself,' uprooted the boy, and by ankle-force dragged him after — up and down and round the Study, stopping now and then to upbraid, rebuke, and finally wallop the *gasúr* for his impudence in following. Next John climbed over desks, forms, chairs, the child still struggling to keep by him. So sorely

127

did the cord begin to cut into his ankle, and so heart-breaking was the drag over obstacles, that the *gasúr* at length yelled with pain. Glimpsing a big knife on a desk, he, when being dragged past, grabbed it, and made a lunge with it at the binding cord. But one of the boys mischievously leapt in, caught the knife's heft to twist it from him, and, dragging the instrument through his fist, unintentionally split open the youngster's palm, from side to side!

Crying aloud, the child began launching poltogs of his fist at his tormentors, who, now grieved for the injury they had unwittingly done, were striving to unleash him. The commotion in the Study attracted the attention of the Headmaster's household — whose apartments were the other end of the same residence — and his daughter, Jeannie, tall, handsome, graceful, young woman, rushed in, to discover what was happening, and to see the boy's blood pouring from him in a stream. She led him away — down the long hall, to their kitchen, where, with a maid's help, and with towels and hot water, the wound was washed, salved, plastered, and bandaged. And, consoled and encouraged, the boy was, by winsome, modest Jeannie, led back again to the Study and set at his desk in calm and peaceful — almost happy — mood.

As Jeannie went away, the lad looked lingeringly after this tall and handsome specimen of the *cailíni* of this Fermanagh country — in dress, style, appearance, so totally unlike the simple girls of Donegal — and he almost thought he wouldn't mind having his hand laid open again, if the wound were to be dressed, and himself cuddled and consoled, by such a lovely *cailín*.[6]

NOTES

1 Once Jaimie's father asked the Master's advice what he should put the boy to, the sorely tried man answered, 'Put him to any trade under the sun exceptin' one that calls for a pen in his fist'.

2 The story-teller died — in his early manhood — in Baldwin's Locomotive Works in Philadelphia. And his stories died with him. Two of these humoursome lads died at home in their late boyhood; two shipped to farway Australia and were lost forever to Donegal; one became a successful shopkepper in his own village; one wandered out of sight in America. One other who went to America became a cab driver in Chicago. Our lad when he himself went to America long years later, discovered him. For years after, on going to, or through Chicago on lecture tour, Jaimie would search out Cormac MacGrady at the cab-stand by Marshall Field's store. Cormac would at once put up 'Engaged' on his cab; both would get into it, and for half-day talk Donegal.

3 The lad, though he became big in manhood, was very slow of growth, and slow of ripening. He carried childhood into his late teens, and boyhood to his nineties.

4   It is proper to set down that, a few years later, when the boy could examine great cities more judically, and more reliably compile statistics on them, he found that Belashanny had:-

Spires	1
Towers	1
Turrets	(What is a turret, anway?)
Domes	0
People	1371
Streets	4 and The Knather

5   They were nearly all of English and Scotch Planter stock.

6   Strange to say, on the very day after this page was penned, a letter to the penman — from a Model School comrade, the Frank MacElroy of the next chapter — said, 'I know you'll be sorry to hear what I have just heard — that Jeannie, who nursed and petted you yon long-ago day that we wounded you in the study, died in Iniskillen last week'. — Go ndeanaigh Dia trocaire uirri!

CHAPTER TWENTY

In Exile

These boys were far from cruel by nature. They were hardy, healthy
fellows, full of life, in whom confinement somewhat perverted the sense
of humour. Nor were they bigoted — even if most all of them were
anti-Irish. The intimate intermingling of opposite elements bred tolerance.
But one thing would not be tolerated — lack of respect from any junior
to any Senior. To make sure that a Junior should know his place the
Seniors sometimes went lengths that might seem harsh — but aback of it
all every man of them was human.

Although Jaimie for some time was stubborn to the Seniors who had
hurt him, he had learnt that it was wise not to speak out of turn; and a week
passed before he was guilty again of positive disrespect. In that time the
other boys became aware that the Child — nickname conferred on him,
on his second day there, and afterwards kept on him — was a great
story-teller: and when, one day, having had the impudence to defy a
Senior, he was court-martialed, Frank MacElroy, eldest Senior, and
President of the Court, sentenced him to thirty nights' story-telling —
sentence to be served in the dormitories, after the Seniors were com-
fortably bedded.[1]

It proved to be a cruel sentence. After a long, hard day's teaching and
studying the Child was terribly tired when welcome bed-time came: and
when, in middle of a story, his voice would begin trailing off, he was
startlingly brought back to cruel reality by loud, angry commands from
the Seniors' cubicles. When a story was very long indeed, and that the
Child, having told two-thirds of it, conceived from the stillness that
everyone but his slaving self had gone asleep, he would, as a test, let his
voice sink lower, lower, and lower — when there was apt to come hurtling
over the top of his cubicle, and maybe light upon his nose, a hairbrush, an
ink-bottle, a shoe, or some other persuasive messenger, followed by some
language — apprising him that at least one Senior was awake, and wanting
his pound of flesh.

Never did any other exile more cruelly suffer from home-sickness, than
did our *gasúr*. Donegal that he had left was poor, wild, and barren.
Fermanagh that he had come to was rich, soft, lovely, abounding in little
hill, many-islanded lake, and waving wood. Loch Erne's loveliness nearly
equals Killarney's — yet gladly would the exile have given a yearful of
their beauties, for one hour on a heathery hillside in Donegal. He searched
out solitary places where he could sit him down and think of Donegal and

130

sob his hearty fill. For months there wasn't an hour of the day, when, studying or teaching, walking out with his comrades, or sitting alone in midst of their uproarious mirth, he wasn't wandering the valleys and roaming the hills of Glen Ainey, or sitting among its kindly, friendly, laughing, story-telling folk around happy turf-fires.

His heart was breaking. A hundred times he made up his mind to run away, resigning the great career that was opening to him — with its prospect of a mastership, ease, and wealth at the end of a couple of years — and go back to Donegal and a life of joyful hard labour, sweet struggle, and happiness everlasting. One and elevenpence, his worldly wealth, was far from enough to pay his way; but, if only his father and mother (now dreaming bright dreams of his future) were not to be brokenhearted by the wiping out of their hopes, everyone of the weary miles from here to the hills of Donegal he would delightedly walk — and beg his bread on the way. At home, with his one and elevenpence — and a penny from a good fairy — he would buy a spade and a scythe-book, hire out by the day, help his people over their difficulties, and ever after, be happy as the day was long. Alone, in loneliness, a hundred times he debated this cure for his woe, and a hundred times decided to take it. But, every time, the thought of his father's and mother's bitter disappointment made him re-decide for Fermanagh and two years of suffering that job never knew — thereafter, a life of ease and easy money, and his people's happiness and hopes fulfilled. The weekly letter that came from home, though longingly looked forward to, drew, when read, a heavier sadness on the boy's soul. — This, even when every couple of months would come a letter from Aunt Cassin, in fashionable hand, worded with elegance, and enclosing, nearly every time, a present of sixpence in stamps. Ill, indeed, could the good poor woman afford such wild generosity — but if she were dying with hunger this true aristocrat would be the lady bountiful. May God bless her fragrant memory!

Curiously, once, with one of his woefullest hours of homesickness the lad bought one of his merriest hours of laughter. On this occasion his agony of suffering — agony is the word — found escape in a burst of 'poetry' — three stanzas of it — the first of which went —

> 'How strange, how wearisome, how sad,
>   The mind doth feel today —
> When all around do seem so glad
>   Why I not glad as they?
> There's something in my inmost heart
>   To check the rising glee,
> Some powerful influence to impart
>   This sadness unto me.'

131

The achieving of such a beautiful poem — the first he had ever been inspired with — not only lifted a load off the boy's heart, but gave him positive joy. Happy, he returned from his place of solitary refuge to the Study, and posed with this first stanza two pupil-teachers who, fancying themselves as literary folk, were constantly talking books and authors — poets especially — and who loved to pose everyone around them with quotations, demanding the author's name. 'I defy either of you to say from what famous poet that is quoted,' challenged the Child. For a very happy, and proud, hour he listened to two literary lights worrying, arguing, all but fighting, over the authorship of the immortal piece. Albert Brady finally decided, and would make affidavit in any court, that the credit was Wordsworth's; but Thomas John MacCreery was ready to lay down his life rather than let Southey be robbed of his due. No wonder it was that, when at length the Child informed them, 'An hour ago, under the sycamore in the backyard, I composed it,' the two maddened men should jump on him, and pound him till they had almost pounded out of his system all the future poetry that was brewing there.

But not quite all. Inspiration again possessed him less than a month later — on the joyful Sunday after a joyful Saturday whereon he had encountered in Iniskillen Seumas Gallagher, Inver fishcadger — with pony and cart of herring, from Inver Bay! Inver! Only three miles from his own home! He slipped away from his comrades and walked the streets with Seumas, selling his fish from door to door — talking of Donegal, getting news, and exchanging memories. Hard it was to realize that here was a glorious man who had stood in Glen Ainey less than forty hours before! And would again joyfully stand on Donegal soil less than forty hours later! The little while he could afford to spend with the ragged cadger from Inver Bay was one of three or four brilliant sunbursts which relieved, almost redeemed, two years of midnight. Sweet memory of beloved Inver possessed him the remainder of that glad day — and throughout the night. And next day the inspiration worked and, to his joy ineffable, expressed itself in —

MY INVER BAY

Och! Inver Bay of a harvest day,
And the sun goin' down the sky;
When with many's a laugh the boats put off,
And many's the merry cry.
To Cork's own Cove though one may rove
He will not find, monchree,
A rarer bay, a fairer bay,
A sweeter bay nor thee.

132

For an emperor's rod and his realms so broad,
I wouldn't swap, not I,
My Inver Bay of a harvest day,
And the sun goin' down the sky.

A purtier boat there's not afloat
Than Donal Rosha's Nan,
A boulder crew, nor boys more true
Is not in wide Irelan' —
A long, long pull, a strong, strong pull,
And one right hearty cheer,
Our Nan so brave she tops the wave,
And our comrade-boats we clear;
We lend the throng, we strike a song,
We rise it loud and high,
On Inver Beg of a harvest day,
And the sun goin' down the sky.

Till we reach away where the herrin's play,
There's neither slack nor slow;
As quick as thought our nets are shot,
On the tafts then we lie low;
And many's the stave rolls o'er the wave,
And many's the yarn is told —
The sea all white with silver bright,
The air all filled with gold —
A scene more grand, God's good right hand
It ne'er reached from on high,
Than Inver Beg of a harvest day,
And the sun goin' down the sky.

O'er far Norway it's give me sway,
With a palace wide and broad,
With silks, and wine, and jewels fine,
And hundreds at my nod —
In robes all gay and golden spray
It's dress me you might do;
But I'd loathe your wine and your jewels fine,
Your gold and your kingdom, too;
For a ragged coat, in Donal's boat,
It's I'd lament of a harvest day,
With the sun goin' down the sky.

Our bravest sons, our stoutest ones,
Have rushed across the sae,
And, God He knows, each wind that blows
Is waftin' more away!
It's sore distress does them hard press,
They drop their heads and go —
Och, Sorrow Queen's, it's you has seen
Their hearts big swelled with woe!
Though gold they make, their hearts they break,
And they oft sit down and cry
For Inver Beg of a harvest day,
And the sun goin' down the sky.

Och! Inver Beg of a harvest day,
And the sun goin' down the sky;
When with many's a laugh the boats put off,
And many's the merry cry.
To Cork's own Cove though one may rove,
He will not find, monchree,
A rairer bay, a fairer bay,
A sweeter bay nor thee!
For an emperor's rod and his realms so broad
I wouldn't swap, not I,
My Inver Bay of a harvest day,
And the sun goin' down the sky.

The fun the lad furnished his fellows by his Donegal accent — which he could no more hinder than he could the bend in his elbow — and by his roaringly funny Donegal words and expressions (barring which would leave him a dummy) helped to make life lonesomer still in the Model School. On top of his mortification in the Study came his difficulty with the town-boys in school, where for five hours every day he had to control and teach a class of thirty. At the start, his child-likeness, his mountainy aspect, homespun clothes, and droll accent and pronunciation, were provocations to their big merriment; and as they were a rowdy lot even for town-boys, controlling them at first was a ficklesomer job far than opening old lea-land. But they didn't know the badger that was hiding within the sheepskin in the so-comical wee Donegal *gasúr*: within three weeks — very sore weeks for the *gasur* — and for a dozen of his charges likewise he had these thirty half-fashionable rapscallions as sweet in their ways as white rabbits — only far more obedient — and actually applying themselves to learn. Even, somehow, discovering that the funny mountainy boy was fond of ballads, some of them, to curry favour, began bringing him sheets and books of these. They turned out to be mostly Orange ballads that these ingenuous Orange boys brought as peace-offerings to a Fenian! But it was the best they knew. And, anyhow, to the *gasúr* they were ballads, embodying rhythm and action.

Easter week vacation came, a respite from hard work and worry; and for the first time the Child was left literally alone in the Model School — all the other pupil-teachers having gone home — a joyful journey which, of course, our boy's treasury couldn't afford. Yet, strange to say, his heart-ache was eased — partly because, for all of the week, he held his mind to intense, unbroken, and prolonged study; and partly because the wonderful stillness in the Study, in the dormitory, in the grounds, brought to his soul a beauty that was balm. Eased of agonizing heartbreak, and steeped for long days in a study that had become sweet, devouring text-books that more and more whetted an avid appetite, a caressing peace sang round and over the boy, and his soothed spirit floated through happy days that where to be memorable.

But the July vacation brought him home. The sights, the sounds, the smells, of the happy morning that he was released to flee to Donegal, are still with him. The grateful aroma of the train smoke in Iniskillen railway station is still in his nostrils. The troops of daisies that twinkled and danced on the hillsides as he journeyed, the gilded armies of buttercups marching the meadows, the sunshine cavorting on the lake waters, are now before his eyes. Never saw he, before, such glorious colours on the earth, nor felt such fragrance in the air — never heard such music as made the most common sounds, nor saw such gladness sitting on the world as on that glory-gilt morning.

He had five hours to wait in Belashanny — for the mail-car to Donegal — which afforded him the joy of exploring and travelling again and again, every street, front and back, of that lovely old ramshackle town — gazing at all the wonders in all the shop-windows, seeing the Knather, the Purt, and the Mall, viewing the magnificent waterfall, the becalmed harbour with its three-masters, and island (Inish Saimer) where landed, before the Flood, Partholan and his daughter, Erin's first inhabitants.

Happiness put out of his head — and his stomach — all thought of eating. Which was well; for, before leaving Iniskillen he had expended all the pocket-money that then remained with him — thirteen pence — for presents that should gladden the heart of friends at home. The drive to Donegal — first through the sunlight, then the gathering dusk, was enchanting. And at Donegal post office, lo, his father waited him!

But, when their greeting was over, and they went to the rear of the car to get the boy's precious bag, behold, no bag was there! At Belashanny he had watched Hughie Manachan, the driver this day, settle it on top of the mailbags, in the car-well — safely and securely, he believed. Yet now it was gone — must have rolled off on the way! The loss of his few personal belongings — few, yet his all, except for what was on his back — was a blow; but sorer to his heart was the thought of his presents gone — and with them gone all the pleasure that was to have been his in surprising and rejoicing the friends whom, with these gifts, he would endow. While it was impossible for any conceivable calamity to take from him the rapture of a Donegal exile's homecoming, still the sense of his great loss formed a cloud rather bigger than a man's hand floating in the moonlit, silver-bright, sky above his home, when, after an hour and a half's tramp from Donegal he sank, with a sigh of gladness, on a stool, in the oft-dreamt-of chimney-corner of his mother's kitchen.

The precious bag was recovered. Nearly a week later, an Inver herring-cadger returning from Donegal market brought news that a Dhrimholme man had found a bag on the post-road two mile beyond Laighey. The lad's father set out the following morning and travelled sixteen miles, bringing back with him the bag, itself unharmed, hid all its treasures untouched. A labouring man had lifted it off the road, and taken it home, to await its owner. There was joy in Israel!

Before he left Iniskillen the Headmaster had spoken quietly to the boy about the need for a pupil-teacher in a fashionable town — Iniskillen was a British garrison town and proud suburb of London! — dressing more formally than he would in the mountains of Donegal; so, when Jaimie returned to school he was arrayed like Solomon's eldest son — in a suit, that, for the first time in his life was *not* homespun. Yet his graduation from homespun didn't overcome the handicap of his littleness and child-likeness — not to mention at all, his persistent Donegal *brόg*. He was still the Child; and because of that, his essays at independence kept earning him sore punishments. On a night soon after his return some act of disrespect to a Senior brought all of them into his cubicle demanding from him an apology — and his stubborn and foolish refusal brought on him one of the great poundings of his school career. He struck out at, and fought, big Tam Clinton, thereby forcing Tam to haul, maul, punch, and pound him, till spurts of blood from his nose, mouth, head, and hands splattered walls and floor. Tam was not only willing but anxious to quit if only the Child would give in and say he was sorry: but the further he was punished, and the bloodier did he become, the more perverse did he grow — till Tam had to stop from fatigue and disgust — and leave the Child still steeped in sin, blood, irreverence, and revolt.

From time to time, too, his persistent nationalistic proclamations and arguments sorely annoyed his loyalist Seniors — all the more, since their magnificent ignorance of Irish-English history put them argumentatively at the mercy of a mere child. In the beginning always he had Frank Scanlan to stand at his right hand in these political shindies — but he, fine, bright, true Irish soul, was a harum-scarum, devil-may-care, chap who after a few months' persistent disregard of all school rules, got himself sent home leaving the Irish fort to be held by the Child alone. It is testimony to the tolerance of the boys, that, though they looked on him as an outlaw, who should — and one day certainly would — be hanged, drawm, and quartered, they came to respect his sincerity, and not resent with bitterness even the most rebel pronouncement he made. One of the Seniors, John Irvine, a loud Orangeman, and drummer-boy in the Orange band of his native village, a big and big-hearted, warm-natured fellow, grew a great attachment for 'the Fenian' and took to teaching him drumming in off hours. For the good purpose they used. the school's magnificent revolving globe on which both of them beat with pairs of school pointers. In a month John taught the Child to beat out The Boyne Water, The Protestant Boys, No Surrender, We'll Kick the Pope before Us, and several other spirited airs — to the detriment of various fine cities, seas, capes, and countries, of the round world. As the globe was guided with pirated British possessions marked in red, our lad, as far as practicable, expended his energy obliterating the lurid patches. Indeed Orange Johnnie raised no objection — but said, 'It's all right. Keep at it. It'll let the Fenian venom out o' your system.'

One Senior there was, however, not absolutely tolerant of the outlaw. That was Barton, a rampant Britisher, who was forever either reading, or ranting about, 'the imperishable deeds of England's glorious heroes.' Which was all right, as long as he stopped there. But he had the unfortunate habit of conceiving the Child to be a benighted native of Asia or Africa, needing badly the blessings that only British heroes could bring him; and, armed with a lance — a long and sharp-ended school pointer — the fellow would put himself at the head of an imaginary squadron of British cavalry, and, crying out 'Charge!' come bellowing and thundering down on the small Fenian — unmercifully spearing him in the stomach, while chanting a wild paean of victory. By good luck whatsoever enmity Barton bore the boy evaporated always with the exaltation of victory — and the Child would be tolerated again, until the British hero was seized by another paroxysm. Happily, one day at length, in one of his hours of exaltation, Barton ran from the school to the town, and to the Soldiers' barracks, where he 'took the shillin', and donned a red coat — duly licensed, henceforth, to introduce civilization, by way of the spear, to natives of all benighted lands, beginning with ignorant Ireland.

Harder on the Child than Barton's British exuberance, was a dislike to him developed by the Headmaster. In the public school one day, in the presence of all the pupils (who enjoyed their tutors' humiliation) the Headmaster rebuked and ridiculed the pupil-teachers — who, by disobeying a ridiculous order of his, had sorely provoked him. Smarting from the Headmaster's tongue and their pupils' laughter, the pupil-teachers stopped their work, turned their back on him and his school, and headed for their residence. Though the Headmaster followed and angrily commanded them to return, they, unheeding, continued their independent march down the school-yard and into their quarters — leaving school and pupils to the Headmaster and his Assistant to do as they pleased with. Dismissing the school at once, the Master descended on the rebels where they sat at their desks in the Study — and passionately scolded, denounced, lectured eight fellows, who, deep in their book, most disrespectfully gave no heed whatsoever to the raging man. Only one of the eight did he single out for particular and personal rebuke — and that was the Child — on whom he laid a heavy tongue. Seemingly, his reason for singhng out for contempt and contumely the Donegal youth was because one so insignificant, a mountainy *gasúr* from the back of God-speed, should have the impudence to stand up in revolt with real young men. 'Impudence,' indeed, was the word he used — 'The impudence, especially, of you, little fellow, who aren't worth your house-room!'

Henceforward, for the greater part of his career in the Model School, the boy lay under his Headmaster's dislike. And, all the harder it was when, after a short time, it settled from an active into a passive form. For, the good man was too high-minded and of too fine principle, to give, again, concrete expression to an intuitive ill-feeling that was maybe as much a pain to himself as it was to its object. Though the boy met the dislike with a show of, sometimes sullenness, sometimes indifference, he always maintained, inside of him, a huge admiration for the man. He liked him for his wit, which was flash-like, often expressing itself in brilliant puns, a form of cleverness that the boy had never before known or heard of. He liked the man for his fine literary quality — was enthralled to listen to him, with apt quotation always at his fingertips, talk on any and every subject with ease, fluency, and a lovely phraseology which, until then, the boy had believed to be attainable only by fictitious characters speaking from book-pages. He stirred the lad's ambition — and determination: here was a man to be admired and imitated. Furthermore, making his brilliance dazzle still more his (secret) admirer's eyes the man wrote poetry — at least splendid songs. And, crowning all, the boy discovered — on occasion when he was sent on message to the Headmaster's private library — that he was a reader of Mitchell, Davis, Fintan Lalor! of Young Ireland! the Spirit of the Nation! — an Irishman at heart — a patriot who, because of the position he held, had to nurse his Irishism in secret. After that, the Headmaster was welcome to wipe his shoes on the boy, morning and night, if he so desired.[2]

He didn't do so — nor wait to do it. But he singled out for favours anyone except our lad. He passed, and kept passing, the boy's juniors over the boy's head. An un-written rule was that when the oldest pupil-teacher moved out into the world — to take charge of his own school — the next in seniority should take his place, and charge of the highest class — and the others in order of seniority, should move, each of them a class upward. Yet the boy was held to the teaching of lower, uninteresting, classes and subjects, whilst his juniors were given charge of worthwhile classes. Making it more mortifying, the juniors who took precedence of him, were not only his juniors in point of service, but weren't half as good as he in either teaching ability or scholarship. Yet the boy bore it in patience. And his patience was, in time, repaid. For in the final three months of his Model School career, the wrong was dramatically righted. William James McCord (we'll call him) our boy's immediate junior, and a favourite of the Headmaster, had charge of the most advanced class in School. Another teacher, the boy's junior, also, had the next class below McCord's. An examination was nearing; and the Headmaster discovered both men unequal to their work. Though they slaved hard to bring their boys forward, they had neither the knowledge nor the knack to succeed. With great embarrassment to himself, and humiliation to the teachers, the Headmaster, at last, found himself compelled to do an unprecedented thing — demote the two highest teachers in the school — even his own favourites. One day he called to his rostrum the impudent lad who hadn't been worth his house-room, and, looking him frankly in the face, said, 'I'm fearful that our high classes are going to discredit us in the coming examination unless we can quickly do more with them than their present teachers seem able to do. I want you to take charge of them and I'll be grateful if you give them all that I believe you can give them. Go to them now. They are yours from this time forward.'

When the examination had come and gone, and that the high classes did not disgrace the school and him, the Headmaster not only thanked Jaimie in words, but thanked him still better by a much-altered attitude.

A radically altered attitude it was. For he soon began substituting Jaimie for himself in the instructing of the pupil-teachers. Whilst the Headmaster was a fine literary scholar he was a sad mathematician — and dreaded taking the pupil-teachers in advanced Arithmetic, advanced Algebra or Geometry. Now, nearly every morning that either of these was the subject of study, he would place Jaimie in *his* chair in the Study, to give the pupil-teachers their lesson. One or other of two convincing excuses he had on most mathematics' mornings — from then till the lad left the Model School: — 'Will you please, Jaimie, take the young men for me this morning, because I have to go to see Barney?' (Barney Gallagher, a character, was man-of-all-work about the place.) — Or, coming into the Study nursing his jaw, and with fearfully wry expression on his countenance, 'Will you please take the young men for me this morning, Jaimie? I've had an awful night with my neuralgia.' Barney and the neuralgia had the perverse habit of picking mathematics mornings for bothering a good man who really deserved better.

Nine months before, the boy had passed his teachers' examination with marks that drew the Inspector's public praise and won his teaching certificate as a First or Third Class teacher — the highest rating that could then be got out of a Model School. The boy was proud of his success. But he was still prouder of the testimonial which his Headmaster wrote out for him before leaving Iniskillen — testifying that he was not merely a rare scholar, 'but has a singular knack, unusual in one so young, of conveying to pupils everything that he himself has mastered.'

Inspired by his Headmaster's example, Jaimie, in his final months at the school, made several bits of humourous verse — of that order of humour whose point is personal. That he wrote with success is proved by the fact that in the case of one 'poem,' a satire upon a fellow pupil-teacher named (we'll say) Watt, the subject made offer of a shilling — in pennies — for the copyright together with all copies extant!

Then also he was offering his services wherever he heard that a teacher or a substitute teacher was needed. A former Iniskillen pupil-teacher, Bob Bannon, who taught thirty miles away, was — by correspondence — on the point of engaging the boy as substitute teacher while he went to the Dublin Training School; but, unfortunately, he took in his head the notion to journey to Iniskillen and see the applicant before sealing the bargain. The man's face fell when he beheld the Child. Then he said, 'Ach, you'd never do!' — and went home. Soon, another chance looked good. Father Pat O'Reilly of Florencecourt needed a teacher, and the Headmaster, a friend of the good priest, told him he had one whom he could most highly recommend. Big and big-hearted Father Pat came to the school in person to give glad Jaimie the appointment. But at sight of the youth he, too, shook his head. He said, 'Your Headmaster spoke of you in mighty fine terms; and from what he said I'm sure you would make a grand teacher entirely — under the proper circumstances. But my school doesn't furnish them. It would frighten you out of a year's growth if you saw the size of the big fellows you came to teach — some of them with whiskers like little fir-trees. And I misdoubt me much if they'd enjoy it either: for, they'd be findin' you too big for one bite, and not big enough for two.'

The *gasúr* left the Model School as he came to it, a child — with a teacher's certificate sticking out of his coatpocket, for all the world to see and ignore.

NOTES

1 Years after, when the young shanachie had become a writer, he dedicated his first book of stories The Leadin' to Donegal, to the hard-hearted judge who had sentenced him to this servitude — and, in the dedication, explained why.

2 Another, rather funny, proof, did the boy, soon after get of the Headmaster's Irishism. On the night that Willie Redmond was elected to Parliament for Fermanagh — first Land Leaguer ever to represent it — our lad, full of enthusiasm, broke bounds with a comrade and stole down-town, to see and hear the fiery young patriot — as then Redmond was — moving and swaying a wildly enthusiastic crowd. Half-way through the enchanting oratory the boy's comrade said in his ear, 'For heaven's sake, hide!' — I see the Master's head showing there beyond'! Frightened, both boys tried to get lost in the depths of the crowd — and when, the speech ended, they were sneaking away, an Iniskillen acquaintance endeavoured to halt them. — 'Don't stop me'! begged the boy. 'We'll be dismissed. The Headmaster is here. We're trying to get away without his seeing us'. 'It's what I wanted to say to you', answered the Iniskillen man, — 'I met him a minute ago ducking and diving, and when I would speak to him he begged me to let him go or he'd get dimissed — for two of his pupil-teachers were here, and he was trying to get away without their seeing him'.

CHAPTER TWENTY-ONE

Kinawley

Larry Meehan's mare that fetched its master to the wedding a fortnight before the christening, wasn't half as long a-coming as the boy's first appointment. He was home from Iniskillen thirteen years before he got it — thirteen years which he spent in farming — at the same time planning, dreaming, scheming, writing to every corner of Ireland wherein (as he read or heard) an exceptionally fine schoolmaster was needed. The almanac to be sure counted this thirteen year gap only thirteen months — because, I suppose, the man who kept tally for the almanac was happy — having a job.

More than ever during these ages did the boy's mind turn to that refuge for Donegal wild-geese, America. As he spaded on Dhrim-an- Aran Hill, both mind and eyes would often flit westward over the glittering track that, starting from the hill's foot and dividing Donegal Bay, lost itself in the Atlantic. He knew well where it led to.

He had a friend in the coal mines of Wilkesbarre, and a couple of others in the steel mills of Alleghany; either of whom would, if asked, gladly pay his passage — and get him a job beside himself. Burrowing like a cockroach in the world's bowels was little to his liking, much though he would wish to be near his Wilkesbarre friend: steelmill labour wasn't so dreadfully alluring either — yet it looked as if he'd cast his lot with it.

At the back of a spade, on Dhrim-an-Aran, when he wasn't picturing himself a Master in the mountains of Kerry or Derry, Burrowing in Pennsylvania's bowels, or frying in front of its furnaces, he was composing 'poetry' — for, now that his mind was freed from study it ran to rhyming — mainly on Donegal and Ireland, their heroes, sorrows and glories. Now and then a humorous subject, too. Frequently he came home from a day's digging or corn-shearing with a whole new 'poem' in his head, ready for the writing down. One long poem he wrote, during a weeks shearing of corn on Dhrim-an-Aran — a moving picture of an exile's dreams and heartbreakings — one which his sailor-uncle, a man hitherto immune to poetry, kept reading for weeks, aloud and to himself. At the end of a reading he would shake his head and say to the blushing poet, 'You must have been inside of me, Jaimie, nights that I stood in the crow's-nest of *The Mary-of-Cardiff* on a time we were trying for three weeks to beat round the Horn.' Mostly, his compositions at this time were short lyrics of a fashion, or little stories that he picked out of the hills like:

CAORA BHIG DHILIS[1]

'O, Caora Bhig Dhilis, the Ware-day is here,
And the sweed, juicy braird has begun to appear;
As, near to my patch I can't trust you, you know,
Till Hallowday dawns to the hills you must go,
        O, Caora Bhig Dhilis!'

'On the mountains, O Patrick, it's hard is the heath,
And tender, you know, are your Caora Bhig's teeth;
They'll put sore, them sharp rocks, on soft wee feet,
O Patrick, so cruel don't be, I entreat.
        To Caora Bhig Dhilis!'

'To stay on the lowlands if me you'll allow,
One blade of your braird I'll thieve not, I vow;
In Ireland a happier sheep'll not be,
Nor a happier man than you watching of me,
        Your Caora Bhig Dhilis!'

'O, Caora Bhig Dhilis, you never will rue
Your visit up yonder, for grand is the view;
From far parts, the rich folks throng there with delight,
And they never be tired, they tell, of the sight,
        O, Caora Bhig Dhilis!'

'But put one of them rich folks to live on the hill,
Only grand views and heather his stomach to fill,
And believe me, O Patrick, nine chances in ten,
But diff'rent the tale he would tell to you then!'
        Said Caora Bhig Dhilis!'

'There's sheep on those hills, too, might teach me to steal,
And there's worse — for, O Patrick, think how would you feel
Some black day you'd come and find, crashed through her
head,
A cruel big rock, and stiff, cold and dead —
        Poor Caora Bhig Dhilis!'

The sorrowful picture soon made Pat comply.
. . . .
In his corn-field next morn a sore sight met his eye —
In the hedge hung a thief, no kick, and no groan,
For, swang by the neck-band — and dead as a stone,
        Was Caora Bhig Dhilis!'

143

One joyous day, at length, there was brought to the boy in the field —
where he was breaking ground for corn — a fateful letter from a schoolmaster in a Fermanagh hamlet that he had never before heard of. The name
was Andrew Anderson, the place Kinawley. He said he had heard fine
things about the boy from the Headmaster of Iniskillen Model School, and
wantcd to know if the boy would consent to take an appointment as
Temporary Assistant Teacher in Kinawley National School.

Though in cold reality the official title of it was the very biggest thing
about the job, the great career of which he had begun to despair gloriously
dawned again on the boy's vision. He threw his spade as far as he could
from him, and, nearly before he knew, was away to Kinawley — which
proved a hamlet hard to find. It was dark night when, bright carpet-bag
on shoulder, he left his train at Florencecourt, and set his foot on the road
in search of a place that was supposed to be six miles off. But after he had
met up with, and been moidhered by, the Five Points and the Seven Points
and a dozen common cross-roads, tried a bit of every way that ran from
each of them, and sampled besides two dozen lanes, boreens, and byways,
it looked to him a deal more like sixteen mile than six. Nearing Kinawley
at last, and learnimg that Master Anderson lived at the end of a mile-long
lane running from the highway, the boy searched to the muddy end every
lane he came up with. At the very tail-end of each of them he found a
lighted cottage — but none of them the one he wanted. It was always, 'Try
a lane a wee bit ahead o' you on the left, for the Masther's.'

When he did find — far in the night — the thatched cottage he was
searching, he found welcome, and rest, a comfortable home, and a Master
of fatherly mien, generous proportions, soft kindliness of speech, and deep
earnestness of manner — an engaging Middle-aged bachelor, reposeful
and confidence-inspiring. Master Andy Anderson, a struggling country
schoolmaster, proved to be a noble-minded, true gentleman whose sterling
character should influence for good the forming character of the boy. God
rest you, Andy Anderson! 'tis many's the prince might have been proud
to be you.

Jaimie had joint charge, with the Master, of a school of about a hundred
pupils. Joint charge, at first it seemed — but often, latter, it turned to be
full charge: for Master Anderson, at once father and mother to the parish,
had, most days, to follow a funeral, settle a quarrel, see a sick friend, draw
a will, abort a threatened law-suit, make a match, sponsor a christening,
give away a bride, sit to a consultation, or take a two-hour walk down the
Swanlinbar road with Father Charles, the curate, who sought the wise
Master's counsel on all parish affairs.

Though the boy was still far from big, here he had to rule a crowd of
lads bigger than himself; but they were gentler far, civiler, and ten times
more tractable than the rioters of Iniskillen. Also they were far less lively,

obstreperous, and harum-scarum than the boys whom he had run with in Glen Ainey. In this low-lying country, pupils were more patient and studious, but far, far from being brilliant as the lightning-quick vagabonds of the Donegal mountains.

Partly from things told him by the Model School Headmaster, and partly because he had heard that the boy wrote poetry, Master Anderson, concluding Jaimie to be a genius, had grown an extraordinary opinion of his Temporary Assistant Teacher even before he saw him — and with his own estimate of 'the new Masther' had imbued both the pupils and people of the country-side; so that the boy, both to his flattering and surprise, found himself on a marble pedestal when he came to Kinawley. From these good simple people he got a reverential regard and respect that meant both pleasure to him and pride. His eminence was profitable, too; for the respect and regard which it won him from his pupils, made a deal easier his ruling and his teaching. The fine order that he soon created in a disorderly school — for, in listing Master Anderson's many qualities above — it was omitted that he was easy-going as Parra Sastha — and the rapid progress of his pupils, made Master Anderson marvel and begin underpinning the boy's pedestal to raise him some perches nearer the stars. The poor man lived and died in ignorance that it was to his good self and the legend he had created, most all of the credit was due.

Regard from this fine-minded man — far up to whom the boy was himself looking — while it flattered and pleased, likewise amused the boy. More especially so when he found that Master Anderson had impressed to the ranks of his admirers rough-and- ready, bluff, blunt, old Father Tom O'Reilly, the parish priest — who lived in Swanlinbar, three miles away — and who grudged respect to his own bishop, if that man didn't work hard for, and win, it.

To win Father Tom's regard was a feat — which innocent Master Anderson's legends about 'the new Masther from Donegal' accomplished. When he brought his new assistant to Father Tom for inspection and approval — or else the good man first inquired about his Kinawley curate, Father Charles — 'How's that lazy slob that I have workin' for me down there behavin' himself, anyway?' He then set about looking the lad over very deliberately — even fingering his homespuns and inquiring how much, if anything, he paid for them. And, after a complete inspection, he who would as readily have said, had he so thought, 'You look to me a rascally schemer and scoundrel. — Take the fellow home again, Master Anderson, and keep a close eye on him' — actually said, 'I believe you're a miraculous teacher, sir. God bless you, and go home! And take good care that Andy Anderson, here, doesn't make you as lazy and good-for-nothin' as he is himself. — Good-bye!' Master Anderson laughed half the way home and was right well pleased that he had succeeded in the rare task of winning Father Tom's approval of anything.[2]

If the boy's days were filled with hard teaching, his nights were spent pleasantly rambling — *céilidhing* it was called here. For Master Anderson was a born and bred *céilidhóir*. Every evening, after school, and as soon as they had swallowed their dinner — a solid one, of potatoes with lashins of bacon and cabbage — the two Masters hied them off on their nightly ramble to one house or other, east, west, one mile away, five mile — some cottage where they sat around the fire chatting half-an-hour with the nice old parents, and then sat around the walls whispering three hours with the far nicer young daughters. At midnight the pair of them would head for home, over ditch and hedge, bog and boreen — through the black dark following paths where the boy couldn't see a stim, but which Master Anderson could trot with eyes closed. Till, reaching the bottom of their own hill of Dhrimlish, they took, at a running-leap, the steep-banked, wide-and-deep stream that washed the foot of the Master's farm. The Master himself knew by instinct just where the stream lay, and could take a run to it and safely leap it in a midnight black as the inside of a cow; but as the boy could only guess by ear — divining the stream's nearer marge by its murmur, and taking its farther bank on faith — more than once he rose up too short and came down too soon — so that by the hair of the head the Master had to haul his Temporary Assistant Teacher from the stream's deepest pool. And, following the rescue, in the Master's kitchen after midnight, they always made a thorough job of wringing out the drownded man's duds — and, then hanging them in the chimney, they'd get into prime condition again before morning. Even if, then, they did smell a bit smoky.

After a splendid supper of thick-milk with oaten stir-about, cold from hours of waiting for them, the Masters retired. And were dilatory about awaking next morning. And would have been more dilatory, but for Master Anderson's aged and worried father. Neddy Anderson, an admirable, and extraordinarily wise and prudent old gentleman, spent his days and nights reading St. Alphonse de Liguori, the Key of Heaven, The Religious Controversy between Pope and Maguire, and other estimable works that were smoothing the way for his soul's soon passing. But the good man's soul meanwhile was disturbed over the late hours — late nights and late mornings — that were the rule with the two supposedly learned members of the household. Every afternoon as the Masters ate dinner, old Neddy Andeison, seated in his straw-bottomed chair in the chimney-corner, spectacles high on his brow, and one forefinger intervening in the half-closed Life of St. Mary of Egypt, preached to the Masters a homily upon sinful waste of time in *céilidhing*, heavily interlarded with quotations from Augustine, Thomas Aquinas, and other indisputable authorities on that subject. Yet, just as surely as came nine o'clock next morning, he would be knocking, pounding, bumping, and thumping with his *croisín* (as, back in Glen Ainey, they called the big helping-stick), on the floor above his head, whereon the bedded Masters slumbered. 'Get up! Get up with ye! ye lazy, good-for-nothin' rakes and roamers, who come home here when the honest half of the worl' is nigh through with their sleepin', and aren't fit to rise at a christian hour in the mornin'. Get up with ye, I tell ye! I'm seein' from the door the white road at Kinawley black-crawlin' with crowds of scholars waitin' for their lazy Masthers to open the school door and let them at their lessons! Get up with ye! Get up with ye! And may the Lord forgive ye — if even He can — for the wasteful lives ye are leadin'! Get up, I'm tellin' ye, again! If the Lord hasn't saved it the pair o' ye will yet wind up like oul' Mickey Maguire.'[3]

The rumours that gave to the boy poetic genius, reached the ears and roused the jealousy of one Frank Maguire whose vocation was stone-masonry, and avocation music and poetry — fiddling and the making of ballads on all great local events. Frank, who, for a third of a century, had been undisputed poet laureate of Kinawley, grew bitter as a magpie against this interloper, and sent the intruder a written challenge to meet him in a poetry- making bout at any place and date he chose to fix. To give the interloper no loop-hole, he supplemented the written defiance by sending two of his ardent admirers on personal embassy, carrying a verbal challenge. The boy arranged, with them, for a meeting of the poets, to decide once and for all which of the rivals should henceforth hold supremacy.

The country-side was agitated over the coming contest. It was their own beloved poet whose songs were sung at every gathering, against the intruder one from Donegal — the poet of known powers against him of only rumoured ones. Though every man ventured his guess, no one could be quite sure just which combatant would survive. Their old idol might be pushed from his pedestal and a new one set up, or the old one be lifted to greater heights.

The two champions met in mortal combat in Pat MacBrien's big kitchen on a snowy February night. The place was crammed with excited neighbours. The combat opened by each poet in turn — Frank Maguire first — repeating the finest poem he had ever given to a gratified world. Then, each in turn, upon any subject he liked, put forth a couplet which his opponent was called on to cap with one that should fit and finish it. After that, a poem, on a subject selected by Pat MacBrien, and entire in eight lines or less, must be composed and uttered within five minutes. His own composition the boy cannot (probably for good reason) recall, but Frank Maguire's is fresh in memory. It became a classic in the country-side. The host had commanded him to satirize an enemy nicknamed Clatty

Moat who provoked Frank by habit of making a near-cut across his small patch of corn-Iand. And Frank's contibution to Clatty Moat's immortality was —

> 'O Clatty Moat,
> You're nothing loat'
> Your habits to maintain —
> Mrachin' o'er my cornfield, and comin' back again:
> But if you do not stop it,.
> And from it don't refrain,
> I'll meet you on some evenin' and tramp you in a drain.''

In years after, the boy was mortal sorry he did not at the time make a full record of the contest — and its inspirations. But he has the poems that concluded the contest — poems which, it was at the time of challenge agreed, should be beforehand prepared, upon a local theme — and submitted to that night's audience.

The new Master's was called for first — given — and appreciated. It was an elegy on the Old Masther, Mickey Maguire — who had passed away just a week before:

> Och, it's cold ye are, poor Mickey and your head is lyin' low
> And above ye, sure, the hare-bell and the daisy soon will blow—
> And the leverock and the throstle will pipe their mornin' call,
> Just as if — God rest ye, Mickey! — ye were never here at all.
>
> And the world will keep a-whirlin' as it was wont of yore,
> And as oft ye demonstrated with chalk upon the floor —
> And the day will follow night, Mick, and the night will follow
>   day —
> And shall we, too, forget you, Mick, for ever and for aye?
>
> No; Teddy may forget to keep a drop of something nate,
> John Murphy may forget to growl, Ned Lynch forget to chate —
> Bold Frank Maguire forget to rhyme, and Terry Mack to pray —
> But, troth, we won't forget you, Mick, although you're in the clay!
>
> The old men, they will mind ye, and will tell us many a yarn
> Of the ructions and the fractions, and the whackin's, in the barn
>   —
> Of the Gough and of the Vosther[4] and of how you quelled a
>   row —
> And they'll shake their grey old noddles, with, 'There's no such
>   larnin' now!'

148

The girls will mind your valentines; the boys, mid heark'ning
  throngs
Of spell-bound ones in distant lands, will fondly chant your
  songs;
And, round the fire in years to come, before their children tall,
They'll boast of how they footed it at Mickey's Christmas Ball.

Och, it's cold ye are, poor Mickey! and your head is lyin' low,
And above ye, sure the hare-bell and the daisy soon will
  blow —
And the throstle and the leverock will pipe their mornin' call,
Just as if — God rest ye, Mickey — ye were never here at all!

Frank's poem was upon The Monster National Demonstration' (of the previous Spring) in Iniskillen. The 'Mimbers' in it referred to were Redmond and other Irish Members of the British Parliament: and the 'Dane' Very Rev. Dean Bermingham, then Parish Priest of Iniskillen. 'Lowry on his monument' in Jail Square was one of the (anti-Irish) aristocrats of the Fermanagh country — statued (misappropriately) *outside* the jail. Barney Maglone, beloved Irish humourist of seventy years ago, used to interview Lowry (on his monument) upon public questions.

Rejoice ye son of Erin, for old Ireland shall be free!
The Bard's inclined to tell his mind, for all that he did see;
On the second day of Feb-ury, right well I mind the date,
Our Mimbers they came over their minds for to relate.

As the bell tolled our that morning to the Chapel we did go,
And fervently we each did pray against the daring foe,
We returned from the Altar, a mark upon each brow —
'With Freedom for our country where is Coercion now?'

With horse and foot we took the road, each shepherd led his
  flock,
And arrived at Inniskillen at the hour of two o'clock;
From Portora gates to Belmore Street was crowded with the
  throng,
No man to yield but for the field in thousands we marched on.

For to make up their number I might go through the count,
But there is no rule in larnin' could tell the full amount.
I saw the hand of Shane O'Neill on the Green Flag from
  Tyrone,
And the royal band of Fintona they played us Garryowen.

> *At the Jail Square I rested, there to take another view,*
> *When Lowry off the Monument he asked me, 'Is that you?*
> *And are these the Derry' Prentice Boys, or when did you*
> > *leave home?*
> *I took you for another man — I thought you were Maglone.'*

> *'We are not the Derry' Prentice Boys, nor yet from Sandy*
> > *Row,*
> *For our Parliament is banded in old Ireland once more*
> *We have the men of Ulster here our cause for to maintain*
> *Our Mimber is bold Redmond and our Chairman is the Dane.'*

> *North and South Fermanagh they made a grand display,*
> *With Kinawley and Kilskeery, and the boys from Lisnaskea,*
> *From Maguiresbridge to Monaghan, and Tempo in the Glen,*
> *With Montiagh lads and Macken men that fought their way*
> > *and won.*

> *We had Belleeck and Belashanny, and the men of sweet*
> > *Roslea,*
> *With Mullaghdun and Arney like an army in array,*
> *And noble Iniskillen with order and command,*
> *Their cry was 'No Coercion! But Freedom for our land!'*

Which champion came our laurelled victor in the great contest?

Reluctantly the boy must confess that it was not he. Some people may credit it to his egotism, but he never could outlive the belief that he failed to carry the crown from Big Pat's less through lack of genius on his part than through local patriorism deflecting the scales of justice. Indeed the judges heartily granted that the boy's poetry was worthy of the very highest marks — remarkably good and neatly turned for one of his tender years — but he was not and indeed couldn't be expected to be, a Frank Maguire![5]

The *bouchal's* new life was blossoming to him in Kinawley when he learnt from Donegal that his own old Master, Master Gallagher, now nearing seventy and wishing to rest for his life's remainder, was giving up Glen Cuach School. At once the boy wrote to the School Manager, asking for the place and learned that, as more than a dozen others were besieging him for it, and he couldn't decide between them, he would hold, for all of them, a competitive examination, three weeks away, and let the best man take it. The lad, who hadn't opened a textbook in more than a year, set himself swallowing books from four o'clock each afternoon till four the next morning. He ran the rounds of the books twice, and on the eve of the day of the contest, started for Donegal with the encouragement and blessing of kindly Master Anderson who would hold open for him his present post till the examination's result was known.

Because his jaunt, that winter morn, had grave result for him eventually, it will be described here. For a week past there had been snow *go leor* — deep layers of it had frozen on the ground. But on the eve of his journey rain began turning to slush all it could of the snow-coat — which was the upper half of it — leaving the rest ice-caked. It was eight or nine miles to the town of Iniskillen where he must this morning catch his train. To hire a jaunting-car he couldn't afford; and an eight or nine mile saunter, anyhow, never daunted him. Light-heartedly he set out, with his bag, at four in the morning — which on that dark winter day was dead of night. He was a light and handy traveller to whom a bag was no bother — and he was much advantaged by the fact that not yet had he promoted himself to an overcoat. The rain had stopped, moreover, leaving only a muddy mist falling and another of the same quality rising to meet it from the melting snow — just the sort of morning (or night) that encouraged a man to briskness. So he tripped joyously over the roads and it only gave rhythm to the jaunt when the caked ice underneath the slush put him half a step back for every full step he tried to take forward. The loss signified little since he had wisely given himself a clear four hours for the journey.

He quickened his step, though, for safety. But, after a few miles he found that the style of going was a deal more tedious — and tiresome — than he had at first thought; and when he had covered half the mileage of his journey, he had used more than half of his time. If he missed his train he couldn't get to Donegal that day, and would lose the chance of a lifetime. So he quickened his walk again: but the faster he would go forward the farther he'd slip back. He fell to running for the final few miles — and reached Iniskillen Station in plenty of time — and a grand lather of sweat. His duds were well soaked, by the co-operative efforts of the moisture from without and the moisture from within. His limbs too, unaccustomed to the double-action that icy roads call for, were telling him they had no objection to a brief rest. He heeded them, and took a platform seat for the half-hour till the train came. And after that gave them a refreshing two-hour rest in a frost-cooled carriage as far as Belashanny — arriving whereat, his legs, feeling they had done their day's work, were loath to carry him out of the carriage. Through humouring and coaxing, however, they bore him into the station-house; and, after a while, inch by inch to the post office, where he had promised them six-hours' ease — that is till the mail-car should start for Donegal in the evening.

But since he found that the more he indulged them the more they objected to start again, he decided it was best to keep them working: so, ignoring their loud protests, he forced them to keep shuffling him, inch by inch, scores of times up and down every highway and byway of Belashanny five hours of it. But he rested them again for the hours on the mail-car to Donegal, through the lovely, frosty, energising night-air that in winter-time makes healthy the Tyrugh coast-road.

In Donegal the bothersome limbs worried less over walking than they had done in Belashanny; and, after he had forced them to shuffle him the first mile of the way to Knockagar, became comparatively compliable. Home was good, and a welcome supper — the first meal since his three-in-the-morning breakfast in Kinawley — and, after that, still better was bed. His mountain constitution brought him up fresh in the morning entirely forgetting that he had an anatomy — and keen for that day's fray.

But before dealing with this and its result, the sequel to the lad's morning jaunt through the misty ways of Fermanagh may be noted. In three weeks' time he was laid down with a mighty aching of his system, a swelling of his joints, and inability to move limb, toe, or finger without exquisite pain — a new complaint in that country-side, which the doctor named inflammatory rheumatism. He had never before known sickness or suffering, but a session with this impressive teacher remedied his ignorance, and fitted him to hold a high head thereafter when he heard people boast of sufferings they had put past them.

He shook off the nasty thing in less than six weeks: but, once every three years or so, for twenty years after, it called on him again, and laid him — out in Ireland a couple of times, but later, in hospitals of New York, Canandaigua, Buffalo, Cincinnati, and New Orleans. Till, finally, when it could teach him nothing new in algesiology, it bade him good-bye. — To God be thanks!

NOTES

1 Pron. Caera Vig Yeelish — Dear Little Sheep. In Donegal, then, the sheep in Ware (Spring) were sent up to the mountains, and taken down to the lowlands again after the crops were harvested. Frequently the sheep have around their necks a twisted-straw neck-band — which may happen to work woe to its wearer in leaping through a hedge, towards forbidden fruit.

2 Old Father Tom hobbled around on, or rather with, a stick — for he used it less for leaning on than for cracking over the head all of his flock who did not do as well, or as rightly, as he wished. With it he chased drinkers out of the public house on market nights, and cleared off the street loiterers who should be usefully engaged at home. The same big, crook-handled stick he also used for pounding down, and finally heaping to a high crown, the tub of oats that each farmer filled for him (part of every parishoner's stipend) in the threshing season. Father Tom stood at his Chapel-door Sunday mornings to insure that every comer put in the box the weekly ha'penny for the church upkeep; and once, when a local shopkeeper, through design or exaltation, slipped into the church without dropping his coin, the good man let the fellow get half-way up the aisle before halting him with a loud 'Misther MacBrien!' which

captured the attention of the whole congregation. And when Mr. MacBrien in obedience turned around — 'Misther MacBrien, when you haven't handy in your shop a ha'penny why don't you fetch a duck-egg to drop in God's box?'

3   Mickey maguire was one of several Kinawley characters who attracted and interested the boy, and sowed in his memory the seeds of future stories. He was known as 'the Old Masther' — having been, before Master Anderson, the Kinawley teacher — his school an abandoned tumble-down barn. He was half-way the old hedge-schoolmaster, without the hedge-schoolmaster's scholarship. He was witty, wrote songs for the countryside, expressed himself in words that dazzled, was fond of his ease, a glass of whiskey, and glad company. He loved with jovial ones to live out the night, had a rank antipathy to work and especially disliked both the day's forepart and its demands. Indeed, he often said it was a sad mistake, anyhow, to have the day begin in the morning. While he was the Master of Kinawley, morning would have long lost its novelty if it wasn't worn out entirely, when he reached his school. Sometimes he forgot to reach it. In rainy weather, when the river was flooded, a strong scholar would wade the stream at mid-day, and mounting the Master on his back, bear him over the flood to the seat of his labours. More than once a rascal among the scholars, undertaking to do donkey for Mickey, would succumb to a weak spell in the stream's middle — with dampening results to a load of learning.

In general the scholars' parents accepted Mickey's unpunctuality as they did the rain and the potato-blight — something that 'twas folly to fret about — but in the police-barrack was a sergeant who couldn't accept Mickey's eccentricities like a philosopher. He was, more by the same token, a miserly fellow, who on Monday mornings too often forgot to send his children the school-pennies that were Mickey's perquisites. Once, this gambler, making up his mind to give the Master what he considered a neat rap on the Knuckles, set down for his child — in the copy-book that Master Mickey examined every day — the pithy headline,

Masters should be punctual in their attendance. When Master Mickey came to read this moral maxim, he said, 'Hem! That's very excellent, chile. — And, now, let me set you another good headline — a small specimen of poetry that you're to copy ten times, under your father's eye —

'Sergeants should be punctual in their pay — Otherwise have less to say.'

Of the old Master's first meeting with the newest Master, our boy — a casual encounter on a stormy day, by Kinawley graveyard, the Old Masther's comment — as later conveyed to the boy, — was, 'The preceptor recently imported from the moun-tain-eous localities to the north-ward I encountered this afternoon inhalin' the salubrious air whilst meanderin' the Shanwalla road adjacent to the local simitery.' When his school was taken over by the Board of Education, Master Mickey was invited to retire from inactive duty — and, at the time that Neddy Anderson was threatening with his fate the two wastrels whom he housed, Mickey was living by the bounty the people, the proceeds of his annual Christmas Ball festivity that crowned all of winter's festivities in the Kinawley country) — and the inditing of poem — valentines for girls in love. He was to die before our boy got to know him as well as he wished.

4   The standard books on Arithmetic in Mickey's days.

5   Yet, partly because of Andy Anderson's propaganda, and maybe more because he proved himself worthy to meet and be beaten by Frank Maguire, the boy's memory became imortal at Kinawley. A weary count of years after, once, when the boy making expedition into the Fermanagh country, was pushing to Kinawley in hope to find again his old respected friend Master Anderson, he met a very old, very poor and ragged man on the road — of whom he made inquiry. 'May God rest his white soul,' the old fellow feelingly said 'The Master's dead and berrid these three years. — Were ye a friend of his?'

'I hope I was. I taught under him long long ago.'

'You did! Would it be imperence on my part to ax what your name was?'

When the boy gave his name, the old man straightened out of the chronic crook that had held his body, lifted high his stick and flourished it. 'No!' he cried in amaze. 'Sure we call you the Miracle Man! For sure you were the most mirac'lous of all the Masthers that ever darkened Kinawley School door! Sure your name was sounded over hill and dale here! Thanks be to God, can it take wan grip o' the Miracle Man's han'? — Harky to this!' And then the poor fellow squared himself in the middle of the road, and, in a voice that the remains of a good one, sang through the Lament for Mickey Maguire, and then sang Frank's Iniskillen Monsther Demmonstration.

'Let me tell ye,' he said in a burst of enthusiam, I don't give a straw what the vardiay of the poetry judges was, that night in Big Pat's; but it's my kindred opinion that for downright poetry you could show your heels to — God rest him! — Frank Maguire any day.'

Though it was plain to a blind man that Terry Manachan sorely needed it he spurned the silver that the Miracle Man would give him — and he had to fling it on the road at Terry's feet as he drove away, feeling prouder that if he had been diploma'd and decorated by the world's foremost University.

CHAPTER TWENTY-TWO

The Master

The tussle among the Masters for the teachership of Glen Cuach School excited Glen Ainey from the mountains to the sea. Every night it was the only thing discussed in the tailor's, in the shoemaker's, at all fire-sides. It came to be known as The Matching of the Masthers. Glen Cuach was a bright prize, by reason it had a slated roof, and was by a village: so, seasoned schoolmasters as well as schoolmasters lately-begun, and some who hadn't yet begun, rushed to the contest. The favourites for the prize were, of course, the older men. They had years of reading behind them, and reputation; and must, of course, be far-and-away better scholars and masters than the young aspirants. Our lad, only a bit of a boy, was sympathized with, but not taken seriously. Being allowed in the running was considered, for the youngster, reward *go leor*.

Father James, the Manager, got Maynooth's Professor of Mathematics to set the papers, to conduct the examination — and afterwards to pass upon the answers. Thirteen Masters and the boy sat to the examination. Glen Ainey didn't set many potatoes that day — nor do much for a week after — till the result came.

About ten days later, on a beautiful, bright, frosty night — vividly the *gasúr* recalls one of the very bright nights of his life — came a summons to Jaimie to attend on Father James at his home in Frosses, three miles away. He didn't let much grass grow under his heels till he was knocking at Father James's door. The good man beamed on the boy and shook his hand right warmly, with, 'Congratulations to you, my hearty! You've snatched the prize! and, I'm delighted to tell you, you've come fifteen points in the hundred ahead of the second champion!'

He led the lad within. 'Though you're mighty young for the job you're now the Master of Glen Cuacli School,' he said 'and it gives me real pleasure to put the key in your — fist. May God gless you, and give you success!'

Only on a couple of other occasions of his life was the boy's heart so suddenly and highly exalted. On that crisp, brisk, beautiful, starlit, frosty night, Jaimie would have been certain but for his shoe's ring on the road that it was floating home on a silver cloud he was. His family was exalted to his own pitch. And nearly so the amazed, happy neighbours. They crowded in to make both his hands sore shaking them, to flail him on the back, and cover him with congratulations. And that, not just because he had won the great contest — though the same was immortal fame — but, more, because now he was settled for life had got the grandest post that the heart of man could desire, with wealth beyond count: and for the duration of his days could sit back with nothing in the world to do but teach a school, carry a schoolmaster's dignity, draw thirty-five pounds salary every year, and do his endeavour to spend it.[1]

For several years Jaimie heartily enjoyed both the great distinction and income and, as heartily, the work that went with them — work which his happy neighbours looked upon as elaborate leisure. The great salary, though a grand thing, was not, to him, the grandest thing about his office: it was that he was now The Masther; and, by high and low, old and young, at wake, at mass, and at market, always as 'Master' saluted; that he had suddenly become a man off eminence, to whom, though only a lad, the parish paid high reverence. No other honour that he could or would win should bring him truer, more permanent, pride.

For his first few weeks in Glen Cuach School, the *gasúr* had an active time, proving to the biggest, strongest, wildest Donegal rascals that he was the Masther. But within ten strenuous days he succeeded so definitely that it wasn't again questioned. Into Bedlam, by virtue of his good right arm and left frequently he had introduced all the repose and decorum of a Young Ladies' Seminary. From the outset he had high enjoyment in moulding young minds. His heart was in the work and he had the knack of knowing how to do it. It is true that in the eyes of the very dignified Masters of the parish he started a scandal by becoming comrade to his pupils actually talking to them outside of school, walking with them, playing with them, taking them on foot-excursions to historic spots holding himself no higher than one of them. He even gave the school a play-hour, and in it, forgetting he was the Master, he became just another of the players. Furthermore, he brought to school with him books that had nothing whatever to do with the curriculum, or with Education as hitherto known — story-books, poetry-books, history-books — talked about these to his classes, and urged the boys to take them home and read them. Worse still because so flagrantly contrary both to the rules and the spirit of the Irish National Board of Education he told his scholars of their own country and her history![2] and, as if that wasn't bad enough, time that should be given to profitable subjects he used to telling the scholars about men who had been transported to the penal colonies in Australia, and other criminals who had been living on the gallows tree. The older, wiser, schoolmasters shook their heads over this startling innovation in a National School and sincerely sympathised with the unbalanced boy who, they rightly foresake, could not last long in the System. The Inspector and other government authorities were bound to hear, sooner or later, that the young Master was trying to expand the curriculum of an Irish National School to include a new, and an immoral subject — Knowledge of Ireland, to wit.

156

But the young Master, all oblivious of error, went forward light-heartedly, dreaming as very, very frequently he did — of halcyon days ahead when, arrived at the age of sixty-five, he would retire on a pension of fifteen shillings and sixpence a year, and be free and able to do all the great things he planned and read, read, read all the books of the world, which his accumulated savings would then buy him without stint. The only shadow now and then dimming the bright colour of his dream, was the sad thought that, to a boy only yet in his teens, sixty-five was so dishearteningly far off!

With spare pennies he began enriching himself — and his evening hours — by purchase, now and again, of paper-covered, small-type, thruppenny and sixpenny classics put out by John Dick of London — God bless him! even if he was an Englishman. Each time that he found himself able to send for a fresh one, and each time that the precious investment arrived, was a time of joy: and for many nights after its arrival a place of joy for him was beneath the wall lamp in his mother's chimney- corner.

For all that they were outraged by the youngster's indiscretions, the older Masters were yet truly, even if condescendingly, kind to him, and partial. Without putting a tooth in it, they admired him for that he, a bit of a boy, had snatched the Glen Cuach prize from a big field of seasoned ones, and felt confident that he was at bottom, all right, and time and kind treatment might win him away from youth's eccentricities. They swore him into the Donegal Branch of the Irish National Teachers' Association; and soon after did him the signal honour of making him Secretary.

Not the least part of the pleasure he got from his new distinction was the contact it gave him with the crowd of originals that were the older members of the organization. There was Master Murray who taught by the sea, little man with large head that was built for a Prime Minister instead of a pedagog — with a mouth tight shut, barred, and double-locked, in desperate endeavour to hold in the high-tide of dignity with which always he was bursting. And sweet, modest, little Master MacGrath of the mountains, who, wet day or dry day, high wind or no wind, showed himself never in public without an umbrella bound midway by black-leather whang, and below and above bulging like a belted Ballykillowen woman. Great, big, stout, magnificently-fed Master Conaghan from the Ainey Water, smiled always the generous smile of a man unreservedly tolerant of this makeshift world and the mediocre people with which it strangely pleased God to surround him — big Master Conaghan who sauntered seven miles to Donegal market every Saturday, scattering his smile on all sides as he went, whilst his admiring little wife humbly walked, worshipping, on his heels, all the way there and back. Prince of them all, Shan O'Cravsey, short up and down but long across, rosy of face as the sun the on Sliabh Liag, beaming like Mayday's morning, and

157

bubbling with genial joke and funny anecdote which made housefulls shake their sides — Shan, whose fellow for story, mirth, merriment, and, still more, true Irishism, the boy was seldom, if ever, to meet again. (And often at whose grass-grown grave — between the ruined Abbey's gable and the sea's edge — the boy still puts up a mouthful of prayer.) Another whose wholesome laugh — his constant companion — was sudden cure for sorest heartache, was Tuathal MacMenamin from Sru-aill Mountain, whose long body was far to fill at meal-time — Tuathal, so tall that to make him companionable to common men, he zig-zagged himself at the more important joints — Tuathal who snapping his fingers at seventy-seven, proved the world was a playground. Once Tuathal, on a Saturday morning, after meandering six miles from his mountain school to the village, dropped in to talk with the boy-Secretary, who, breakfasting, invited his visitor to a bowl of tea, a slice of toast, and a boiled egg. The provender was accepted — and a second round of it — and a third. But the boy began to be downright surprised when Tuathal answered 'Surely,' to a fourth entreaty. As a matter of form a fifth helping was suggested, but Tuathal promptly and firmly replied, 'No, no! I mustn't take any more. — If you'll excuse me,' getting up from the table, 'I'll be hurrying on to Larry Gillespie's where I ordered breakfast half-an-hour ago and it'll be getting cold on me!'

The greatest character, and most original of all, in the Donegal Branch of the Irish National Teachers' Association, was the boy's friend, patron, and admirer, Manus MacClusky, from the Nick of the Balach — ugly as Socrates and almost as sage — a man as solid as Muckish mountain, of wide reading, who, though scorning to swallow every tuppenny theory put to him by book-writers, always gathered profit from everything he perused — Manus, who read *The Nation* every Saturday night to a kitchen-full of neighbours — not only read, but expounded it: for, after giving out a paragraph or three paragraplas he would put down paper and spectacles, and, striding back and forth, looking now at the rafters, now at the floor (never at his spell-bound audience), explain, interpret, and qualify by his own opinion, what his audience had just heard. Manus was man of choice words and flowing, flowery style — who, when he spoke, said something worth listening to, dressed in large language appropriate. Of sturdy opinion and inflexible principle ever, Manus, in the matter of a trifling dispute that cropped up in the Association and which a compliant one tried to smooth over by compromise, with a thunderous No! negatived the base proposal — 'NO! There's a principle involved, and I proclaim that Heaven itself could be too dearly purchased at a sacrifice of principle!' Manus whose great dissipation was letter-writing, found frequent opportunity to indulge it, in communicating with the boy-Secretary. Each of his productions was a rare specimen of the epistolary

158

art. A sample may here be set down — a letter of apology for himself and wife (his Assistant Teacher, and mother to a large brood) unable to attend a March meeting. The epistle is exactly as penned by the eloquent one.

My Dear Brother:

One week from current date our serried hosts [There would be eleven members at the meeting if all attended] should be assembling in history-crowned Donegal, with banners floating to the breeze in the noble Cause we all have at heart. [Chief aim of the Cause was to obtain for its humblest member a minimum wage of seventeen-and-sixpence a week]. But I most regretfully beg leave to apprise you that left wing of the regiment is unable to march. My modest spouse reluctantly intimates to me that for reasons which feminine delicacy forbids her specifically to define, it will be, if not impossible, at least impracticable and inadvisable for to move on the rendezvous that day; and I hereby affirm that all appearances tend to corroborate if not substantiate her statement.

For my humble self, I am hors de combat — having been again outflanked by my inveterate enemy, the rheumatism, induced by undue exposure to the unpropitious climatic conditions prevalent on the fourteenth ultimo whilst I was engaged in the strenuous occupation of turf-cutting on the bogs northward of Loch Nam-Ban-Finn.

Praying our Heavenly Father to direct by his divine spirit, and guide by His benign wisdom, the grave deliberations and momentous decisions [Most momentous of their decisions, in their meeting-room, — the back-parlour of Larry Gillespie's public house — usually was, whether they would have their drinks punched or raw] of my brethren-in-arms, at their august assembly in Lawrence Gillespie's Council Chamber, on the imminent Ides of March,

I beg to remain, My dear Brother,
Your very obedient, humble servant,
Manus MacClusky.

In Larry's back-room the Masters pleaded their grievances with an eloquence which convinced every ardent one of themselves that their claims were justified and must not be refused. They proposed, and, everytime, passed (unanimously), five resolutious that had been proposed and passed (unanimously) at all meetings since the oldest member joined the organization and drank five rounds that promoted grateful good fellowship. The young Master — who scandalised them by drinking ginger-ale — walked the merry miles home with older members to profit by the learned debates which Larry's poteen was ever sure to provoke. Before coming to the parting of their ways, a mile beyond Knockagar, all five (there would, then, be left about five) roused from his second sleep old Master Gallagher of Turas Hill — Jaimie's predecessor in Glen Cuach — where the reinforced, learned company settled to weighty discussions which ended only when the streaks of dawn began assaulting the little window. They posed one another with their prize posers — the problem of the tinker and the kettle; the tethered ass; the seven grains of wheat; the forty-pound stone smashed in four pieces by an idle fellow's sledge; the eight gallon, five gallon, and three gallon kegs; whether to pronounce *it is* as spelled, or as *Eet ees;* the spelling of the turf-boys' halt-call to his donkey, Phthrough!; the irresistible force meeting the immovable object; and scores of equally fascinating problems.

For the Master many other things combined to make life pleasant. Much joy he got from time to time penning a new 'poem' which lifted him for days to another world. His hunger for the folk-tales, great throughout childhood and boyhood, grew even greater when he was the Master. In scholar-days his spare time was mostly filled with field-labour, but from a Master with a millionaire's income, manual labour couldn't be expected. So, his afternoons and evenings now, and his week-ends, were taken tramping the country and roaming the mountains, garnering more of the stories and absorbing more of the life. His week-ends were his chief joy — when he could hie him straight from school to the far-away, lore-filled glens and mountain-sides — losing himself to the world and living in Heaven till came Monday morning and the return journey to the world and his school.

Some sweet Donegal *cailíni* there were, too, who for him tinged life's cup a rosy red — pleasant, playful, winsome, merry- eyed ones, who liked the young poet and Masther, were by him liked much, and for him often made sweet summer twilights a song. — And a literal song for, to, or of, one of these winsome ones occasionally would he pen — such as —

THE PATHER ACROSS THE MOOR

One harvest evenin' as I took the road from Glenties fair,
I o'ertook a freshlipped cailín of modest mien and air,
So pleasant our discoursin' was, it grieved me, to be sure,
When she said at length 'Good-bye, kind sir, my path's across
  the moor.'

I looked upon her wistfully — her gaze fell on the grass.
It's lonesome walkin' is the moor,' I said, 'mo chailín dheas;
And the path is not so narrow, but there's room for two, I'm sure;
If you don't object I'll take with you the path across the moor?'

'The moon is up, the path is straight,' she answered courteouslie.
And I never do feel lonesome when crossing of Tiree:

160

I thank you very kindly, sir, but to my father's doore
I've always took the path alone,' she said, 'across the moor.'

'That the path's both safe and pleasant for one, I'm sure is true;
But you guess not its delights,' I said, 'when jogged along by
 two.'
'A kind good-bye, pray, gentle sir! My father he is poor,
And I, a humble maid, have never been beyont the moor.'

'You do father wrong,' I said, 'for his is wealth untold,
The king of royal Spain is not so rich, for all his gold.
And, rank and worldly riches for me have little lure —
I'd barter both, with you to walk, henceforth, across the moor.'

I looked into her tender eyes; she blushed and cast them down:
I touched my lips upon her hand; still Nuala did not frown;
I took her hands in both of mine, and prisoned them secure,
While she murmured, 'You may join me on the path across the
moor.'

Ah, then, his years were happy years. The world held no joys that
weren't enclosed by the great circle of the Cruach Ghorm mountains.
Much schoolmastering, a little poetising, and a great deal of glad
wandering, made life rich and full and very desirable.

Only one bar — and that a trivial one — to complete felicity did he
find. The great man of the National Board of Education, the Inspector,
who had the happiness of all Masters in the hollow of his hand, had learned
— as he couldn't help — of the young Master's political heterodoxy —
for which crime however he couldn't directly punish him, through lack of
circumstantial proof. But there are more ways of killing a dog than
choking him with butter: this Inspector, a small, fine, very handsome, and
very anti-Irish man, in proper fulfilment of his duty mightily strove to
harass the boy by petty persecution; and, far more, year after year, denied
him entrance to the Second Class Teachers' Examination, stepping-stone
to First Class. Getting the higher classification would have meant both
moral and material advance for the boy — adding fi'pence (price almost
of a coveted paper-covered book!) each day to his income. But, now, he
must content him on the lowest rung of the ladder — be satisfied to remain
a Third Class teacher till that grand, but, alas, far-off day when he'd get
his pension! Yet, God bless him! the simple lad, forgetting the ladder-foot
and imagining out of existence English-Irish National School Inspectors,
and English-Irish National Boards of Education, blithely went his lilting
way.

NOTES

1   One of his rejoicing neighbours, Tam Stewart, would enthusiastically impress the boy, 'Jaimie, if you were to begin at wan end o' your salary, and the devil at the other, ye could never meet in the middle.'

2   Under the Irish National Education System, as by England established, Irish pupils were then zealously shielded from the contamination of Irish history. Such an objectionable subject was not to be mentioned in an Irish 'National' School.

CHAPTER TWENTY-THREE

The Bocadeen

Rumour of a dorcu[1] having been seen on Cruach-an Airgid came to our schoolmaster's ears. A man crossing the mountain from the Big Glen of Glenties to Glen Ainey had first seen him; then Shemishin O'Gallagher of Cloch-Fionn had glimpse of him disappearing among the rocks of Carn; and, after that, two or three sheep-men on the alts caught a waft of him going over the hip of the hill. The dorcu was in everybody's mouth, and all the country was concerned. Excited by the intelligence, our school-master *bouchal* set out for the hills one March week-end to see what he could see. — And, setting out in search of the dorcu, he discovered, instead, the Bocadeen.

In the upper end of Litirfad, before facing the mountain, the Master sought company — and found Ned Haughie, returned diamond-miner from South Africa, glad to pull on his great mining boots, take down his gun, and join. It was still early when they started up the mountain, headed for the Cruach. There they spent hours tramping, wandering, screening among rocks, firing into caves — but the devil a dorcu did they find. Finally, concluding that those who started the rumour had in reality got glimpse of an extra big broc they set out for home; and on the way dropping into a lone recess of the hills, Cron Ciaran, they came on the habitation of the Bocadeen.

His history, as the Master learnt it, was interesting. His real name was MacDaid. His nickname — and the only name by which he was known — he had got in his far-away young days. He was a child of the mountains, born on them, spending all his life on them, and because as lad he was so agile, climbing and running the hills, bounding from rock to rock, the men who went there after sheep named him the Bocadeen (little goat). There had been four brothers of the MacDaids and one sister — living in a poor cabin their father had put up at the head of a lone little rock-strewn valley pocketed in the hills. By sheep on the mountains they had supported themselves, and a very little bit of cropping on pocket-handkerchief pieces of soil between the rocks. Their life was hard, and constantly they knew hunger, but they were wedded to the sorry spot that was their own.

Ten years before this time, the Marquis, claiming rent for the hut their father had built, and the patches of land they had made on the mountain side, evicted them when they weren't any longer able to pay — were barely able to hold body and soul together. A regiment of English red-coats came[2] — for the evicting of many poor creatures in Glen Ainey

— and under guard of England's army the bailiffs and crow-bar men stamped out the fire on the hearth of the MacDaids, broke down the roof-tree, smashed the door and window, and broke the walls — after flinging the family and their sorry few articles of furniture on the hillside.

Digging from the bogs limbs of the ancient fir-trees there buried, the MacDaids laid these, aslant, to a standing gable of the hut that had been their home, covered the logs with sods, thatched with rushes, and in this lean-to (which was entered by creeping on hands and knees), they lived. All of them were over seventy at the time they were evicted — but were healthy, hardy people. Grief for their home, which they dare not rebuild under pain of prison, and added hardship and hunger, carried away three of the men. Now the Bocadeen, in his nineties, and his aged sister, in the eighties, survived: but when Jaimie and Neddy came to their habitation that day, they could see only the old woman. The Bocadeen, on a bed of rushes within, had been ill for over a year, and could not come out — whilst the visitors could not easily creep inside. Through the hole in the roof that was window and chimney, the deep-wrinkled, cheerful sister told the Bocadeen that strangers were here; and to them he called warm and tender Gaelic greeting from his rushy bed. In spite of the fact that death was expected and prepared for — he had got the Last Rites a week before — his voice was strong and hearty, and filled with pleasure at welcoming strangers to his hills and home. So rejoiced was he at the coming of human beings that he grew voluble both in Gaelic, which was his proper language, and in English, which he had acquired. He wanted to know all about his visitors, their friends and relations. When he learned that one of them was son to Pat, the famous fighter, he put up a cheer from his sick-bed, death-bed. When, furthermore, he learned that his hero Pat's son loved and was searching out the old lore, there was grand gladness in his voice as he shouted, 'Then *cead mile fáilte!* it's a hundred thousand times welcome ye are! There was never a man in the mountains either this side of them, or the other, could tell tale for tale of the *sgeulachta* with me, nor recite with me, verse for verse of the old *laoithe*. Och, it's wish I do that I had a year to live on this bed and you a year to stand there listenin' to me! Such a sack of the old tales I could deliver you, as would bend you to the heather, going home. — Do you know all about Oisin? Do you know about Gol and Fionn? and Conan and Oscar and Diarmuid? Cuchullin, himself, and Conal Cearnach? and all the rest of them? Ach! ach! sure I know them hairoes as if I got up and lay down with them all me life long! There wasn't a deed one of them ever done but was as familiar to me as the grey rocks on the side of Cruachan-Airgid! The Fenian *laoithe* were as near to me as me skin — and with a flake of that same I'd part before I'd lose one of them. — Do you know about the time Oisin went to Tir na'n-Oige? the beautifullest of them all. — Hear to this! just listen to this!'

And, through the hole in the roof he began chanting the Lay of Oisin in the Land of Youth — in ancient Gaelic, now and then interrupting himself, to give English translation.

In very condensed summary, this way went the long, grand poem poured forth through a lean-to roof from the dying man on his damp rushy-bed: On a beautiful May day, when Fionn and his Fianna were hunting, they sat them at noon to rest on the brow of Gleann-na-Smoil whose flower-decked slope eased itself down to the Irish Sea. A genial sun beamed on them, the thrush and the blackbird chanted in the grove, and the lark trilled in the blue sky overhead, while their hounds made music in the covert — and, like Homer listing his ships, Oisin chants the names of all the famed Fenian hounds, Bran, Ceol, and the rest. As Fionn and his lieutenants sit, drinking the beauty of the day, behold a dazzling maiden on a white horse, with retinue of fifty other maidens, rides from under the sea! Up the valley they come, toward the wondering Fionn. The radiantly beauteous one who leads, announces to Fionn that she is the Queen of Tir na'n Og, and that, desiring a mortal husband, she has come to choose him in Eirinn, the land of brave men. And since among all of Eirinn's brave ones the Fianna are bravest, and handsomest as well, to them she has come — and to him, Fionn, their leader and chief — that he may let her choose among his men. But Fionn's men are fighting men, and all of them he needs. However, of his many sons, one of them, Oisin, is a poet, and she may have him.

Oisin, bidding farewell to his comrades, is mounted on a steed and rides off with the Queen to her land of enchantment. The charms of this magic land where the old become young, and the young grow never old — where spring and summer with autumn go hand in hand, and are eternal — its songbirds, of beauty never known on earth, making music such as never on earth was heard — its woods and waterfalls, its hills and dales and shadowy lakes, its loveliness, surpassing the power of the poet to describe — the eternal beauty reigning here — is chanted in intoxicatng strain, and the happiness unending, unabating, of those whose blessed lot is cast in this enchanted land. And all was Oisin's. (And oh! the richness of feeling, the ring of joy and glow of soul with which the dying man from his damp rushy-bed, through hole in the sod-roof, sang the beauties of that beauteous land!)

Then, a sequel: Oisin, ere he had been twenty-four hours (as it seemed) in this magic land, fell homesick — for Ireland and for his comrades — and begged his Queen to let him return for one hour's visit with his land and his people. His hunger would not be allayed, till at length, sore against her wish, she had to consent to his going. On an enchanted white steed she mounted him, with warning that while he remained in Ireland he must not touch earth — which faithfully he promised. And he promised to return, soon, satisfied.

When Oisin, on his magic steed, emerged in Ireland, he rode forward till he met a man from whom he sought news of his comrades — 'Where shall I find the Fenians?' (For, living in encampment, they constantly moved from place to place over Ireland.) This man, looking up in wonder at the mounted stranger, exclaimed, 'The Fenians? The Fenians? I never heard of any such.' Oisin, angered to meet a creature who had never heard of the bravest, most undaunted, fighters Ireland had ever known, spurred his horse and rode past him — almost over him. Meeting a second man, he would enquire again for the Fenians. This man looked at the rider in wonder and said, 'The Fenians? The Fenians? Who are the Fenians?' Contemptuously waving this one out of his way, Oisin spurred on again. Meeting next, an old, old, bent, grey-bearded man hobbling on two sticks, Oisin drew rein, and putting his hand on the old man's shoulder, asked, 'Can you tell me where I'll find the Fenians?' The old man, throwing back his head, looked at his questioner, the radiant youth on horse-back, and exclaimed, 'The Fenians! The Fenians — Yes — I remember! — My father told me how his father told him that his father before that used to relate wonderful tales of a wonderful band of men, the Fenians, who lived in Ireland three hundred years ago!'

The twenty-four hours Oisin thought he had passed in Tir na'n Og measured three hundred years of earthly time! And he had returned to a land peopled by little men, who had let perish from memory the name and the fame of the noblest band of heroes earth had ever known! In intense disgust he wheeled his horse — now to speed him back to Tir na'n Og and his beauteous Queen, and put from memory evermore a land that had proved itself unworthy of a man's regard.

As he rode, he saw, on a hillside where a house was about to be built, sixteen of the creatures who now peopled Erin struggling to push into the foundation-pit a large stone. Oisin, riding up, waved them aside and said, 'O puny ones! let a man show you what a man could do in Ireland three hundred years ago, when the gallant Fenians walked your hills.' Bending low in his saddle, he put to the rock one hand to push it to its place — but with the strain the saddle-girth broke, and he fell to earth — and, to the amazement of those who looked on, the radiantly beautiful youth who had spoken to them from the saddle was now a wrinkled, weazened, old, grey man!

When they came to find that this was one of the pagans of old time, come back to Ireland from the land of enchantment, they sent for Patrick — a man who had recently brought to the land a new faith, and converted to it all of Ireland's people. And Patrick came hurrying to convert and baptise him. But the holy man found that it had been easier to convince and convert all Ireland, than it was this former one returned. Gladly did

166

Oisin listen to argument, but hard it was to understand, or believe, that Patrick's Chief, above in the skies, whom he was asked to bow to and worship, could be worthier or nobler or braver or more powerful, than the great Chief, Fionn, leader of the Fenians. Long were the arguments, each of them chanting the merits and the powers of his own chief — till almost Patrick despaired of converting this stubborn pagan.

But he succeeded at length: and baptised Oisin. This, his greatest victory since setting foot in Ireland, the Saint resolved to mark by some signal miracle. And what could be worthier or more appropriate than releasing from hell those whom his convert loved most, his kin and comrades, the Fenians? — thence condemned because they had not known the true God. And what could be grander than to make the new convert the instrument of their release!

So, saying, 'Now, Oisin, I shall show you the place of torment that through your baptising you have escaped,' he opened that place to Oisin's vision and let him see his comrades there confined — but fighting, as on earth had been their trade. They were leagued against the devils, and, led by the most powerful of their number, Oisin's old comrade Gol MacMorna who wrought destruction on the demon host with a great flail. Following Gol's terrific onslaught, Oisin saw, the Fenians prevailed over the devils, beating them back, back, back, till, having forced them into hell's last corner, they were on the verge of victory complete — but, alas! at the critical moment the tug (leather hinge binding the hand-staff to the soople) of Gol's flail gave way! The conquering weapon gone useless, the devils, taking heart, rallied and threw back the Fenian host — back, back and back, until they had driven them to hell's opposite corner — and defeat — almost! But Oisin, to his joy, now saw Gol, a new tug on his flail, take the lead again, and turn the tide. But alas! on victory's verge again the cursed leather gave way and the tide again ebbed for his friends — who were once more only saved from annihilation by Gol's having fitted to his flail still another tug.

When he considered that Oisin was properly impressed by his comrades' suffering, and the moment had come for working the miracle, Patrick said, 'Oisin, to mark your conversion, I ask you to name the wish dearest to your heart, and through me God will grant it.' Oisin's face lighted with joy. — 'Then, Patrick, ask your great Chief for one hour only to let Gol MacMorna have an iron tug to his flail!'

And now the enjoyment and triumph that rang in the voice coming through the hole in the roof, must have measurably approached Oisin's anticipative joy.

A few months later, the Master heard of the Bocadeen's exchanging his damp, rushy-bed under the lean-to in Cron Ciaran for a fitter one in

Heaven. And at his coming there, surely a gathering of mingled saints, sinners, and arch-angels crowded him, seeking to drink from his lips the honey-store of Oisin's lays and Ireland's legends, whereof they had so much, and often, heard — and which, to Ireland's impoverishing and Heaven's enriching, the Bocadeen carried away with him from the hills of Donegal.

NOTES

1 A fabled, or half-fabled, animal, the dorcu — Irish equivalent of the unicorn — was said to have lived in the Irish forests centuries ago. In the Master's day many of the old people believed that it still haunted the hills; and now and again reports flew round of someone encountering him.

2 The boy himself had seen them come. The eviction procedure, in every such case, was as here described.

CHAPTER TWENTY-FOUR

The Matching of Billy MacCailin

Matchmaking was one of a Master's duties, by custom established — helping a man to ask the wife — which meant, eventually, asking the wife for him. A Master's aid in wife-getting was worth half a fortune. His very company to a would-be groom entering the home of eligible girls meant that a lucky one of the girls was already half-married. Not only did his companionship on such occasion add another hundred pound to the man's worldly worth, but it made it more than embarrassing for the girl's father and mother to say No to the proposal. They often yielded to the Master's intercession sooner than put a slight on the intercessor: because to a Master, from all the world was due reverence and respect the highest.

Matchmaking the boy had known well, even in his childhood — when it was more general than now. Often, as child and lad, seated, on a night, by the fireside of one or other home that boasted marriageable girls, he had witnessed the excitement when two strangers or half-strangers — not usual ramblers there — walked in, dressed in Sunday clothes, with a bottle of whiskey sticking out of the pocket of the older, more collected, of the pair. — And, as an unheeded child, he sat on, listened to the preliminary sparring, and then the listing of assets, the fortune-bargaining, and final settlement and jollification. Several times, too, it had been a treat to him to follow in a fair the many-daughtered Shusie MacCalliog, as she collected marriageable boys, got a few friends as helpers, headed the whole party to a room in Larry Gillespie's public house, and there set about matching on the captured boys a couple of her daughters whom she considered ready for the road. For during a good span of our *gasúr's* young years Shusie's matching of her girls had been an attractive feature of every fair.[1]

It was of an evening on the hinges of Lent that Billy MacCailin called to our Master, with request that he'd help him to ask the wife. He was a *rallianach* of a fellow—big, lumpy, untidy, uncultivated, loud-voiced, and with a shock of straggly red hair like a thatch-roof after an October hurricane. Billy owned a farm half-way to the mountains, and having nobody to help him wrastle with it, was usually stuck both ends in the earth from June to January and round the year again. He was as heavy-minded as he was heavy-heeled — hadn't any of the country-boys' airiness, never tripped the hills to a spree nor had time to do so. He had got enough schooling to know that book-learning was beyond him and had best be left to idle-minded ones. Not but he respected learning in cases where — as in the Master's — it earned a man a living without bending his back. Billy, for all his lumpiness, was good-hearted and well-intentioned — not a bad bone in the body of him.

'Masther,' he said, when he had settled himself by the Master's fireside, 'I'm thinkin' of takin' on a wife.'

'Maybe the thought's a good one,' the Master answered him 'and maybe it isn't. — Aren't you leading a peaceful life as you are? — and for five-and-forty years back?' Billy was no chicken.

'I am. — But bekase I've come to believe the old sayin' that contintion is better than solitude, I've made up my mind to marry.'

'Oh! — Do I know her?'

'I misdoubt me if you do. — I don't know her meself.—

It's why 've come to you — to ask two favours. — I want you to oblige me with the loan of your Sunday throusers — these that I'm in aren't daicent enough to ask the wife with. — Then I want you to come with me and do the askin'.'

'I'll lend you the trousers and put a prayer on them that they may win the wife for you. But I'd be obliged if you didn't ask me on such an errand.'

'Are ye not me own blood-cousin?'

'I suppose I am — unfortunately.'

'My great grandmother and your grandfather were own brother and sister, weren't they? And doesn't that leave us second-and-third cousins?'

'But, Billy, *a thaisge*, why don't you take with you one of your own comrades and neighbours?'

'The divil a trust one o' them blaguards I'd do. They'd come a Mattha MacCabe over me and you're too daicent to do that.'[2]

There was no refusing Billy. The Master got him into his own other pair of trousers, which, as Billy was both very big and very tall, were too tight and too short for him. But the delighted wearer pronounced, 'They're just dandy. And I'd like to see the woman could say No to me, in them.'

Billy was setting about the asking of a wife with the same hap-hazardness that he farmed — and his neighbours and friends said that was 'by bull force and no brain.' Billy said, 'The dark's only droppin', and as we have a long night afore us, and can cover a deal of ground afore mornin', it will be mighty *dauny* work on our part, if we can't collect a wife from some house or other between here and the Fall of Sru-Aill, ere the morrow's sun sees us.'

'But you must have some particular woman or other in your eye?'

'I have twenty — and if I only get the worst of them, she'll maybe be double as good a woman as I desarve. — But I'll marry divil a one o' them that 'ill not bring her worth with her.'

'You want to marry the money, Billy, and bid the wife to the weddin'. — But you aren't going to ask twenty women?'

'Faith, no! Maybe it's tired I'll get afore I ask two. And maybe I'll have luck the first shot. — There's little Bridget Dunnegan of Cluanboran, a likely *cailín*, a bit young maybe, but snug-built and able to hold her own on any farm. She's of daicent family, moreover, and I'll be lucky if I get her. — Let us try for her first, in God's name.' He was changing into the Master's coat-pocket, from his own, the necessary bottle of whiskey.

They set out for Cluanboran — for Bartley Dunnegan's there. Because Billy had had no help *footering* with his farm, and wrestling with cattle, he had been 'too throng' ever to go courting. Going and coming from mass, howsoever, he had had his eyes open, and among many likely ones favoured little Bridget. The Master objected that Bridget was too fine and soft for him and his mountainy farm; but Billy pointed out that on his place the softest and finest girl would soon roughen and harden. 'They say,' he commented, 'that even the consaitedest people will get inured to hell, if you give them time.'

'But Bridget won't go to your hell to try the inuring.'

And the Master was right.

Bridget's house was as neat and warm as a bird's nest—in every way the opposite of what Billy's was sure to be. Bridget, who was both young and winsome, stopped tidying the hearth to give the visitors greeting. Her father and mother, seated one in each chimney corner, were much respected people. The Master quickly saw for himself that their visit was wasted. But he must now go through with the form. So unlikely for Bridget was Billy as a courtier that it was plain no one of the inmates suspected the visit's object till, after several minutes casual conversation, the Master pulled the whiskey-bottle from his pocket and asked Bridget for a cup. Then it was all out. The old couple coughed, and Bridget, after handing over a cup whose side pictured a boy and a girl standing among willows, significantly said that she must finish the cows' milking, took down a tin-pandy from a nail on the wall, and, picking up a three-legged stool, went to the byre. The Master's elbow jundied Billy in the ribs, signifying, 'Don't let her go — Engage her in conversation.' — But sign-language was too recondite for bucolic Billy, who just looked about him bewildered.

If there had been in the Master's mind the merest doubt about their mission being a failure, it was gone like a puff when Sally Dunnegan, instead of drinking down the thimbleful he handed to her, just touched her lips to it for good manners, saying, 'Here's to your good healths, gentlemen!' — and passed it across the fire to Bartley, who, wishing the ramblers health also, swallowed half a spoonful, and gave it back. As the Master was now bound to go on if the gallows was at the end, he filled a full glass — for Billy and he, drinking to the household's health, tossed it off like a teaspoonful. He then treated himself to the smallest sip that

171

politeness called for — and began telling their business, to have the hanging quick done with. When he finished there was the kind of a pause that stuck pins in him. At length Bartley coughed — which was saying to the wife, 'You tell them.' Sally coughed back, signifying, 'just undertakke it yourself, Bartley.' But Bartley would persevere, to put the burden on the woman. — 'You have heard the gintleman, Sally. — What have you to say?'

'Oh, just whatever you have to say yourself, Bartley.'

Bartley coughed, with anger at the woman. 'Well don't you think, Sally, that our Bridget is young?'

''Tis the identical thing I was thinkin',' Sally concurred.

'Ay, that's so,' confirmed Bartley. — And then, 'Gintlemen, we're everlastin' obliged to yous for the honour ye do us — highly obliged to Billy for the particular compliment he pays our Bridget as well as ourselves; and if she had only a couple more years on her back, we wouldn't be asking the Lord to send her a braver man, or us a son-in-law we'd be prouder of. — And for you, Masther, we crave your pardon for refusin' any request in the worl' you'd make. It's mortal awk'ard to both Sally and meself to say No to you, and we wouldn't if we could. Teetotally again' our will, we just feel that we have to, and we hope you'li overlook our bad manners, and feel certain there's no slight intended.'

'Bartley and Sally are correct,' Billy commented when they had left Dunnegan's behind. — 'Bridget I now see isn't the girl for me. I noticed on a near view that she's entirely too tindher. — 'Tis a seasoned one me and my place necessitate.'

He proposed, then, two seasoned ones who lived in adjoining townlands nearer the mountain. Both of them, it is true, had forgotten when they cut their wisdom teeth, but they were what he called 'a hardy scantlin' that could not be harmed by the toughness of his townland. 'They're well foundationed, and a creel don't break the back of either of them. Moreover, rumours give the two o' them cattle as well as cash.'

The Master tossed a penny to find which of the two should be offered the honour. Cassie McCadden was the fortunate one. 'But we can't offend the family with a broken bottle of whiskey,' objected the Master.

'I'll show you,' said Billy, 'how to hold it that no one 'ill be any the wiser.' And he did so. However, coming up the boreen that led to the McCaddens' door, they met a *gasúr* coming from it who was able to inform them that both Cassie and her parents were at home. 'But,' he added, 'there's two men just come in with a bottle of whiskey — and old Molshie told me I could be runnin' home with meself.'

Since some more fortunate fellow had got ahead of them to Cassie there was nothing for it, now, but try for the girl who had lost the toss. She was Ellen Mary Branigan and lived a mile off. She was on the frosty side of forty — but had ten head of cattle of her own, if rumours didn't lie.

The Master didn't relish going to ask Ellen Mary. Her people were cross, and a sarcastic people. Besides, he didn't like one bone in Ellen Mary's body, least of all her tongue. But she was hardy all right, sound and strong, with no risk of breaking in the middle (as anyone would say who saw her), and fit in a field as a man — which suited Billy. So, he'd be glad to try to get her for him.

They went to Condy Brannigan's — Condy was the father's name. There was a welcome and twenty before them there. When it came to the Master's disclosing of the bottle — held in the skillful way Billy had coached him —Ellen Mary, after handing him the requested cup, did not take herself out of the house as had done the modest Bridget, but bestirred herself to household duties in room and kitchen — always within earshot — like the wise one she was. Both Condy and his wife, Anne, did justice to their drinks — a good sign. The Master wished Ellen Mary were as favourable — but he sensed otherwise.

He said, 'We're on an errand here tonight.'

'Arrand or no arrand,' answered Condy Brannigan, 'both of ye are hearty welcome.'

'That they are,' clerked Anne.

'My friend Billy, here, has taken the notion on him to marry a wife.'

'Neither blame nor shame to him,' encouraged Condy.—'There were men in the world afore him that took the like notion and I'm misdoubtin' there'll be ones after him the same way.'

'And looking around him to pick a worthy one, he asked me if I'd come with him to your house, Condy Brannigan.'

'Well, I'm sure, anyhow, we're forever obliged for the compliment.'

'Of all girls in the parish he considers your Ellen Mary a fine, bouncing, sensible girl, and the makings of a good wife.'

'Well, maybe so, maybe so. — Anyway it isn't for us, her own father and mother, to go slighting her.'

'No, we wouldn't slight our own daughter,' Anne clerked.

Ellen Mary was now confining herself to the room and making great rattling at furniture — pointed proof to them in the kitchen that she was as innocent as a tom-tit of what was transacting here.

'So, we've come here tonight to ask if you'd let us have Ellen Mary?'

'Humph!' said Condy, and 'Humph!' echoed Anne.

They were noncommittal — wouldn't object to hearing more.

'My friend Billy's house and farm will be a good sittin' down for any woman.'

'What has he exactly?' asked Condy.

'What way is on him?' Anne translated the query.

'Well, he has a good thirty acres of land to begin with.'

'I don't care,' interposed Condy, 'if it's thirty thousand. — What I want to know is, how much of it's *land* — able to support man and baste — and how much is feedin' ground for snipes?' Condy worthy father of a worthy daughter, wouldn't be driven in blinkers.

The Master had to confess that the real land was less than a third of the whole; but, Billy reared and sold more cattle off his ten good acres than many another did off twice as much. He counted Billy's stock — two milkcows and a strapper, two two-year- olds and three year-olds, two pigs, with hens and ducks and geese *go leor* — and he was in nobody's books, but had in the stocking seventy pounds of dry cash. 'And now, friends Condy and Anne, I'll make bold to ask you what you can match that with, on Ellen Mary?'

'Beggin' your pardon,' said Condy, giving the demand the go-by — 'but in the first place, if we consent to give him our Ellen Mary, what work would he be expectin' of her?'

So far, so good. The Master was relieved to find the outlook promising. — 'There Billy,' he said, 'speak up for yourself.'

But the Master soon could bite his tongue for letting Billy into the business, when he heard the list of requirements in field work that fellow expected of a wife. He had made himself such a slave to work that he couldn't conceive of any sensible body ever objecting to work while he — or she — was able to stand up. Condy coughed now and again as Billy unfolded his list; and Anne coughed a couple of times. The Master got into Billy's ribs several unseen nudges — but he might as well have been nudging the Stannin' Stone of Drimbith. The Master's heart sank.

'Aisy, aisy,' said Condy, at length. 'Aisy, me friend. Don't ye think ye may be makin' a mistake, and that it isn't a wife you want at all, at all?'

'What do you mean?' asked Billy.

'I mean,' said Condy, drily, 'that I believe it's a good, excepshally strong donkey you're needin'. But we'll hear what Ellen Mary says. — Ellen Mary!' he called.

Ellen Mary came down from the room with the innocence on her face of a fox's grandfather. 'Ellen Mary, these gintlemen are lookin' for a wife for Billy here, and they're doin' you the honour of asking us for yourself. What do you think?'

'Aren't the gintlemen too kind, to do me the honour! But, if it isn't impident o' me, may I ask if Billy's farm is that haggly- straggly stripe of granite rocks and heather that runs up and down the hill of Tullin-na-Tha — to the clouds and back?'

'In troth, that same is Billy's farm,' replied her father.

'And what stock does he starve on it?' the sharp one asked next. Her father enumerated the stock for her. 'Ach!' she commented. And then, 'And what slavery would he be expectin' of me?' As if she hadn't heard and well noted every word of Billy's listing.

As Billy balked at repeating the list of duties, her father enumerated them. There was an awkward pause, after and her father, to relieve it said, 'I told him, meself the first thing he should do after the weddin' — *in case he got any woman to take him* — was to trot the wife to the forge and have her shod. — But I likewise advised that a *rale* donkey would be convenienter for him.'

'And what did the donkeys ever do to you, father?'

It was getting too awkward for the Master. He rose up, saying, 'Well, I suppose Ellen Mary isn't intended for our friend Billy, and there's no use in our delaying.'

'Masther,' Ellen Mary said, 'I'm mighty obliged to you for the honour you do me — and to Billy likewise — I'm mighty obliged to yous both — but I think it'll do me no damage to take another saison out o' meself.'

Poor, uncultivated Billy, getting up some ill-timed spunk here, remarked as he, too, arose, 'Och the divil a borsel o' damage, Ellen Mary, will a year more or less do ye, *now*' — putting just enough stress on the *now* to make sure it would get through a well-seasoned skin.

The clever Ellen Mary, not pretending to notice the emphasis, went on, mild as mare's milk, 'Maybe Billy, you'd better take me father's advice and do with a donkey this saison. A good donkey will be handier and cheaper, and just as aisy fed as a wife — and will maybe leave ye more time for makin' your soul which it's high time ye were thinkin' of, instead of meditatin' a wife.'

A battle of wits between the pair was only stopped by the Master on one side and Ellen Mary's father and mother on the other stepping in to trade compliments — so that the pair of men carried from Condy Brannigan's door a load of thanks and apologies.

'I didn't miss her, Master, did I?' queried Billy. 'Did you notice the shot I give her?'

'If it was shots that were being exchanged,' said the nettled Master, 'I'm afraid I'd now be walking with a corpse. — Where do we go next?'

Said Billy, 'The night's young yet. With God's help we'll try another throw. A likely girl is Nuala Gillespie of Augherbeg, and if you aren't yet tired askin' women, I want you to come with me and ask her. — If we fail again this time, I swear on the Book I'll never marry, but buy an ass as Condy advises.'

The Master suggested he might do like Charlie Dearg who long ago kept a fine shop in the Kelderry. Made mad by the refusal of the woman he wanted, he swore he'd marry the first *cailín* came into his shop in the morning. And, when, next day, a simple country girl, with shawl over her head and a basket of eggs on her arm, walked in, she was dumbfounded by a proposal from Charlie. But when she collected herself, she whispered him Yes. They raised the finest family in the country-side, and were happier than anything told about in the story books. But Billy wouldn't have this. It was now Nuala Gillespie or the donkey. For Nuala's they headed, after giving a *gasúr* tuppence for himself to run to Molshie Brennan's shebeen and bring them a fresh bottle of whiskey.

There was welcome before them at Nuala's. She was a practical girl — but far from being as hard as Ellen Mary. She had a practical father and mother likewise. Billy was acceptable to the parents — after the Master had listed his assets, and that Billy himself had, now more wisely than before, stated his modest requirements in a wife.

But the Master had to battle much — driven on by continuous and vigorous pressure from Billy's knee and foot — to coax Nuala's father and mother to fortune her with a cow, a calf, and fifteen pounds, more than they at first proposed. He failed to get, in addition, a two-year-old bullock that Billy's knee kept insisting on. But when, about the bullock, they proved themselves as unshakable as the Rock of Carn, Billy, in a gallant outburst of generosity, exclaimed, 'To hell with the bullock, Masther! — Do you think I'd give the go-by to a good girl like Nuala for sake of a two-year-owld?'

The bargaining for the fortune was, to be sure, done after Nuala had been called in and hesitatingly yielded her consent — after first generously, but vainly, suggesting that her younger sister, Annie, might better fit Billy. Annie was not there to ask: but her father gave an emphatic, No.! he couldn't see his family brocked.[3]

The match was made, the wedding day settled, everyhing fixed. And lo, on the second night after, Nuala made a runaway with a boy of her liking! But she kindly sent a message to Billy asking him to the Runaway — and holding out the inducement that Annie, 'a double better girl than meself, any day,' would be there, — and she and he could match.

Her parents came for Nuala and her boy, before morning — to bring them home. There they found Billy and Annie courting. At their home, then, two matches that satisfied all parties concerned were fixed up before day broke. It was a great celebration. At the feast, the Master was the most honoured man.[4]

NOTES

1 Because matchmaking was common then, it must not be thought that there were no love-marriages. Far from it. But even when a bouchal had already wooed and won his cailín, he still had to win her father and mother. With his friend and intercessor — or, sometimes, his own father and mother — he must work out the business end of the matter with her parents — after 'asking' the daughter of them.

Were the young people in love, and the match or setlement not pleasing to the girl's

176

parents, the solution maybe a Runaway. Secretly arranged between the lovers, the Runaway would be held at the house of a relative who favoured the match. The boy with his friend, the girl with her friend, met after night and 'ran away' to the rendezvous. The news of the Runaway went round the country like wildfire, the country rallied to the romantic ones, bringing a fiddler with it; and dancing, singing, and merry-making — with the lovers the centre of all — filled the night till day broke. Word of the Runaway was sent at midnight to the objecting parents — who, if they now relented, hastened to the rendezvous, and invite to their home the boy and girl and all the company. Headed by the fiddler, diddling his elbow for all it was worth, the joyful party danced and sang its way over the hills to the home of the bride-to-be, there played and danced till morning — and were invited to come again for a merry wedding a week or a fortnight later.

But if, after the summons had come to them, father and mother, still unrelenting, glumly kept their seats by their own fireside, then in case the boy was enough in love with the girl to take her without dowry, the marriage was arranged for an early day, the girl remaining with relatives meanwhile. But in case the boy's parents also objected to the match, and that consequently he had 'no way on him' to support a wife, the matter had to be suspended or dropped. Which was ill for the girl — for if a Runaway did not end in marriage the girl was socially compromised, and cheapened in the marriage market. Spirited young men, who, before, would have been delighted to wed her, would now hesitate to pay her serious court.

Almost, but not quite, extinct in the boy's early days, was the professional matchmaker — usually a woman of very small possessions, or a wandering beggarwoman or beggarman. These rovers, travelling wide, had a more extensive field of observation and selection than the match-maker of fixed abode — and knew the details, means, and circumstances, of every family in two baronies. At the request of either a practical, or mercenary, mother of a marriagable girl or boy, the far-wandering bacach searched out a desirable mate of proper social standing and circumstances. Good matches in one part of his territory he advertised in other parts — and accepted proposals. Only preliminary negotiations were his to carry on — enough to convince two families that it was worth while coming together for detailed discussion. Some of the better-off and harder-headed ones in our boy's territory of Glen Ainey, where soil and people were poor, coveted mates for their children from the rich barony of Tyrugh beyond the Bay, where more money went with the marrying one. But Glen Ainey people in general — those not maritally connected with Tyrugh, nor aspiring to be — had contempt for the people of the richer territory, who, they held, were slaves to outward show. And there grew up in Glen Ainey and became common on its people's lips, the jibe, 'Tyrugh, the white house and the yalla blanket!'

In that time, besides Tyrugh another foreign source of matrimonial supply, for Glen Ainey (as indeed, for hundreds of territories), was Loug Dearg, St.Patrick's Purgatory — a lone loch in the loneliest mountains of Donegal — to whose Holy Isle went on pilgrimage all good people from over the North of Ireland (not to mention many from Ireland's other three-quarters, and Irish from Scotland, England, America, and Australia). On Holy island during their three-day pilgrimage, young men from one county met and made acquaintance of young women from another county — acquaintance that often led to marriage. 'Lough Dearg matches,' as they were called, were noted throughout Donegal. Many a time the lad listened to Billy Martin, who had got his County Armagh wife out of Lough Dearg, in her presence exclaim, with rueful voice but twinkling eye — 'Ach, sure what could I expect? I got her doin' my pinance, and sure it's doin' my pinance I still am!'

Most wives were asked, most matches made, in the week before Lent, especially in the few days immediately preceding it. And, Lent's first Saturday — first Lenten market of Donegal village — was known as Puss Saturday: for it was held that, in the market that day, you could tell at a glance every girl of marriageable age who still remained unmarried — by the puss she carried on her lips

2   Mattha MacCabe was now an old man, but two generations before, when he was a likely young fellow, a comrade chose him for the wife — asking. — When Mattha discovered the

177

intended wife to be not only a winsome girl in her own right, but blessed with a fine fortune, he proceeded to put in one word for his friend and two for himself — with the result that he got himself matched and married on the woman whom he went to woo for his friend.

3   When one sits down to eat from a pot of stirabout it is good form to take it 'out of a face' — working one's way across the pot spoonful by spoonful in an orderly way. An unmannerly fellow, however, is as like as not to broc the pot, digging here, there, everywhere. When it comes to matching and marrying, good fathers and mothers don't like even the best man in the world to broc their family!

4   Annie, a fine girl — really much better than Nuala — made Billy a remarkable wife. Before many years went over their heads she had him a much less uncultivated clown, more human and Christian-like, tidier, smarter — and gathering some enjoyment from the world he had been slaving his way through.

CHAPTER TWENTY-FIVE

Breaking into Literature

The boy was now well settled for life as a school-master — and in it as happy as the thrush in the bush. Except, of course, for the far-too-far-offness of that sixty-fifth birthday. And the happiness of school-mastering, as shown, was now and then heightened by the creation of a new 'poem.'

But he was to fare farther and dig deeper in literary fields. A new county-paper just started, it was, that led his footsteps on. Donegal had had no paper of its own, and for news looked to *The Derry Journal*. But now a clever little newspaper man of Donegal blood in Glasgow, Eoin MacAdam, came to Belashanny and started *The Donegal Vindicator*. Searching out literary talent and hearing that the young Master of Glen Ainey was a bit of a writer and bit of a poet, MacAdam journeyed to him, and asked his help to make the Vindicator a success — 'And I'll publish to the world all the poems you make.'

It was an alluring opportunity — only — as the Master put the objection to MacAdam — 'I haven't any spare money.'

'That's all right, I never charge for printing good poetry.'

Very grateful, the young Master opened his school-desk and gave him a piece he had just written — on Shan the Proud — the great O'Neill, who was the scourge of Elizabeth.[1] The man read it there and then, and grew so flatteringly enthuastic over it that the boy took him home and counted out to the amazed, almost overcome, man thirteen other pieces.

As these pieces appeared from week to week — over *a nom de plume* — the young Master's pride and happiness grew — and he felt stimulated not only to further poem — distilling, but trying his hand at prose, also. Reflecting on the glamour and the humour of the fairs that used to be, the boy wrote and sent to Eoin MacAdam his first prose sketch, An Old Irish Fair. When the next *Vindicator* arived, his joy was large to find a full column given to, not the printing of the piece, but its announcing!

'LOOK OUT! LOOK OUT! LOOK OUT!' was printed in letters an inch high a full line to each of the three. And then 'COMING! COMING! COMING!' in three full lines also.

'SEE NEXT WEEK'S VINDICATOR'

It besought its readers to make haste to the nearest newsagent, and place their orders — because on next week would be printed the extra-super-attraction of all the super attractions which *The Donegal Vindicator* ever did or ever would present to the public it loved — 'an article replete

179

with humour, charm, literary grace and excellence, the first prose effort of the already- renowned poet, 'Mac of Glen Ainey,' who has enshrined himself in the hearts of *Vindicator* readers the world over, and whose patriotic poems are stirring the souls of Irishmen from the Giants' Causeway to the Cove o' Cork' (The paper circulated 287 copies — all in the southwest of Donegal] 'the *Vindicator's* own poet laureate! Ireland's only poet! The justice famed Mac of Glen Ainey!'

Naturally, after that, the Master gave most of his spare time to writing for the *Vindicator* — verses, sketches, reports of big happenings that happened around Donegal Bay, reports of still bigger happenings that never happened around Donegal Bay — or elsewhere. Each week for three years he contributed from one to five columns of all things imaginable, and some things unimaginable — and at the end of that time was amazed and made happy by a money order for ten shillings from a grateful editor. It was accompanied by a letter of heartiest thanks for the work Jaimie had done in putting *The Donegal Vindicator* on its feet. The frivolous may laugh at the recompense, but that ten-shilling honorarium for three years' work meant more to the lad than cheques for one hundred times that amount paid him in later years for work done in one day.

With the thanks and payment came two bits of advice: one, 'Write a couple of stories and send them to America, to a paper called the *New York Sun*. If it takes them it will pay you five dollars apiece' — the other, 'Collect your poems and publish them in a book. There isn't a reader of the *Vindicator* who won't go without his breakfast to buy it — and every last one of them will nag his neighbours to do likewise.'

Quickly Jaimie wrote two little Irish snatches and sent them to the New York paper — whose editor returned them with thanks. With enthusiasm unslacked he gathered his verses, and, under the title Shuiler[2] from Heathy Hills had them printed in a slim, green-paper-covered shilling volume by gallant Tom Irvine in his printing-house on Derry Walls. And through the enthusiastic aid of *Vidicator* readers in Donegal, and schoolmaster admirers in other parts of Ireland, he sold, in three months' time, the full issue of twelve hundred copies! Overnight, not only had he become a wealthy man — twenty pounds clear profit in his purse but likewise a famous book-author!

Now a letter from an admirer in Fermanagh told the Master that a Dublin paper called the *Weekly Irish Times*, about to bring out a Midsummer Number, was offering valuable prizes for (a) the best poem submitted, (b) the best fiction story, and (c) the best description of a ride on an Irish jaunting-car — 'You'll win one of these prizes if you try.'

His verses were, he knew, too Irish for the anti-Irish *Times*; stories he could not write, never had written; but the jaunting-car article appealed to him, remembering a funny and eventful, long car-drive that he had had the summer before in the Fermanagh and Cavan country. For this particular contest was offered as prize, 'A Week at Rostrevor with Railway and Hotel Expenses Paid.' The lad wrote his article, bristling with humorous incident, and sent it with a prayer to Dublin. After four impatient weeks the Summer Number of the *Weekly Irish Times* arrived with him one bright morning as he was stepping out for school. Opening the paper with trepidation, he beheld — on its very front page!—

> *The Prize for the best sketch of*
> *A RIDE ON AN IRISH JAUNTING-CAR*
> *Is awarded to*
> *'Mac of Glen Ainey'*
> *Knockagar, Glen Ainey,*
> *Co Donegal.*

And there too was the prize article itself — spread over the front page of one of Dublin's leading papers! He wrote the editor: 'If, instead of wasting good money on railway companies and grand hotels, you will be so kind as to send me a cheque for the amount you would expend on me, I'll make it go farther and fetch me more fun.' And by return of post he had a cheque for four guineas — prize beyond dream!

Now, he burned to burst into the writing field. He was advised that it was fiction the publications wanted. He had just heard in the hills a good tale of a poteen-maker out-witting the peelers. He turned this tale over and over in his mind, amending it, strengthening it, rounding it out. After school, and dinner, he sat him down in the family circle, in the chimney-corner with a copy-book on his knee, wrote out, and finished, far in the night, his first story, Dinny Manachan's Last Keg — and next day sent it off to one of the two leading penny story-papers in Dublin, *The Irish Emerald*. Within the week came a letter from the editor who was to prove a truly good friend to the boy — with cheque for a guinea. — 'I am paying you the very highest I give even to a well-known author, so pleased am I with your story which is unlike anything else the *Emerald* has ever got. If you can send me others like it, I may be able to print one a month.'

The jubilant lad sat down in the chimney corner the very next night, and wrote, complete, another merry story — sent it off, and drew another warm letter and guinea cheque. Then a third story — which quickly brought its cheque, likewise. 'Now I'm provided for three or four months' wrote the kind *Emerald* editor, evidently afraid that the mill was going to grind too fast for him.

The other weekly story-paper of Ireland was *The Shamrock*. The boy would try it. He selected a character, Corney Higarty, a long dead, old

181

pensioner who had fought through the Peninsular War, and, who, nightly around his Knockagar fireside, would hold a houseful of the neighbours spellbound over his glorious deeds and hair-breadth 'scapes. A story of Corney, the Master now put in a copy-book and launched at the *Shamrock*. The editor answered, 'This is a capital yarn that *Shamrock* readers will love. If you can do me seven or eight more, about Corney Higarty, and as funny as this one, I'll pay you ten shillings apiece.'

It happened that just then Glen Cuach School needed to be closed for repairs. That very day he shut the school, and gave the day's remainder to imagining Corney Higrty incidents, feats, adventures—in the Peninsular War. The Englishman Wellington couldn't conduct the campaign without him; and Buonaparte — Boney, as he was affectionately known in Knockagar — would, but for Corney, have overswept Spain. More than once he saved Wellington from the results of his own stupidity, extricated him from inextricable positions wherein his eternal blundering had landed him, and, after, led him and his army to victory. Boney, whom Corney walloped in single combat in view of both armies, hated the heroic Irishman like the devil hates holy water, and offered ten thousand pounds for his head. Spanish heiresses fell head-over-heels in love with the undaunted hero, and oftentimes he had to fight duels with too-persistent fathers, just to keep their heiresses off him.

On the day, a week later, that the Master opened school, he sent to the *Shamrock* editor eight new stories, making a series of nine Corney Higarty's Yarns — wherefore, by return mail he got a cheque for four-pound-ten ! *The Shamrock*, the boy thought a good name for an Irish gold mine.

Into his hands, at this time, fell an English magazine called *Great Thoughts*, with an article that gave him high ambition, encouragement, and stimulation. It was about a Scotchman by the name of Barrie who had come out of nowhere and was suddenly making name, fame, and fortune, by showing to the world the characters of a simple Scottish village, and weaving quaint tales around them — the self-same thing that the Master had begun to do for Knockagar! The boy was fired with inspiration and determination. No Thrums could be half as rich in character, atmosphere, incident, lore, as his own Knockagar; and — as in honesty of heart he had to admit — no Barrie could present the quaint life of little places one quarter as well as could he. Though in his heart he really wished the Scotchman no ill, Jaimie could see no reason why he, within a couple of years, wouldn't have people saying, 'What in the earthly world, anyway, did we see in that, fellow, Barrie?'

He had found he could write stories as easily as he could teach—and liked the new work just as much. Which was well: for in his school-mastering he was now feeling a bit discouraged: the harassments of the

Inspector had become more constant and provoking. As the edge was thus worn off his teaching-eagerness, his writing-eagerness increased. Every evening, now, after school, after dinner, he was under the lamp in the chimney-corner, covering copy-books with his imaginings. — This, too, in midst of a, noisy family, and rambling neighbours who were coming and sitting and chatting, telling news, discussing politics, arguing history, singing songs, telling stories. It occurred to him that the old folk-tales, of which he had such rare store, had literary value — and ought to be marketable. A sample one of these he set down, The Leadin' Road to Donegal, and sent to *The Weekly Freeman*, Dublin newspaper that liked to print a story or two in each issue. Mr. MacSweeney, editor, replied that the tale pleased him indeed: he would be glad to take a series, and pay a pound apiece for them. In little more than a month's time, by the fireside, neighbours coming and going on their nightly visits, and discussions raging around him on Irish politics, he penned twenty old folk-tales for the *Freeman* — giving them a title in every way fitting, *In Chimney Corners*.[3] When it began publishing them the *Freeman* discovered that the old fireside tales, which people had been forgetting, were hailed by its readers with joy. So, in short time after he had leapt the fence from the little Donegal field of the *Vindicator* he was at home in the wide Irish field, and the name Mac of Glen Ainey was as familiar at cottage firesides in Cork and Kerry as it had been in the land of the O'Donnells.

'Try a book of stories with a London publisher,' advised Eoin MacAdam. The Master did so. A London publisher soon brought out a book of his short stories, *The Leadin' Road to Donegal* — on a co-operative basis which conditioned an equable division of receipts the fame to go to the author and all money to the publisher. Considering that fame and money were better than fame alone, he next put out on his own responsibility, and in Ireland, a book of stories, *'Twas in Dhroll Donegal* — which brought him a small amount of both fame and fortune.

At this time, when, just succeeding the Parnell *debacle*, nationalism was at its lowest ebb in Ireland, there was founded in Belfast a monthly journal for the fostering of Irish patriotism, language, and literature, *The Shan Van Vocht* — the work of two gallant Belfast girls, poets, of whose names and writings the boy had been till then ignorant. He received a copy of the first number, with a letter, informing him of the object these girls had set before themselves, and asking if he felt it his duty to help — and to do so, as they were doing, just for love. The boy still recalls admiring the beautiful penmanship, and marvelling at the strange and lovely name to the letter signed, Ethna Carbery — little dreaming that the lovely name was soon to be sweet-sounding on every truly-Irish tongue and music-making in every Irish patriot-heart the world around — and also to be strangely, almost tragically, interwoven with his own.

Pleased with the Irish feeling that glowed on every page of the little paper, the Master sent a hearty reply, together with a poem and a story — and assured the girls they could count on his unstinted aid. And henceforth, for the career of that journal through whose influence these brave girls revived Irish nationalism when it was perishing, heartened again the disheartened, and rallied to mother Ireland the far-scattered fighters at earth's ends the mountain schoolmaster never missed a month without contributing his little share to the work: and his writing for *The Shan Van Vocht* was to him, after the joy of his first few years schoolmastering, the happiest work of his maturer years.

During all this time he was never forgetting the hills and their treasures. His father and mother were upbraiding him for two things — wasting his weekends on the bogs and mountains, and moidherin' his head and murdering himself, doubled up in the chimney-corner from after-school till bedtime, spoiling clean packs of good copy-books with idle tales. His mother would solemnly warn him, 'I've known people whose brains turned with work not half as foolish.'

NOTES

1

SHAN AN DIOMAS

(Shan the Proud)

On they wild and windy upland, Tornamona,
    High above the tossing Moyle,
Lies in slumber, deep and dreamless now,
    A warrior weary worn with battle-toil.
On his mighty breast the little canna blossoms,
    And the scented bog-bines trail,
While the winds from Lurigaiden whisper hush-songs,
    Round the bed of Shan O'Neill.

Time was once, O haughty warrior,
    And you slept not to the crooning of the wind —
There was once a Shan whom daisies couldn't smother,
    And when bog-weeds couldn't bind —
Once a Shan widh death-shafts from his fierce eye flashing,
    With dismay in fist of mail —
Shan whose throbbing pulses sang with singing lightning,
    Shan our Shan, proud Shan O'Neill!

Him the hungy Scot knew, and the thieving Saxon,
    Trait'rous Eireannach as well,
For their mailed throats often gurgled in his grasping
    As he hurled their souls to hell.
Sass'nach now, and flouting Scot, and Irish traitor,
    Breathe his name and turn not pale,
Set their foot upon the warrior's breast, nor tremble —
    God, the breast of Shan O'Neill!

> *Will you never, O our Chieftain, snap the sleep-cords?*
> > *Never rise in thunderous wrath?*
> *Through the knaves and slaves who bring a blight on Uladh*
> > *Sweeping far a dread, red, swath.*
> *O'er the surges shout, O you on Tornamona!*
> > *Hark the soul-shout of the Gael —*
> *Rise, O Chief, and lead us from our bitter bondage!*
> > *Rise, in God's name, Shan O'Neill!*

2   Shuiler (from siubhal = walk) is Irish for vagrant. — The only fly in the ink, when this book was put out, was that printers throughout the land conspired to refer to it as Shinlers from Healthy Hills.

3   Several years after to be published in book-form in America, under the same title.

CHAPTER TWENTY-SIX

The Wake

In his mountain rambles at this time, which brought him very much farther afield than those of his earlier days, the young Master met many strange experiences but maybe none stranger than a particular wake in the far away Cruachs — where he witnessed a weird custom that he had thought gone for a century.

Wakes and wake customs as he knew them, might have been treated earlier in this narrative, for they were important in his life, in all mountain life in Donegal.

When, in his boyhood days, news of a death winged over a district, all work was instantly suspended — the man stuck his spade in the ground, the woman dropped her rake, the lad threw from him his pitchfork. The dead must be respected. Neighbours began dropping in to the death-house when the women had been given time to wash, dress and lay out the corpse; but it was after nightfall that the wake took on its proper character and proportions. Kitchen and room would then be thronged till morning with the many whose common duty it was to sit in the death-house the night through.

When a neighbour entered a wake-house he, noticing not anybody, picked his way through the throng to the room where the corpse was laid, knelt by the bedside, and said a patter-and-ave for the soul that had gone. Standing up, then, he looked for a while in the face of the dead, before seeking out, and extending sympathy to the bereaved ones. Returned to the kitchen then, among twenty men who are sitting smoking and chatting there he finds a seat, accepts a clay pipe well-filled with tobacco, and is ready to contribute his share to the conversation.

At a table here are a couple of young men, friends of the family, seated before a roll of tobacco and pile of white pipes, cutting one and filling the other, and passing them to all comers. Where the women sit, in the room, snuff is being passed for those who indulge in it, and subdued conversation fills the place.

Among the men in the kitchen conversation will probably start with someone inquiring, 'What age, now, would poor Padraic in the bed above be, God rest him?' Half a dozen of his contemporaries volunteer replies but no two agree. A debate begins, each man dipping into memory, and proving his point from certain events common to the life of the deceased and himself — 'I mind well the harvest day, in John Andy's meadow in the Longbottom, that Lame Billy McCue from Altcor (who was afterwards married on Sheila Brennan of Loch-na-mBanfin) that Lame Billy was kilt off the top of a cart of hay givin' down the rope to Condy Melly of the Moor. For Billy was a powerful man and the rope wasn't powerful enough — and it broke and he came down. God save us all — on the crown of his head, missin' by a hair the points of a pitchfork but breakin' his neck. It was Padraic — Lord be marciful to him! — lyin' in the bed above, who run for the priest. I watched him that day meself takin' the hills like a hare; and a brave *gasúr* he was, just the size and height and age of little Dinny Macain, there in the corner — and Dinny is thirteen if he's a day—and that would ha' been within a kick of the shin, of Padraic's age that day. Well an' good. That was the Year of the Big Drowndin', when Francey Dunyon's dullin' boat, filled to the brim with too big a load of herrin', went down off Doorin Head, and Mickey's son Jimmie was the only man saved of the crew. Which would be in October, within six weeks or two months after Lame Billy, God rest him! was killed; and Mickey Dunyon, when his body was cast up two months after at the Burnfoot, was buried in Old Inver graveyard. I went to Mickey's funeral myself, me father holdin' me by the hand (I was a brave slip of a lad). — That was the second winter before Waterloo — and five before the Dear Summer. And Waterloo, as all the worl' knows was in '15 ; and as all the worl' knows likewise, '18 was the year of the Dear Summer. Now poor Padraic, in the room above, may God give him rest! was thirteen years of age then, or we'll say for argument's sake twelve, or even eleven — and them of you who are better scholars than meself — which wouldn't be hard — can calculate for yourselves how long it was from Waterloo to this present year and clap on top of that thirteen years — or twelve, or even eleven as I said — ye'll have Padraic's age — and ye'll find that, for an ignorant man, I'm not far wrong when I say that Padraic was within a kick of the shin of eighty.'

From Padraic's age they branch out into discussing the ages of the oldest men in the parish — relating them to great national or local events — the Year of the Turnout, the Year of the Dear Summer, the Year of the Blight, the year that Dan (O'Connell) brought home Emancipation, the Day of the Straws, the Night of the Big Wind, the year the big tree fell on Tam Kerrigan's, the Day of Rory na Rogaire, the summer that Paddy Managhan travelled to Dublin bringing 'the Rent' to Dan, the Year Dan died.[1]

The floodgates of memory unlocked, fascinating are the stories of olden time that now the old men unfold — the way that things were long ago, the wonderful happenings, the extraodinary men that were then, their powerful feats, the ghosts they saw, the fairies they encountered, the romance, the drama, the tragedy of the years!

Till midnight the old men hold the center of the floor, and the young, who will get their innings farther in the night, hang upon their words. Then the rosary is chanted for the dead. All in the house, room and kitchen, kneel, and chorus the responses as an old man, a celebrated leader of rosaries gives it out. Some of these, vain of their praying powers, mortify the young when they draw the rosary out to inordinate length, garnishing it with too many trimmings, improvisations of their own, and prayers for too many objects outside their immediate concern: till frequently it is great relief to youth to hear one of these pedantic prayers arrive at the final prayer, 'The angel of the Lord appeared unto Mary' — to which they joyfully give its proper, prayerful response. But our lad recalls one trying occasion when a great prayer, Conal O'Gallagher of the Old Road, having indulged himself in extra prayers that nigh broke the hearts of all in the house, at last made the joyful announcement, 'The angel of the Lord appeared unto Mary,' and drew from a sorry rascal, Jimminy Haig of Killian, the dumbfounding response, 'Faith, he was a taijous time on the way.'

After the rosary, tea was set up, and after tea they that were going to sit out the night —most of those present — set them to make the long hours pass lightly. So, the old men began recital of the ancient Finian tales, and the young began their games —a perpetuation of the ancient pre-Christian funeral games — the Sittin' Bróg, the Stannin' Bróg, and so forth. Games were practiced only in wake-houses where the death had been a natural one from old age, and no inordinate grief sat upon the survivors. Sometimes, in the house of one who had lived alone and died of old age, leaving none to mourn, the spirit of youth expressed itself in uncontrolled games that might run to recklessness. Of one such occasion our boy was a witness. It was the wake of old Peter the Ghost in the upper end of Glen Ainey. As Peter left no relative to take control at his waking, a band of half-wild youths from Over-the-Hill, to whom life meant only action and devilment, there presented themselves, and when game-time came proposed a sport to Glen Ainey hitherto unknown — what they called Making Freemasons. The Over-the-Hill boys divided themselves into two parties, one of which went outside to conduct the initiations while the other remained within to pass to them all ambitious candidates. Soon after the going out of a candidate, screams, pretended or real, were heard from him — which thrilled, excited, and made more eager the waiting candidates within. When the initiated returned he pretended to be shivering and trembling, was certainly very pale, and pushed to a place very close to the hot fire: but he never parted his lips — a proper course for one to whom solemn secrets had just been divulged. At length after big, rough, and powerful Paddy Haughey, of Clochan, had gone out and was, apparently, being initiated, there began to be heard tremendous bellowing and mad swearing, followed by a scuffling, thuds, whacks and blows, wild cries and shouts. The Over-the-Hill boys who held the door within had hard time restraining the waiting candidates who strove to burst out and have their share of whatever fun was going. But all were freed when the already initiated ones who shivered by the fire suddenly rose like one man, made a mad rush for the Over-the-Hill boys within, whipped and walloped and pounded them out through the door — and then jumped into the melee outside, where big Paddy with his wrists bound together was, double-handed, laying about him right and left, knocking down like ninepins the Over-the-Hill Boys who, dancing around him, went down and came up and went down again like rubber balls. In an instant all of the Glen Ainey lads, those already initiated as well as prospective Freemasons, were smashing and crashing the Over-the-Hill boys, scattering and chasing them for their lives over ditch, hedge, bog and moor — till the last of them was cleared out of the countryside.

After the rope was cut off Paddy Haughey's wrists, every-one learnt how Freemasons were made. — A candidate's wrists were tied with a stout cord, and he was bodily raised till the bound wrists, stretched high overhead, were slipped over one of the stout thatch-pins at the house-eave. Thus suspended from the thatch-pin, a bucket of water from an ice-bound pond nearby was gently, slowly, poured inside his coatsleeves at the wrists, went trickling down his arms, over his shoulders, and caressingly around and clown his body and legs, till it reached the toes and backed up at the shoe mouth. 'Twas small wonder that the wake of Paddy the Ghost witnessed both the birth and burial of Freemasonry in Glen Ainey.

One other rather remarkable happening of those olden times in Donegal, occurring at something akin to a wake, was the Race of Rory na Rogaire — Rory the Scamp. At that time, when there died a poor man who left nothing for his waking and burying, the corpse was laid out by the wayside, covered with a white sheet, and a plate placed on the breast for the pennies and thruppennies of the charitable passersby. Now, Rory na Rogaire who living by his wits had used up all other stratagems for making a dishonest living, at length conspired with Barney MacCunnegan that he should be found dead on a certain Saturday night, and that Barney would dress and lay him out at the Chapel-gate on Sunday morning; the proceeds to be divided between the two rascal-conspirators. The parish was surprised, streaming to mass on Sunday morning, to learn that the vagabond Rory had at length been called to his account — suddenly, too, as many a wise one had prophesied. But now, under the white sheet at the Chapel gate, everyone forgave Rory his many rascalities and contributed to the plate on his breast. Came along Mickey the Miserd, from the hip of Carn- na-Maoin mountain, who, besides being a miser, or because of it, had, under his skin, nigh as much roguery as the dead man — only, was more cautious in exercising it. The two rogues, moreover, had never loved each other. Now, the sight of the plate of money going waste whetted Mickey's avarice. He had never been able to profit by the rascal Rory, alive — but he would, with a good deal of pleasure, profit by him dead. Under pretense of putting a penny on the plate, Mickey the Miserd grabbed as much silver as his fingers could conceal — his one eye, meantime, spying one side of him and his other eye the opposite side. But a sudden wild yell went from him and he went up in a jump when he found his guilty hand grabbed and the silver shaken from it — by — the hand of the corpse! Three more yells he put forth — and ran for his life. The corpse, swearing vengeance against a rogue he had never loved anyhow, bounced from his bier, and, disregarding the shower of coppers and silver that he scattered, gathered the white sheet about him, and away after Mickey! If Mickey had feared at first he might lose his senses, his plight was piteous when he beheld the corpse pursuing him. In horror the crowds coming to chapel scattered right and left, and took to their heels at sight of the shrieking pursued and his ghost pursuer. The whole countryside was soon in mad stampede — and that day proved one of the wildest Donegal ever knew. And the Day of Rory na Rogaire was added to the other remarkable epochs in the Donegal Calender.

But the wake that figures largest in the boy's memory — the one this chapter set out to tell about — was a fearfully solemn, almost a tragic, affair. It did not occur in his own parish, but over the mountains, in the Cruachs. This was a wake in which would be, could be, no games, no stories, no reminiscences even — only silence and great sorrow — sorrow for the fine young man who was underboard, and sorrow for the grief-stricken ones he had left. It was the wake of Donoch Og Mac Aloone, a brave fellow suddenly cut off in his prime. His death was tragic. He had gone on the mountain of Cruach-an-Airgid after sheep, on a spring morning, and did not return home that night. In the moonlight searching parties went seeking him, but it was next day that he was found — his dead body at the foot of a precipice — mangled and broken. Terrible was the grief of his old mother and his four sisters. His father was dead. One thing that made their grief still wilder than ordinarily it would have been; rumour of possible foul play — unusual in Donegal — had spread, and horrified everyone; but more especially the family of the dead man. He had been in love with, and expected to be married to, a lovely cailín of the countryside, Rosha Mac Aloone, no kindred of his own, though a name-sake. A young man from the other side of the mountain, Eamonn O'Boyle, had been in love with Rosha too. He had met her at a dance once that she visited on his side of the hills — had been smitten with her and courted her, and had made many a day's journey over the mountains to see her after she went home. He had hoped to marry her. But Donoch Og fell in love with, and won, Rosha — ousting Eamonn. Six weeks ago the three parties concerned had met in the same dance-house in the Cruachs. There arose a difference, and hot words, between Donoch Og and Eamonn. But they did not come to blows. Their dispute, such as it was, quieted down, and, people thought, was almost forgotten ere the dance was over.

Boys from both sides of the mountain often met on the mountain when searching for sheep: and on the day on which Donoch Og on the Cruach lost his life, two sheepmen from Glen Mor, climbing the Cruach, had seen Eamonn on the hill, and, an hour later had seen Donoch Og travelling in a direction that might bring him across Eamonn's path just about at the spink over which Donoch was supposed to have fallen. That the two might have accidentally met — and fought — a fight that had dread ending — was to Donoch's friends and neighbours, but particularly to his family, a horrible possibility that made far more painful their grief.

Under common circumstances the wake would have been solemn — but a dread cloud of doubt made it infinitely more so. The Master had wandered into the Cruachs the day after the finding of Donoch's body — on one of his wonted wanderings — putting up at the house of Shemus Gildea. He attended the wake on its second night — as in duty bound. Although wakes were not without their attraction for him, this one, because of the grief he must witness and feel, he would gladly have forgone — but could not without risk of giving hurt.

It was a sad and painfully silent affair. When the silence was broken, it was by sobs from one or other of the women of the family, or from Rosha MacAloone, the dead man's sweetheart, who sat bowed by the bedfoot, her face almost completely hidden in a shawl — or by hushed whisperings, which instead of relieving the silence made it sorer still. Toward midnight, after the bursting into the house of a breathless barefoot boy of fourteen, a lad from the outer Cruachs — everyone was startled, electrified, by a rumour going from mouth to mouth round kitchen and room — that Eamonn O'Boyle and his party, from beyond the mountains, were making their way to the wake-house. Young men there, the dead man's friends, grew restive, murmuring. When it had turned midnight, and the second mystery of the rosary — it was the Five Sorrowful mysteries that had been chosen — was being given out by Para Mór MacAloone, uncle of the dead man, the door opened and a band of young men, headed by Eamonn O'Boyle looking wild-eyed, entered. Inside, they dropped on their knees, and joined in the rosary. At the next Mystery — the third, to everyone's thrilling Eamonn O'Boyle took the decade and led it in a clear, bold, loud voice, that differed startlingly from the soft, pathetic tone of preceding and accompanying prayers. Before he had finished his decade, the answering voices of the women were being broken by sore sobs — first sobbing heard since the rosary began. When the prayers concluded and people were arising from their knees, Eamonn O'Boyle, arising also, picked his steps through a throng of dazed men and women to the room — and to the bedside, where kneeling, he prayed with bowed head for several trying minutes. Everyone was seated and everyone was silent — and tense — when he arose. A strange something pervaded the house — part of it was a gripping apprehension. For a minute Eamonn stood looking silently into the face of the dead. Then, turning, he addressed Donoch's mother. He said in a clear, calm voice, 'I'm Eamonn O'Boyle from Deisard beyond the hills. Myself and Donoch, may God give him rest, had a little difference about' — here he turned toward the sobbing girl at the bottom of the bed — 'about Rosha here. I believe we were both on the mountain at the same time, the day Donoch died. That started rumours that reached me in our Glen. I threw from me the spade I was working with when I heard it. I went home for my coat. I took neither bite nor sup but headed for the hills instantaneously — and these boys here came after and joined me. The first house we struck on this side of the hills was Manis O'Melley's of the outer Cruachs. There we learnt the rumours were real and deep. We hurried on. Here I am now to face this dead boy, God, and you! — And,' he added, squaring himself toward the house, 'to proclaim for myself that I neither met nor saw Donoch MacAloone on the hill that day. That, moreover, if I had met him, I'd have seen my right hand cut off, ere I'd do the boy hurt, harm, or offence. Before the God at whose feet the dead man's now sittin' I proclaim the truth. And after that I challenge you to give me what test you choose.'

Everyone knew the real test he had in mind — one not invoked in these hills for the most of a hundred years. Only a couple of the very oldest there had ever witnessed its invoking — though, of course, all were familiar with the tradition of Touching the Corpse.

The dead boy's mother must have had it in mind even before Eamonn made offer — for she answered at once as she rose up, controlled and calm, 'Then, Eamonn O'Boyle put your hand on the boy's breast and ask God to witness between you and him.'

Eamonn, turning, placed his right hand on Donoch's breast saying, 'May God who is the judge between dead Donoch and myself be now the livin' witness of my innocence.'

The mother, who had stepped close to the bed, gazed in the face of her dead son for a minute, during which Eamonn, in silence, still kept his hand on the breast of the corpse. With a burst of gratefulness, that almost seemed joy, she then said, 'No blood shows — thanks be to the good God and His Blessed Mother. — Eamonn O'Boyle, there isn't a straw's weight of suspicion left on your head. As you go home to your own glen may God cross the hills with you.'

Eamonn eased the woman into her seat; then standing up, and facing the house again, said, 'Before I go back to Glen Carn I want to say about

Donoch, that in spite of the little difference come between us I never met a cleaner boy or manlier man, or one in my secret heart I admired more. He was a brave *bouchal* whose life again didn't exist between Donegal and Derry town. — And,' now turning to the bowed Rosha, ''t was small wonder Rosha, that he won you from me. Small blame to you for lovin' the man of us that was best. And of yourself, Rosha, before I go I'll say the same word now that I've lost you — the same that I said to yourself when I believed I had you — Your like, again, for goodness as well as comeliness, is not on the green sod of Ireland this day. — God's blessin' go with you wherever you go! God rest Donoch's soul, and comfort and strengthen them that are grievin' him. — If you'll excuse us, we'll be settin' our faces to the hills again. 'Tis a long hard way, and it will be well in the morrow when we reach Glen Carn. — Goodbye!'[2]

NOTES

1   The years of the Turn-out signified the 1798 rebellion Year. Dan's Rent was the people's contribution to Dan O'Connell's campaign whilst he fought for Repeal of the Union (with England) — after he had won the battle for Catholic Emancipation.

The Day of the Straws (at the beginning of the last century) has ever remained a day of mystery. On that day one of your neighbours appeared breathless at your door, in his hand three straws which he had pulled from his thatch-eave: one straw he handed to you with directions to draw three from your own thatch and with them speed with all your might forward to your three father neighbours, giving one straw to each and commanding him to act as you have done, and speed the chain onwards. The only possible explanation of the day of mystery which the boy ever heard was, that it was a plan of Dan O'Connell's brain — to test how speedly he could get his message to the ends of Ireland, in case he had to call on the people to rise in rebellion again. The straws went to every cabin in Ireland within one day.

The Night of the Big Wind was January sixth, 1839, Ireland's most memorable night in the nineteen century. It marked an epoch from which were counted minor events for a decade before and nearly a decade after. It still figures large in Irish minds, and is a familiar phrase in the mouths of even Irish-Americans who are the children's children of exiles who left Ireland soon after. Father John Cavanaugh of Notre Dame University (may God rest that grand priest and great man, famed orator and prime wit!), once was asked by a group of fellow Irish-Americans what should be done with a certain bonbastic and prolix would-be orator who was making himself a very menace at the meetings of the Irish Fellowship Club. 'The man deserves to be signally honoured for his persistent industry,' said Father Cavanaugh. — 'Let us make him the (K)Night of the Big Wind.' And the Knight of the Big Wind he was henceforward.

2   Touching, as a test of innocence or guilt was practiced in the mountains down to the nineteeth century. It was believed that when a guilty person laid his hand on one whom he had killed, blood would ooze from the mouth and nostrils of the dead one.

CHAPTER TWENTY-SEVEN

The French Ambassador

The career of the Master as a master was nearing its end. By the Irish National Board of Education paid an enormous salary to put National education into his pupils' minds, he was endeavouring, instead, to put into their minds and souls national education, uncapitalised. And, aggravating his sin, he was trying to do the same to the adult population — who, just now, sorely needed such. For, from a mistaken idea of loyalty, following misleaders who sought to trade, for a parochial 'parliament' in Dublin, Ireland's claim to freedom, the people had fallen into a sad state of national degradation. Without public rebuke — even almost without Irish murmur — Mr. John Redmond, leader, speaking at Oxford University, proclaimed to the world 'An independent Ireland is not only impossible, but undesirable'!

Only a pitiable handful throughout Ireland now dared to stand, against the multitude, for the true national ideal — and by the misleaders whom they dared oppose these few were held to public obloquy, as traitors in the enemy's pay.[1] Because these were so few and so hard pressed the Master — despite that his nature craved a life of quiet — not only could not afford to shirk his duty, but must intensify and redouble his activities.

More persistently he put forth national propaganda — both by word of mouth and pen. In Glen Ainey and elsewhere he formed nationalizing clubs of the young. He founded '98 Clubs for adults. He organized a national demonstration, for which he brought speakers from other parts of Ireland — a few of the few who held to the Irish ideal, Freedom, and could vigorously present that ideal to his people. In every possible way he strove to do his part in propagating and strengthening the national spirit that was either dead or dormant throughout most of the land. And he did these things quietly, through earnest ones who worked with and for him — thus withholding from the attentive authorities any direct proof of his moral turpitude.

To worsen matters, he committed at this time an offence more heinous than usual. It was when a Queen of England, Victoria, was being groomed to make a tour — in reality a Boer War recruiting tour — through Ireland and showers of preparatory propagandist matter, in the form of newspaper articles, pamphlets, books, were deluging the land. For purpose of countering the evil propaganda, and of impressing impressionable youth with the fact that *their* allegiance lay with Cathleen Ni Houlihan, the evil-minded schoolmaster — under his semi-protective pseudonym spread in print —

MY QUEEN

One Queen I own, and one alone
    Commands my meek obedience;
No sovereign named by human law
    From her draws my allegiance.
For her I live, for her I strive,
    And shall, till life is ended;
And with my latest parting breath
    Her name it will be blended —
                            Cathleen,
Your dear name will be blended.

I love God's peace upon our hills
    And fain would not destroy it;
I love sweet life in this fair world
    And long would I enjoy it;
But when my Sovereign needs my life
    That day I'll cease to crave it,
And bare a breast for forman's steel,
    And show a soul to brave it —
                            Cathleen,
For your sweet sake to brave it.

O, glorious death on battle-plain
    Our foemen oft hath baffled;
And proudest lovers of Cathleen
    Have holy made the scaffold:
Not mine to choose, nor mine to care —
    The cause the manner hallows —
I'll court the steel, or kiss the cord,
    On green hillside, or gallows —
                            Cathleen,
For you I'd woo the gallows.

My life is then my Queen's, to leave,
    To order, or to ask it,
This good right arm to fend or strike,
    This brain, is hers, to task it.
This hand that waits, this heart that beats,
    Are hers when she shall need 'em,
And my secret soul is burning for
    Her trumpet-call to Freedom —
                            Cathleen,
O sound the call to Freedom!

Naturally the pressure on the evil man was redoubled — by both 'the Authorities', and his Inspector. The latter was now haunting him — to find, or make, reason for giving him a long furlough. He browbeat the Master's pupils into fright and failure at examinations. On every one of his continual surprise visits to Glen Cuach, the good earnest man, determined to catch his victim in crime, gleeked into the very mouseholes, searching pretext for reprimand and Report. Once, after spending an hour in vain search he found that the Master was using in his Roll Book a sheet of blotting paper that had printed on its center an Insurance Company advertisement — just three lines — as —

THE SO-AND-SO LIFE INSURANCE COMPANY
Established 1851
Capital £2,500,000

The little man triumphantly commanded the Master to his presence, and, exhibiting the evidence of flagrant crime, demanded, 'Why, sir, will you persist in breaking the rules of the Irish National Board of Education?'

The puzzled Master said, 'I don't understand you, Sir.'

'Come with me.'

He led the way to the card of Rules and Regulations hung at the head of the school. 'Please read for me Rule No. 15a.' The still puzzled Jaimie read aloud a rule regulating the use of textbooks in National Schools — 'No Publication other than those approved by the Irish National Board of Education shall be used in this school.'

Thus, the rascal was caught red-handed. He was rebuked before his pupils, and then reported to Dublin headquarters, for two mortal offences—

1. Ignorance of the Rules and Regulations of the Irish National Board of Education.

2. Breach of Rule No. 15a!

But the pot came appreciably nearer the boil-over, when, one January day a new, strange Inspector, sent down from Dublin, bounded into Glen Cuach School, summoned the Master to the desk, and announced,

'I am come to question you on two serious matters.'

'Very well.'

'Do you, sir, a teacher salaried by the Irish National Board of Education, promulgate the doctrine 'English laws are made for Irishmen to break'?'

'Will you kindly help my memory, with occasion, place, and date?' Well the Master knew that the good man had his information by hearsay, at fourth-hand.

'Have you ever said it? — I demand that you answer me whether you ever uttered those words.'

'And I respectfully request that you help a man to answer whose memory isn't good.'

The good man shifted his position. — 'Do you *think* that English laws are made for Irishmen to break?'

'I'm very sorry, sir, but I really must object. It is your privilege — which I heartily grant — to examine my acts, but, you know, you really must leave me a little privacy in my thoughts.'

The man flushed. Then drawing from his pocket a notebook, he took out of it a newspaper clipping, a bit of verse entitled A Call, signed 'Mac of Glen Ainey.'

'Do you know whose signature that is? — appended to this treason-jingle?'

The Master took the clipping and very earnestly examined the signature, holding his head first this way, and then that, in resolve to wring from it the writer's identity, or perish. But he didn't seem to succeed in his desire for revelation. — 'I could of course give a guess' — he was returning the piece 'whose signature it might be, but if I guessed wrongly some man might sue me for slander. Besides, sir, I feel sure your guess is worth more than mine.'

The good man's face flushed. — 'Summon here your Sixth Class.'

The Master called up the class, and the Inspector read them the piece — a hortatory piece, which the Master had recently put out for stimulating of laggard young Ireland.

A CALL

Sons of Bamba,[2] *Wake! 'Tis day-break!*
  And the stars are off the sky.
All the worlds awake and striving,
  While in torpor still ye lie!
Heard ye not reveillé playing,
  Voices calling, watch-boys baying,
Quick feet tramping, horses neighing,
  Songsters choiring in the blue?
Sons of Samba, Rouse ye! Rise ye!
  There is work for men to do.

Sons of Banba, Wake! 'Tis morning!
  Long the bell for work has pealed,
All around ye droops the harvest,
  Lone the steward waits in the field.

197

Oft his call — nor were ye hearing,
  Men are needed for the shearing,
Men toil-loving, men unfearing,
  Brave of heart, and hard of thew,
Sons of Banba, Rouse ye! Rise ye!
  There is work for men to do.

Sons of Banba, Wake! 'Tis broad day!
  High the sun rides o'er the hill,
Gold grain's bursting, blades are rusting,
  And ye steeped in slumber still.
Brave men worked when ye were weeping,
  Wise ones sowed while ye were sleeping,
Now a harvest's for the reaping,
  Sickles many, labourers few —
Sons of Banba, Rouse ye! Rise ye!
  There is work for men to do.

Sons of Banba, Wake ye, Wake ye!
  Passing, fleeing, is the morn!
Let God's harvest fall and wither,
  And Ye'll wake the shame and scorn.
Hear ye! Hear! the cry for workers!
  You men! True men! — Loungers, shirkers,
Slaves and knaves, and low-born lukers,
  Them let stupor woo.
Sons of Banba, Rouse ye! Rise ye!
  There is work for MEN to do.

When the Inspector had finished the reading he tested the pupils on its easy symbolism — and with marked pleasure heard them answer — correctly, instantly, eagerly. By grimace and gesture, from behind the Inspector, the poor Master endeavoured to discourage them; but the earnest lads, misinterpreting his distress signals, only redoubled their efforts and eagerness! The Inspector, getting suspicious, asked the Master to take his stand behind, not him, but the pupils.

The poor boys were highly pleased and proud — for their Master as well as for themselves — when, at the end, the Inspector congratulated them upon what he termed, 'perfection amounting almost to brilliancy in this particular branch of study. — If your next annual examination shows you only half as perfect in the more prosaic studies that the National Board prescribes for its schools, I'll be not merely pleased but very much surprised.'

It was plain that the Master must go. And, indeed, it must be admitted that, in view of the requirements definitely *not* required by the 'National' Board of its 'National' Teachers, he had earned his way out. His Inspector's surprise descents became more frequent — and more surprising. A detective sergeant was brought to, and stationed in Donegal village. The local police, from whose garden the Glen Cuach School could be commanded, were supplied with a spyglass; the Master's movements day and night were, every one, meticulously recorded — and special note taken of all who companioned him. If no direct evidence could be got on him, his position and his life might be made uncomfortable.

But the wayward young man had his own perverse point of view. To him it was all in the day's work — and as such light-heartedly accepted. And then, considerate as he always was of his friends, rather than impose on the Irish National Board the cruel pain of dismissing him, he decided to dismiss the Irish National Board.

Which he did. At eleven o'clock one March morning the scholars were mystified to find the Master omitting roll-call. And within the next hour he dumbfounded them with the announcement that he was letting-go school and themselves from under his charge. From noon that day he would no longer be their schoolmaster — or *a* schoolmaster.

The children went away, amazed. Within half-an-hour the countryside was in amazement, too. Immediately he had closed the school- door for the last time, and turned the key in it, he walked to Frosses, to Father Pat (the school's Manager now), and handed him the key, saying that he was giving up school and schoolmastering — and going to try his hand at something else — anything else.

Since never before in Donegal's history had a man in his right mind voluntarily resigned a sinecure that paid him nearly two shillings every day the sun dawned on him — dry day, wet day, Sunday, Monday — the good priest was as dazed as the rest of the country. In his own kind way he did his best to wheedle and coax the errant fellow into taking back the key and re-opening his school. But as he could only draw from the strange man a smile and a headshake, he eventually concluded — as all the world of Glen Ainey consented to conclude that the Master's writing had at last flown to his brain! Such being the case, nothing could be done about it except give him silent sympathy and await his return to sanity.

The Master had, that day, taken with him from the school three dozen fresh copy-books — and now every night he was trying to fill these books with stories. To the neighbours, dropping into his father's house on their nightly visits, and, with tail of eye, as they talked, taking in the lad's feverish fireside scribbling, certain proof was provided that their gravest suspicions about the state of the boy's brain were, alas, only too true!

Since a few stories a month was the most that the Dublin papers could take from him, and that he owed a fresh duty to his family after throwing to the winds the regular family income, something more he must do than story-making. As he could think of no possible opening for him in Ireland, America, which had been in the back of his mind for long years, now more insistently pushed itself forward. At length, without telling anyone — even his parents — he decided to slip off to the land whereto, alas, all the Irish boys were now hurrying. He was hardy and strong and fit to face, there, any kind of work whereby he could make necessary money. And, though hard labour would be welcome enough, he mightn't, after all, have to tackle it; he had a ready pen, and might get a job on some country paper in a land where, he understood, papers were frequent.

Just then occurred something odd — and utterly foreign to the spirit of his life — something, too, that could never have entered his dream, wild and wide as it was. Though, as it happened, it did not affect his future course, but went out of his life again as suddenly as it had come in, it is worth setting down for the embellishing of the boy's iliad.

A very few days after he made his decision to emigrate, there came to him, by a devious route, a letter from Paris, from the Director chief of *Le Petit Journal*, asking if he would accept the editorship of an English-language paper in Singapore. A militant Irishman was wanted for the post: he had inquired about such person from a patriotic Irishman and a patriotic Irishwoman then resident in Paris: they had heard of, and recommended to him, the Donegal schoolmaster.

The boy was more than amazed by this extraordinary offer — come dropping out of the sky. He saw at once its (political) significance —which appealed to his instincts. He saw, too, that it wasn't without danger — but was willing to disregard that. But, Singapore, besides being a notoriously unhealthy place, on the burning Equator, was so far from Ireland and from everything and everyone he loved, that it looked like transportation for life. He would take a few days to consider it, meantime saying nothing about it to anyone. Before he had yet reached a decision, lo, another letter came to say that M. Hippolyte Marinoni (of Le Petit Journal) had now a new propostion — one that he did not wish to put into writing; but would the boy please come to Paris to hear it?

The boy's curiosity was awakened. Most of the few pounds he had behind his hand he was willing to gamble on the great journey into the unknown world, after an unknown proposition. He went off hastily. To him, from the Donegal mountains, the journey into the world and the world's capital was an exciting one, surely. The Irishman who had recommended him met him on his arrival, and took him direct to *Le Petit Journal* — to M. Marinoni in his private office.[3]

Now, the time was just following the sensational Fashoda Incident — in which France, having occupied Fashoda in the Sudan, had, to her great

200

humiliation, to evacuate it in response to a twenty-four-hour ultimatum from England. And she was feverishly equipping herself to face England and try to wipe out her recent shame and recoup some of her lost prestige.

So, the Singapore proposition which had been put to the boy was one of ten thousand details that were a necessary accompaniment to her preparations. But M. Marinoni informed the lad that, acting for a government department, he had, now, a more urgent and very much more important proposition to make to him — namely, that he should journey to America and interview there five men who headed the big Irish organizations, secret and open, in that country, discuss with them certain proposals of the French government, get their decision, and also an estimate of the number of men they could furnish for either a Canadian or an Irish battlefield, in case France declared war on Britain. Jaimie joyfully accepted the great mission — and was given on the nail his own asking for expenses. As the mountain-boy had both quaint and scant idea of money's value in travel, he only asked a hundred pounds — which was paid him in gold. He was ordered to set out as quietly as possible.

As he foresaw that when he had fulfilled his mission, he must settle down in America — maybe never to return — he went back to Donegal to put a few things together, and say goodbye. With thirty-nine of his hundred pounds he paid a debt he had incurred for publishing of his *Leadin' Road to Donegal*, gave fifteen gold sovereigns to his grieving mother, threw his few belongings into a bag — not the original rainbow-hued receptacle — and with them an armful of story-filled copy-books. For Liverpool he set off, and at Belfast, enroute, spent the evening between train and boat with his friend Ethna Carbery, and her family — who were as puzzled and grieved as his Donegal friends at the boy's sudden departure for the Land Beyond, to push his fortune.[4] He took steerage passage in the old-time Majestic, — and with nearly forty pounds in his pocket, was gone a great man on a great, secret, diplomatic mission.

The nine-day voyage was not pleasant to the diplomat — for the conditions in the more modest quarters of Atlantic liners of those days were trying to anyone of moderately sensitive tastes. So it was happy to him to be disgorged on Ellis Island amid a motley crowd of many nationalities — very like, he thought, the animals being emptied out of the ark — if only the latter had carried bundles. Met by the muscular, strong-lunged reception committee which the American Government in those days maintained for welcoming visitors to her shores — herded through the cattle-pens of The Island, his initiation into Americanism — was France's first Ambassador to the Irish Republic as in America Established.

NOTES

1 An amusing instance of the carefully spread rumour that Dublin Castle (seat of the British government) was his secret paymaster and backer, the Master met with one time that, having formed the youth of various districts into national clubs, he organised a grand gathering to parade through Knockagar, caman on shoulder, singing The Risin' of the Moon and other such stirring songs. As the brave lads tramped and sang in unison down the village street, with the police on their barracks-steps taking record of all their names, one or two good simple, wandering old mountain women, standing by the young Master — whom they did not know by sight — commented to the order, 'Tchuck! Tchunk! Tchunk!! I'm thinkin' this'll make a gay payday for the young Masther of Glen Cuach. Half-a-crown a head for every caman-man I understand the Castle pays him. — See the polis takin' the tally.'

2 Bamba is an ancient poetic name for Ireland. It may be noted that shearing is the term used in Donegal for reaping corn.

3 This M. Marinoni, by the way, was the inventor of the rotary press.

4 About the boy's going Ethna Carbery wrote in a lament — under a purposely misleading signature — 'E.D.M.' in America the boy read the poem, Páistín Fionn, in the next month's Shan Van Vocht, but did not know nor even guess its author's identity till a coupld of years later. — It may here be noted that the head of the one-time Madairín Rua had changed from red to fair.

PÁISTÍN FIONN

O, Páistín Fionn, but it vexed her sore,
The day you turned from your mother's door
For the wide grey sea, and the strife and din
That lie beyond, where the ships go in.

There was always peace in the little town—
The kindly neighbours went up and down,
With a word to you, and a word to me,
And a helping hand where might be.

The sheltering hills and the rainbow skies,
Set the dreams alight in your boyish eyes,
And the shrill sweet singing from every brake
Stirred in your heart a restless ache.

So you left our glens and our fishful streams,
To follow the lure of your boyish dreams;
Through the lonely cities you wander long,
Far from the moors and the blackbird's song.

Has the world been good to you, Páistín Fionn?
Has the yellow gold that you sought to win
Been worth the toil and the danger dared?
Has plenty blessed you, and sorrow spared?

Your mother sits in the dusk alone,
And croons old songs in an undertone,
Old cradle-songs that your childhood knew,
When her folding arms made a world for you.

Her sad heart, loving and hoping on,
Awaits your footsteps from dark to dawn—
The thin cheeks paler and paler grow,
With hunger for you as the hours drift slow.

Then, Páistín Fionn, come back, come back—
A homebound bird o'er the glancing track;
The door is open — the hearth is red —
And our love is calling you, Dear Fair Head.

CHAPTER TWENTY-EIGHT

And he lived happy ever after

Only that this book is meant to be a record of the boy's career in his own land — with, for its rounding out, the very least touch of Beyond — it would be sore temptation to give here the rare account of the French Ambassador's experiences in the New World — his first night there — in a hotel in lower Greenwich Street — whereto he had been directed by a kind man on Ellis Island — and indeed a hundred other highly rare experiences that befell the mountainy lad in the Great Land. But so long have we dallied on the way that, now, it is better to push quickly to the end of the rocky road. (Was it so very rocky?)

After three weeks in New York, Boston, and Chicago, conferring with Irish-American leaders,[1] and finally furnishing details to Paris — which completed his diplomatic mission — Jaimie found himself an ex-Ambassador, in a lodging house in Brooklyn, with seven dollars and thirty-five cents in his pocket — and before him a wide world calling to a brave boy to come and conquer!

For several days he journeyed afoot over Brooklyn Bridge to Park Row, there to offer his valuable services at every newspaper door. He did not get much beyond the door. Most office-boys to whom our lad applied for a job mortally regretted that they had their staff complete. One of them, wishing to encourage obvious merit, said he would have a suitable opening twelve months and one day from next Christmas and particularly desired the homespun-clad *bouchal* to call on him at twenty-five minutes after nine of that morning. The *bouchal* recalls with amusement that at the *Tribune* the office-boy was darned sorry he had not presented himself two hours earlier, for he had had to fire the managing editor that very morning — but unfortunately, had just re-filled the post. The New York press could not, seemingly, afford an opening to genius come a-begging — but it afforded the boy, through its files, free reading of its advertisements — wherein he diligently sought distress-calls for help from owners of country newspapers. But vainly.

Then the boy thought he would tempt American magazine editors with some of his stories. Considering, after due inquiry, that a magazine called *The Century* was most deserving of his literary support, he dug out from his bag, on a morning, a handful of the least turf-smoke-stained of his manuscripts, treated himself to a three-cent ride over Brooklyn Bridge — and from its terminus walked all the way, via the Bowery, to Union Square and the *Century* office there — where, as usual, he had to content him with interviewing the office-boy, and with him left the copybooks. But, to his disappointment they were returned, with regrets and thanks, two days later — seemingly unread.

He realized that he should have insisted on seeing the editor, and interesting him in this new, fascinating kind of work which America should have opportunity of enjoying. He would go to *Harper's* — which, he heard, was worthiest of American magazines — and do this. Stuffing his pockets with copy-books next morning, he walked Brooklyn Bridge, and went down under, to old, dirty, forgotten Franklin Square, and to a very old, very dirty, cobweb-windowed building — the strange domicile of the great *Harper's* publications. He wrangled with the office-boy to get to the editor in person — till the office-boy, bothered, at length took his message. That very genial, lovable, beautiful character, old William Alden, was then editor of *Harper's*. His curiosity aroused, Mr. Alden asked that the Irishman be shown in. Our boy still sees vividly the grey-bearded, genial-eyed, glowing-faced old gentleman in his swivel-chair, and the strange, yet very kind, surprised smile that over-spread his face at sight of a raw, tow-headed, homespun-clad, pocket-bulging young Irishman come striding into his office. But he gave the boy warm handshake, gracious welcome and a chair. 'And now,' he said, 'tell me what I can do for you.'

The boy proceeded to unfold his tale to the genial man — informing him he had come from the mountains of Donegal, where he had been born and reared, and had lately been a schoolmaster; that he was of the people, had lived their life, become saturated with their lore, absorbed their character, and, having ambition to write, had been trying to crowd it all into stories. Mr. Alden's face showed increasing interest as the boy spoke. He now offered the boy a cigar, which was declined, lit one himself and laid him farther back in his chair, to listen more at ease. 'Go on!' he said — 'Go on! Tell me more.'

The lad went on — giving details of his own life in particular, and Donegal life in general. The kind old gentleman still more and more interested as the narrative unfolded, kept encouraging the narrator with compliant nods of his head — and didn't seem to mind if the boy should talk round the clock.

'Now,' the Donegal *gasúr* said, after he had talked for an hour, 'I think I could do stories of our Donegal life that would interest *Harper's* readers.'

Mr. Alden smiled another of his very genial smiles — for a full, silent minute. Then he said, 'This is a mighty interesting thing. I'm tremendously interested. — But,' he went on, 'I need to tell you that *Harper's*, which I naturally think is the leading magazine here, is published for a class of sophisticated readers who look for what I might call the finished product — stories written by leading writers of the day who've had long experience with the pen. These writers, almost all, spent years of apprenticeship in the pages of other magazines before they qualified for us. I see — I know — that you have a very rich mine to draw from, and I feel sure, too, that you could set down very, very interesting stories for readers of Irish magazines — and maybe for *Harper's* too, when you have more experience — you have so interested me that I want to watch your progress. I somehow feel that we may be proud, one day, to have you in our pages. Meantime if I can do anything to help you get a footing in America, I'll gladly do it. If you could let me have a couple of your stories I'll read them, and advise you on them — criticise them if you'll permit me, and tell you just what you might do with them, or where you might offer them.'

'That's very kind of you,' said Jaimie. 'And I have some here.' Diving into his pockets he began drawing forth his smoke-stained copy-books and counting them down on the desk of an amazed man, till, when Mr. Alden's mouth was opening wide with wonder, the boy finished his labours at the count of seven. When he got his breath Mr. Alden lifted onto his desk a little black bag that had been sitting on a chair, and re-counted the seven copy-books into it.

As he was putting them in, he more than once raised one near to his nose, sniffing. Then he said, 'Would you mind my asking you what is the remarkable scent that I get from these books?' The boy told him it was turf-smoke — and at the same time apologised for the discoloration of the leaves. Mr. Alden, delighted as a child, now felt at leave to treat himself to several long, deep sniffs. He said, 'When you entered my office I even felt the same scent coming, it must have been, off those nice homespuns you wear.' This pleased the boy much — for, so constantly had people on the streets turned to look after him that he felt uncomfortable coming into the office of *Harper's*, so clad. But it was his Sunday suit — and Monday one.

Mr. Alden said, 'When stories come into this house they do not come to me to be read, till two or three others read and weed them out. I have only time to read the very likely ones. But you, and the story you tell me, have so interested me that I'm going to take these manuscripts right home with me to Jersey this afternoon, and read them for myself. — Let me see now,' he went on, 'today is Wednesday. Tonight and tomorrow night I'll get through them. — Would you come here on Friday morning? and I'll have ready for you both the stories and the best advice I can.'

On Friday morning the boy was in Franklin Square nearly before the janitor had opened *Harper's* front door — and was tramping round and round the Square observing everyone who went into the cobwebbed edifice — till at ten o'clock he saw good Mr. Alden enter — with his little black bag. He gave the old gentleman time to get settled in his office before walking in and presenting himself again to the office-boy — who, smiling and gracious this morning, volunteered to tell Mr. Alden that the Irishman was here to see him.

Our lad can again see Mr. Alden's kindly sweet smile of greeting, on this morning. He didn't speak a word — but shook the boy's hand cordially, and motioned him to a chair — then took up the black bag, opened it, and counted seven copy-books from it onto his desk. From the pile he seperated one. — The lad's heart bounded. The man, O joy! was maybe going to take this one for *Harper's*. — Still without speaking, the old gentleman proceeded to light a cigar. And then, leaning back in his swivel chair, swung round to face the lad — at whom he looked steadily for nearly a minute. He then said, 'Well, as I promised, I read through your seven stories.'

The boy nodded his thanks.

'I have brought them in here again today.'

Then he reached out and lifted the single one which he had separated from the others — one wherein the lad's hopes were now bound up.

He fingered it in silencee for a minute, turning it over and over. — The lad's heart was actuallv thumping!

'This one,' said Mr. Alden slowly, 'I have read over three times. I wanted hard to take it for Harper's.' — The boy's heart seemed nearly to stop. — 'But, very reluctantly, I had at last to decide against it.'

The heart did now stop for a full instant, the boy really believes.

'The other six stories,' the good man drawled on, 'I'm keeping for *Harper's*.'

The boy very much doubts that he even said, Thank you. He doesn't, and didn't, know what Mr. Alden said during the next few minutes. But he came to consciousness when he heard the kind man suggest, 'Now maybe you would like to have a little cash this morning.'

'Indeed and, thank you, I would,' the lad — that day living on his last dollar — replied; and so eagerly that Mr. Alden's smile changed into a discreet, very kind, little laugh.

'Well, suppose I now give you a cheque against one of them, and we'll fix up the others later. — Now here's a story,' he lifted one, Alley Cannon's First and Last Duel (which was, later, to be the first published in *Harper's* — and, moreover, was to get front place — with remarkable illustrations by Keller) — 'How much shall I pay you for this one?'

Aware that *Harper's* was one of the biggest, richest publishing houses in New York, the boy wasn't going to be so unwise as to tell that he was paid from two-and-a-half to five dollars for stories in Ireland. *Harper's* wouldn't be hurt if they paid double, treble, as much as the little *Shamrock* or *Emerald*. He answered, 'I don't know. I leave that to you to fix. You know better its value.'

'Then,' said Mr. Alden, 'how would a hundred dollars strike you?'
It struck the boy dumb!

When, in a fog, Jaimie had got his cheque and with it stumbled out of the editor's office, he hastened to cash it ere rumour should reach the Brothers Harper of what a fatuously kind editor was doing to their bank account.

News of a new writer runs quickly round the publishing houses of New York. Only a few days later came a message to the boy from Robert Underwood Johnson, of the *Century*, asking if he would let them see again the stories that he had submitted a week ago — or any others that he wished. The boy brought to the *Century* office ten copybooks. He rode all the way to Union Square now. Both Mr. Johnson and Richard Watson Gilder, the two poet-editors, received the lad graciously, chatted with him long, took his manuscripts to read, and took himself to lunch. Three days later they sent for him, and told him they were accepting eight of the stories for the *Century*.

McClure's followed by accepting three stories — and asking also for a book — which he put together for them out of the bag that couldn't be emptied. Under the title *Through The Turf-Smoke*, this book appeared on St. Patrick's Day — dedicated to the friend whom he most esteemed in Ireland, Ethna Carbery —

> *'Your fond heart throbbed for our country's story,*
> *Your great heart glowed for our country's glory —*
> *Because it was so, O Banba's daughter!*
> *This tribute take, o'er far far water.'*

In two weeks McClure, Philips and Company had to go to press with a second edition of the book — when Sam McClure (who left Antrim a child) slapped Jaimie on the back, with 'No, my boy, they can't keep us Irish down!'

Interviews with, and articles on, the Donegal Mountain lad who had crashed the gates began appearing in the New York papers, others were syndicated over America; receptions were tendered him, dinners given in his honour where everybody was in black-and- white with the exception of one, who was a study in mixed tweeds by the table's head. Other magazines wanted to know if there were still other stories in the bag — until one or more was placed with every story-magazine, except either two or three, then published in New York, Boston, and Philadelphia.[2]

When this success-fever was at its height the boy heard the call of the hills of Donegal — and harkened! Then, one night, at one of the rare salons of the rare Baroness du Monde, getting his share of fêteing and congratulating (where he recalls the courtly hostess counting; representatives of seventeen nationalities, from a be-feathered Medicine-man of the Sioux all the way up the social and racial gamut to a long-robed Chinese philosopher — and where, too, he witnessed the play-boy son of New York's most noted publisher of the day laying in the lap of every guest leaflet forewarnings of an impending book of his own brewing) his noble-hearted friend Sam McClure who attended with a branding-iron under his coat in hope of meeting mavericks — came up, with dilated nostrils, and hurled at him,

'Are *you* mad?'

The *bouchal* looked astonishment at the publisher.

'Someone just said that you're going back to Donegal! That's not so, surely?'

'Well, I've been thinking of it.'

'And I repeat, Are you mad?'

To say Yes to such an insinuation was, of course, out of the question. But, on the other hand, to answer No would be the very surest mark and sign of the hopeless madman. After a moment's thought he replied modestly, if hedgingly,

'I — I can't say, just off-hand. But why do you suspect me?'

'No man in his right senses would run away from showers of the finest publicity got by any foreign writer come to America in my memory. We have big and noted writers here who would gladly hand over the best of their two eyes to get half the advertising that's being hurled at you.'

Ignorant of the value of publicity in this new world, the boy felt he had got all of it that was necessary. He told Mr. McClure that a little was as good as a load. And, anyway, he said, he thought they had about exhausted all the good things they could say about him, and there was just the danger, now, of their beginning on his other side. Indeed, only the very day before, there had come to him a clipping from *The Cleveland Plain Dealer* wherein he was described as 'an ungainly, red-headed, rustic-garbed, ex-schoolmaster, whom no jury in its right mind would ever, on the looks of the thing, convict of genius, unless the case was stiffened by plenty of suborned perjury.' — 'So I think,' he said, 'I'm seizing the psychological moment for getting away — if, God help me! I haven't already over-passed it. — And if I depart with colours still flying it will be an easy thing for you to proclaim my retreat a victory-march.'

As had ended all his old folk-tales so ended the *bouchal's* own tale: After slaying the slews of giants and dragons who would have stayed him, and gaining his quest, the victorious hero won home with wagons of gold (some thousands of dollars at least), wooed and wedded the beautiful Princess for whom all previous champions, princes and knights had contended in vain, built a castle with a window for everyday in the year, and lived happy and well ever after![3]

NOTES

1 And getting guarantee of a speedy first draft of 100,000 fighting men — if any way could be worked out for getting them to a scene of action.

2 The number of story-magazines in America at the time was about fifteen. The boy had stories or poems accepted by Harper's, The Century, The Atlantic, Youth's Companion, McClure's, Cosmopolitan, Lippincotts, Saturday Evening Post, Frank Leslie's Monthly, Leslie's Weekly, Munsey's, The Independent, The Criterion — and Sunday supplements of the New York Newspapers.

3 Although it was the usual for a returned American to bring back riches, yet to bring such wealth as did the gasúr, after a mere seven months in the land of gold, was startling to many honest ones of Glen Ainey. They wished the boy well, they liked him, always had had a high opinion of him, and he came of decent people, but — well — they were really sorry that he hadn't given a more colourable explanation of his sudden opulence. To expect them to believe that bright Americans crammed his pockets with gold for telling them old stories that the very child on the road could have for the asking in Glen Ainey, was presuming just a little too far on their credulity.

Yet, one of his neigbours, Tam Stewart, rough and warm-hearted man of the Planter people, coming to welcome the boy home, shook both his hands with powerful handshake, saying, 'Jaimie, lad it's a thousand welcomes ye are back to Glen Ainey! and I want you to know that, no matter a dam how you got your money, it's hearty gald I am that you got it.'

Because of rumours that arose a few months after his quitting America, to the effect that the homespun boy, ere beating a safe retreat to his native hills, had cleverly taken in all the bright American editors with stories plagiarised wholesale, the house of Harper was put in panic. And the row over the matter divided into two hostile camps the house of McClure. When assumed proofs from books of continental and eastern folklore began to convince the majority that the Donegal mountain gasúr had sold the Americans editors a gold turf, large-hearted Viola Roseboro, McClure's chief literary adviser, and stoutest champion of the mountain boy, shed tears — Heaven bless her! The boy, at length coming to learn of the storm that had broken, returned to America in September to face his rather innocent accusers and their rather amusing accusations. He comforted the troubled editors, sold them another bag of his stories — which he had written around the summer — and, after a four months stay this time, sailed for Donegal again — with forty-five hundred dollars in his bag! To the still greater perplexity, not to say consternation, of Glen Ainey.

And its involuntary suspicions were confirmed by the fact that now he shunned America — gave it time to forget both his misdeeds and him — for five years, before sallying forth again. Then, following the foot-steps of the rest of Europe's surplus population — he came to America to lecture the natives.